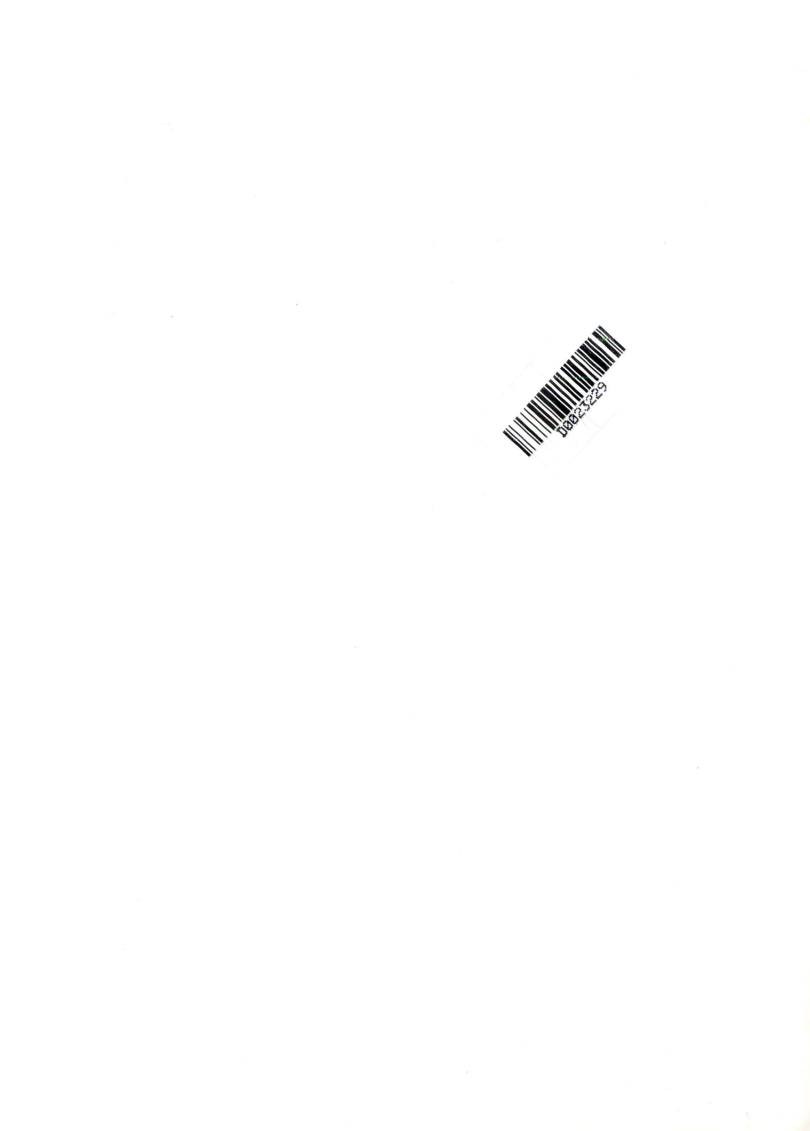

HISTORICAL
ATLAS
OF THE
Celtic World

HISTORICAL
ATLAS
—OF THE—
Celtic World

Angus Konstam

Checkmark Books
An imprint of Facts On File, Inc.

Historical Atlas of the Celtic World

Text and Design © 2001 Thalamus Publishing

Checkmark Books
An imprint of Facts On File, Inc.
132 West 31st Street
New York, NY 10001

Library of Congress Cataloging-in-Publication Data
Konstam, Angus.
    Historical atlas of the Celtic world / Angus Konstam ; [maps, Roger
Kean ; illustrations, Oliver Frey].
        p. cm.
    Includes bibliographical references and index.
    ISBN 0-8160-4761-8 (alk. paper)
    1. Civilization, Celtic—Maps.   2. Celts   I. Kean, Roger.   II.
Title.
    CB206 .K66 2001
    911'.364—dc21

                                    2001042102

You can find Facts On File on the World Wide Web at:
http://www.factsonfile.com

For Thalamus Publishing
Project editor: Neil Williams
Maps and design: Roger Kean
Lay-out: Joanne Dovey
Illustrations: Oliver Frey
Four-color separation: Michael Parkinson and Thalamus Studios

Printed and bound in Italy

ISBN: 0-8160-4761-8

Jacket design: Cathy Rincon

10 9 8 7 6 5 4 3 2 1
This book is printed on acid-free paper

PICTURE CREDITS
Picture research by Image Select International Limited and Thalamus Studios
Lesley and Roy Adkins Picture Library: 10, 14, 34, 70, 85, 106, 122, 130, 131, 132, 155 (top), 186; AKG London: 58, 66, 119; AKG London/ Erich Lessing: 57, 87; Ancient Art and Architecture Collection: 146; Art Archive/ Archaeological Museum Brescia/ Gianni Dagli Orti: 37; Art Archive/ British Library: 160, 161; Art Archive/ Dagli Orti: 65, 88 (left), 182; Art Archive/ Musée Alésia Alise Sainte Reine France/ Dagli Orti: 29, 36, 104, 105; Art Archive/ Musée Borely Marseille/ Dagli Orti: 171; Art Archive/ Musée des Antiquités St Germain en Laye/ Dagli Orti: 100, 168; Art Archive/ Musée Lapidaire Avignon/ Dagli Orti: 19 (top), 169; Art Archive/ Museo Nazionale Atestino Este/ Dagli Orti: 2–3; Art Archive/ Prehistoric Museum Moesgard Højbjerg Denmark/ Dagli Orti 112–13; British Museum, London: 18, 19 (bottom), 26, 46, 47 (left), 48, 49, 59, 71, 73, 81, 99, 103, 111 (both), 114, 116–117, 118, 120 (both), 127, 128, 129, 136, 138, 139 (top), 142, 147, 172, 180, 181, 183; Celtic National Museum of Ireland, Dublin, Eire/Bridgeman Art Library: 141; Clwyd/Powys Archaeological Trust: 61; Collections/ Geoff Howard: 63; Collections/ Brian Shuel: 52; Crown copyright: 75, 125 (bottom), 156–57; Richard Cummins/CORBIS: 170, 175: Dominique Darr: 41; Dominique Darr/ Ann Ronan: 43; Robert Estall/CORBIS: 22; E.T. Archive: 45; Macduff Everton/CORBIS: 94; Image Select International Limited/ Ann Ronan: 1, 5, 17, 42, 44, 92, 107, 110, 162, 163, 177; Martin Jones-Ecoscene/CORBIS: 165 (top); Caroline Knight-Edifice/CORBIS: 155 (bottom); James Murdoch-Cordaiy Photo Library Ltd/CORBIS: 164; National Museum of Ireland: 72, 134, 140, 159; Dr. David Nicolle: 11, 30, 31, 74, 76, 77, 79 (both), 80, 91, 98, 124, 125 (top), 133, 148, 150, 151; Gianni Dagli Orti/CORBIS: 40; Pictures Colour Library: 173; Post Office, Republic of Ireland: 174; RMN: 15, 67; RMN/ Arnaudet: 32, 33; RMN/ Gérard Blot: 47 (right), 53 (top), 139 (bottom); RMN/ Loic Hamon: 21; RMN/ R.G. Ojeda: 7; RMN/ J. Schormans: 6, 54, 67, 88 (right), 89, 114 (left), 115, 117 (right); Kevin Schafer/CORBIS: 12, 53 (bottom); Richard Hamilton Smith/CORBIS: 187 (left); Spectrum Colour Library: 101, 184, 185; Ted Speigel/CORBIS: 107; Superstock: 149; Patrick Ward/CORBIS: 165 (bottom); Werner Forman Archive: 23, 60, 102, 143; Werner Forman Archive/ National Museum, Copenhagen: 64; Wild Country/CORBIS: 123; Adam Woolfitt/CORBIS:13, 187 (right).

Half title page:
Fragment from the
Book of Kells (*see
pages 162–163*).

Previous page:
A 4th-century BC
Celtic votive plaque,
depicting mounted
Etruscan warriors
from a time when the
Celtic Venitii were
penetrating Etruscan
territory along the Po
Valley in northern
Italy.

Facing:
Decorative elements
from pages of the
Book of Kells.

Contents

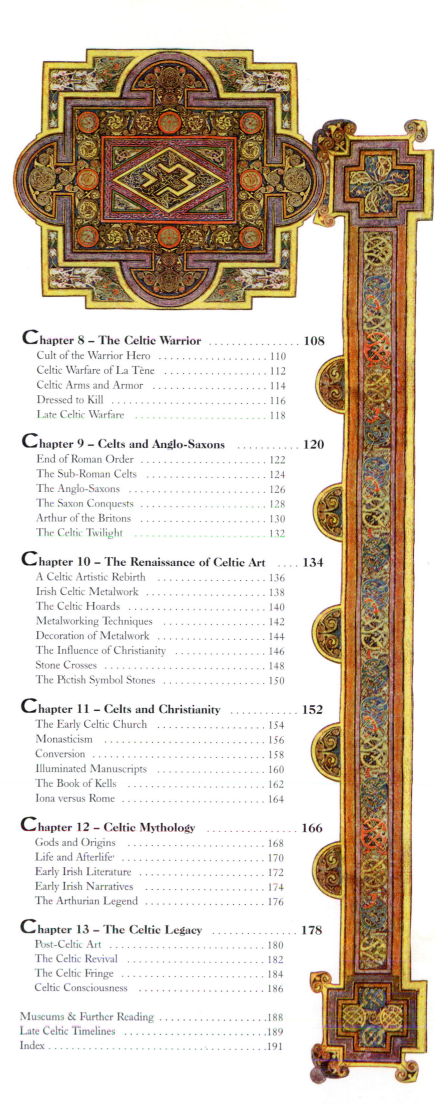

Introduction

Some three thousand years ago, an Indo-European civilization emerged in central Europe that came to dominate the north of the continent. Possessed of an advanced culture, the structure of their warrior-society allied to their ability to produce well-crafted metal weapons made them a force to be reckoned with. The Greek traders who first encountered them during the sixth century BC called them the Keltoi or Galatai. Today, we know them as the Celts and Galatians.

Right: Sword with a human head. The pommel is made from bronze, but the blade is forged from iron, making this Celtic weapon from the La Tène III period more fearsome than the purely bronze swords of the Celts' enemies.

T he Celts have variously been described as "the conquerors of Europe," or, less flatteringly, as "the barbarians of Europe." They were certainly the first northern European people sufficiently organized to be labeled a civilization. At the height of their power during the second century BC, the Celtic world stretched from Turkey to Ireland, and from Spain to Germany. Other Celtic settlements have been traced as far away as the Ukraine. Celtic peoples inhabited the banks of the great rivers of Europe; the Danube, Rhine, Rhône, Po, Thames, Seine, and Loire. Consequently these people established trading links with their neighbors in the Mediterranean, and goods from the Middle East have been found in Celtic grave sites in modern France and Germany. The entire continent of Europe north of the Alps was joined together in a loose confederation of tribes who shared a common Celtic culture.

Much of what we know about the Celts comes from accounts by the Romans and Greeks, as well as from the archaeological clues the Celts left behind them. To the civilizations of the Classical Mediterranean, the Celts were a people to be feared, and Celtic armies swept into Italy, Greece, and Spain before the Romans were able to contain them. Celtic warriors were recruited to serve in the armies of the enemies of Rome, and they became Rome's most implacable foe.

The Celts were a warrior aristocracy, and military prowess was considered one of the strongest virtues of a Celtic ruler. They were also impetuous, and their eagerness to meet the enemy in battle proved to be a weakness, which the Romans exploited to the maximum. Celtic civilization on the mainland of Europe was all but extinguished in a single decade when Julius Caesar invaded Gaul during the mid-first century BC. The only group of independent Celtic peoples left were in Britain, and a century later the Romans launched a conquest of this last Celtic bastion. The Romans were followed by Germanic conquerors, and by the tenth century the Celts were reduced to a shadow of their former glory. From then onward, the Celtic world comprised of a handful of small, poor nations clinging onto the Atlantic rim of the European continent.

The Celts have a reputation as one of the greatest artistic peoples of the ancient and early medieval world. They have left behind them an artistic legacy in their metal artifacts, many of which are seen as some of the most beautiful objects ever produced. They possessed a creative drive and vibrancy that survived through the centuries. When the Celts converted to Christianity, this artistic ability was channeled into the production of exquisite devotional objects, including illuminated manuscripts which still stun people with their color and complex beauty. Above all, the Celts are remembered for their enigmatic artistic signature; complex patterns of intertwined scrolling decoration that graced Celtic artistic endeavors for over a thousand years.

Through this artistic legacy, and also through the myths and legends written by later Celtic scribes, we can understand a little of the world of these Celtic people; how they lived, who they worshiped, how they fought, and how they celebrated life. Their civilization touched most of Europe at some stage in its history, and it remains one of the most enigmatic and misunderstood of all the world's great cultures. Be prepared to fall under the spell of the Celts as you journey through their rich and colorful world.

Movement of northern European peoples
from the Urnfield Proto-Celts (1000 BC)
to the pre-Roman conquests of the last
century BC.

ATLANTIC OCEAN

NORTH SEA

BALTI

Celtic expansion

Slav/German migrations

NORTHERN
BRONZE AGE
(Proto-Germanic)

MIDDLE BRONZE AGE CULTURES
(Outside Urnfield cultures)

Hallstatt

La Tène

extent of Proto-Celtic Urnfield groups c.800 BC
early Slavic
early Celtic
early Italic tribes
precursors of Illyrians
early Hallstatt culture (iron producers)
extent of Hallstatt culture
original territory of La Tène civilization
expansion of the Celts
Celtiberians

VENETI

Celtic expansion

Latin migrations

LIGURES

ETRUSCANS

PICENTES

UMBRIANS

ADRIATI

SABINI

VOLSCI

LATINI

SAMNITES

MESSA

LUCANII

GREEKS

IBERIANS

MEDITERRANEAN SEA

Chapter 1

Celtic Origins

Pre-Christian Celts left no written records, so all the accounts we have of these people are from prejudiced Mediterranean writers, the first by Greek historians, writing in the fifth century BC. Fortunately, a wealth of archaeological material has survived that has allowed us to come to a closer understanding of Celtic society, and its origins.

The Celts dominated Europe for over 500 years, and their roots can now be traced to earlier European societies of the Neolithic and Bronze Ages. Historians and archaeologists have established that the Bronze Age "Urnfield" people were the direct ancestors of the Celts, and in the period between the tenth and the seventh centuries BC the foundations of Celtic culture were established in central Europe. These Bronze Age people seem to have assimilated the earlier indigenous inhabitants of the continent, and also managed to form a union with a mysterious wave of equestrian warriors who swept into Europe from the east during the eighth century BC. Archaeological evidence suggests a period of instability in Europe, as settlements were destroyed, religious offerings and human sacrifice increased, and whole populations sought safety in remote areas. The end result of all this turmoil seems to have been the creation of a new ruling caste, a group of outsiders who became closely linked with the Bronze Age people of the "Urnfield" era.

By the beginning of the Iron Age in the eighth or seventh centuries BC, these people seem to have merged into a unified culture, based in modern Austria, Hungary, Germany, and the Czech Republic. A burial site at Hallstatt, Austria has provided the name for these people. The "Hallstatt" culture (*see pages 16–17*) was the first true Celtic society, and within two centuries these early Celts had managed to extend their influence throughout much of Europe.

Like the La Tène period Celts (*see pages 20–21*) who succeeded them, these people were part of a warrior society, where conquest and military prowess were exalted. Although they were unable to resist the pressures created by Germanic incursions from the east, these Celtic warriors succeeded in carving out a unified European civilization that would dominate the continent until the ascendancy of the Romans in the first century BC. Far from being a "barbarian" culture as portrayed by the Romans and Greeks, the Celts formed one of the great civilizations of the ancient world.

Slav migrations

Proto-Celtic expansion

SCYTHIANS

DACIANS

BLACK SEA

Illyrian migrations

ILLYRIANS

Celtic expansion

THRACIANS

Celtic expansion

GALATIA
276 BC

AEGEAN SEA

GREEKS

Neolithic Europe

During the late Stone Age, immigrants to Europe settled along the network of rivers that cross the continent. These Neolithic people were farmers, and their society amalgamated with the indigenous hunter-gatherer peoples they encountered. By the third millennium BC these farmers had developed into a society capable of working in metal, and had established the cultural framework that would characterize Bronze Age civilization.

Below: The best known and most widely visited stone circle in Europe is Stonehenge, in Wiltshire, England, built approximately 5,000 years ago.

Knowledge of farming was brought into southeastern Europe by migrants about 6000 BC, possibly by people looking for a refuge from the soil exhaustion or climate change in the Middle East. During the following millennium, farming spread westward into central Europe and beyond. The most widely used arteries for migration were the Danube and Rhine rivers, a series of waterways that pass through some of the richest agricultural land in Europe.

These farmers brought new practices and techniques with them, or adapted older ones to suit the climatic conditions of Europe. These included their own distinctive methods of pottery manufacture, tool-making, and construction. All of these had developed into identifiable forms, distinct from their earlier non-European styles. These Paleolithic people were augmented by further waves of Eastern incomers during the early Neolithic, from about 4000 BC onward.

Celts and the Iron Age

The terms "Stone Age," "Bronze Age," and "Iron Age" were created by Danish academics during the 19th century, who used them as a means of dating their museum collections, and the terms are still widely used as a form of reference. The more modern the era, the more accurately defined its chronological brackets become. The "Iron Age" is generally acknowledged to have lasted from around 700 BC until around the mid-first century BC in France, the mid-first century AD in England, and the fifth century AD in the regions encompassing the Celtic Fringe (principally Ireland and Scotland). This "Iron Age" period closely parallels the era of the Celts, and although the end of the Iron Age varied from place to place, for the purposes of this study the Scottish-Irish terminus will be adopted.

These ages, periods, and eras are really little

external enemies.

About 2500 BC, a distinct cultural group emerged, and their roots have been tentatively traced to the Iberian peninsula. These were known as the "Beaker" people, from the distinctive bell-shaped beaker or drinking vessel found in their gravesites. This was often buried alongside weapons, such as flint-tipped arrows and occasionally small metal daggers. A second group emerging about the same time were the "Battle-ax" people. Once again, the people were named after distinctive objects found in their graves. These people buried their dead individually, under earthen mounds, a tradition that may have originated in the steppes of the Ukraine. A stone battle-ax was often found in the graves. Eventually the two groups would unite, creating a new European society capable of metalworking; a people who would usher in a new cultural age in the continent.

Above: At Carnac in Brittany, France standing stones were placed in a series of concentric circles.

more than convenient slots in which to place archaeological and historical information. To the pre-Celtic or Celtic peoples of Europe, the boundaries between the eras passed without notice.

The people who inhabited the European continent during the Neolithic period were farmers who still relied on hunting to augment their diet. Since agricultural techniques were primitive, land development was limited to the most fertile areas, primarily along the banks of rivers. Subsequent waves of Eastern migrants created a population increase that led to tension. Archaeological evidence suggests that during the later Neolithic period, some villages were fortified for the first time, a sure sign that these European farmers felt threatened by

Bronze Age Europe

The introduction of metal-working technology into the European continent altered the status quo. Regions that could supply the raw materials needed to produce bronze weapons, domestic items, and tools prospered. Trade links developed between these areas that reached as far as the Middle East. As these cultures prospered, Bronze Age society became more stratified, and grave artifacts provide evidence of an emergent aristocracy of warriors and chieftains.

Below: One of the standing stones in the Ring of Brodgar, Orkney. These stones formed part of an interrelated network of stone circles in the area.

These are the people who left behind them the incredible legacies of Skara Brae in the Orkney Isles (a well-preserved Neolithic village), and the monument of Stonehenge, along with many other stone circles. Evidently their society was sufficiently advanced to undertake complex construction projects. Scholastic research suggests that the initial spread of the Indo-European language throughout the continent took place during this period, a linguistic root for the Celtic tongues, as well as for Greek and Latin.

By about 2000 BC, these people began to produce metallic objects cast from a copper alloy, ushering in the start of the Bronze Age in Europe. This new technology spread rapidly throughout the continent, making it hard to identify exactly how or where bronze-working first appeared. Although its introduction in the Middle East resulted in a more spectacular change of social and cultural life, unlike the Levant, Europe had all the copper and tin it needed. During the second millennium BC, areas such as central Europe and southern England profited from the supply of raw materials, and trade links developed throughout the continent.

The three cultures

In central Europe, the Bronze Age has become identified with three successive cultures. The first was the Únêtice culture, which emerged about 1500 BC. The culture centered around the metal producing regions of Moravia, a center for trade as well as production of bronze objects. Únêtice period merchants initiated trade between Europe and the Mycenean culture of the eastern Mediterranean.

The Tumulus culture became the dominant society in central Europe about 1200 BC, a people characterized by an increasing social stratification between chieftains and the general population, and in a spread of political and trading links through parts of Europe and into the Mediterranean. While they replaced the earlier Únêtice culture, and were based in the same general geographic area, the Tumulus people appear to have been more warlike than their predecessors.

Grave remains provide evidence of the importance of beaten bronze arms and armor, some of which was clearly ceremonial rather than functional. There is also evidence that they were more expansionist than the Únêtice people, as Tumulus-type graves have been identified over much of central Europe. This indicates a level of military activity that was absent from earlier European societies. Archaeological evidence shows that at about the same time many settlements became heavily fortified, with completely encircling walls and ditches. Part of this military activity, political expansion, and evidence of an increasingly stratified society may be linked to a more widespread disruption of society.

At this time, powerful Mediterranean civilizations such as those of the Myceneans and Hittites were almost completely destroyed, and while some historians blame social and economic factors, others suggest military disruption from barbarian raiders from the north and northwest. In Europe, a similar upheaval seems to have taken place, although its effects were less spectacular. While the reasons for this remain unexplained, the result was the decline of the Tumulus culture, and the emergence of a new central European society, known as the Urnfield culture.

This society was the direct ancestor of the Celtic civilization, and historians have referred to it as being "proto-Celtic." The Urnfield people emerged during the first centuries of the millennium bearing all of the social and cultural attributes of the "true" Celtic cultures that would succeed them. All they lacked was the technological ability to produce iron—the primary identifying feature of the early Celts.

Above: Remains of the Neolithic village of Skara Brae, Orkney (c.3,000 BC). It was uncovered by a storm in 1850.

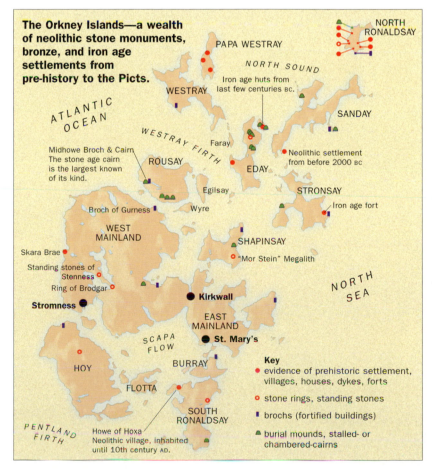

The Orkney Islands—a wealth of neolithic stone monuments, bronze, and iron age settlements from pre-history to the Picts.

NORTH RONALDSAY

PAPA WESTRAY

NORTH SOUND

Iron age huts from last few centuries BC.

WESTRAY

SANDAY

ATLANTIC OCEAN

WESTRAY FIRTH

Faray

Midhowe Broch & Cairn The stone age cairn is the largest known of its kind.

ROUSAY

EDAY

Neolithic settlement from before 2000 BC

Egilsay

STRONSAY

Broch of Gurness

Wyre

Iron age fort

WEST MAINLAND

SHAPINSAY

Skara Brae

"Mor Stein" Megalith

Standing stones of Stenness

Ring of Brodgar

NORTH SEA

Kirkwall

Stromness

EAST MAINLAND

St. Mary's

SCAPA FLOW

HOY

BURRAY

FLOTTA

SOUTH RONALDSAY

PENTLAND FIRTH

Howe of Hoxa Neolithic village, inhabited until 10th century AD.

Key
- evidence of prehistoric settlement, villages, houses, dykes, forts
- stone rings, standing stones
- brochs (fortified buildings)
- burial mounds, stalled- or chambered-cairns

The Proto-Celts

During the first millennium BC the "Urnfield" culture emerged as the dominant society of central Europe. These people were seen as the predecessors of the Celts, and their society has therefore been described as "proto-Celtic." The only difference between these people and the Celts of the Hallstatt era is that the latter developed the ability to produce iron. This technological achievement ushered in both the Iron Age and the dawn of the Celtic world.

The Urnfield culture emerged about 850 BC, and its similarities to the "Celtic" culture of two centuries later are striking. Place-names suggest a linguistic connection between the two cultures, and it appears that the two societies were based on the same social, military, and political structures. The Urnfield people differed from the Tumulus society that preceded them by their burial methods. Their dead were cremated, then placed in urns and buried in

Below: The reconstructed interior of a Celtic dwelling, showing a central hearth and domestic ware.

designated areas; level sites that lacked the mound that gave the Tumulus people their name. It has been suggested that this new form of burial was introduced into the European continent by an influx of people from the east, but it now appears more likely that the development was a result of internal change, probably the result of a shift in religious belief. Although the society was identified by its burial methods, its principal characteristic was expansion through military conquest.

The Urnfield people produced a battle-winning weapon; a long, heavy, straight-bladed sword designed for cutting or slashing. Together with the armor, helmets, and other pieces of military equipment that have survived, they point toward an increased emphasis on warfare. Settlements became more heavily fortified, and the first evidence of hilltop fortifications using ditches, palisades, and timber and stone walls can be traced to this time.

This increase in military activity was partly a result of an increased level of bronze production in central Europe, a result of improved mining and metalworking techniques. Archaeologists have been able to determine where objects were produced, and to identify the differences between local centers of production. There is also some evidence of specialization, with some areas becoming known for the production of weapons, some for bronze sheets or domestic ware, and others for decorative objects. Agricultural implements such as sickles and plows also suggest an improvement in agricultural production. If agricultural techniques improved, and this was combined with the introduction of methods such as crop rotation and animal husbandry, then living standards would improve and population would increase.

The crucial step forward

The development of iron-working technology took place about 700 BC, marking the transition between the Urnfield culture and the civilization known as the Hallstatt culture. While the former

has been identified as "proto-Celtic," the latter was truly Celtic in nature. Together with its successor, the La Tène culture, the two periods mark the span of the Celtic age, a time that almost exactly mirrored the era known as the Iron Age.

There is a danger in making too great a distinction between peoples of the late Bronze Age and those of the early Iron age. Both peoples occupied the same geographical area in central Europe, and exhibited the same patterns of society, culture, and political structure. The only essential difference was that the Hallstatt culture Celts used tools, weapons, domestic items, and equipment made of iron. In the past historians tended to overlook the evident transition from one culture to the other. Certainly, the advent of iron-working technology was a significant technological milestone. It allowed for the production of more reliable tools and weapons, it made these items more widely available and less expensive, and it revolutionized warfare and agricultural production.

Because iron was a far harder metal than bronze, both swords and plows became more efficient. The economic and military implications were that the people who controlled metal production or produced the best quality iron objects possessed a significant technological and military advantage over their rivals.

Above: This prestigious bronze funerary urn dating from the 8th to 7th centuries BC, was recovered from an Urnfield burial mound in France.

Hallstatt Culture

During the 19th century archaeologists uncovered a host of early Celtic graves in a remote valley in Austria. These discoveries were given the name of the modern village where the cemetery is located. The "Hallstatt" people came to represent the earliest identifiable Celtic society in Europe. Although they were the descendants of the Urnfield culture, these people had progressed to become an Iron Age society.

Hallstatt is a small, isolated community situated in a mountain valley in the Salzkammergut region of central Austria. This remote area was one of the earliest centers of salt mining, which led to a significant level of activity in the region from the eighth century BC onward.

The Austrian Alps of the Salzkammergut provided a rich source of readily available salt. Local names such as Hallstatt and Hallein were derived from *hall*, a word of Celtic origin that became linked with the later German term *salz* (salt). Salt was used to preserve food during the winter, and provided a valuable trading commodity for the local Hallstatt peoples. With the discovery in 1824 of the ancient cemetery at Hallstatt a string of excavations over the next century revealed the presence of some 2,000 graves and cremation remains dating from the eighth to the sixth centuries BC.

Like the Urnfield people who preceded them, the Hallstatt people cremated their dead, at least until the seventh century BC. About that time there seems to have been a return to the inhumation of the dead in wood-lined burial chambers, which reflected the earlier Tumulus civilization tradition. It has been suggested that this was prompted by a change in the nature of the early Celtic aristocracy. Horse harness fittings and bits were also found in grave sites from Eastern Europe to the British Isles.

Mysterious equestrian invaders

A steppe people known as the Cimmerians migrated west under pressure from the Scythians. It is considered possible that these people were absorbed by some of the late Bronze Age peoples of central Europe. Horse furnishings appeared in several warrior graves from the eighth century, including some of the Hallstatt sites. Contemporary engravings also depict sword-armed equestrian warriors. Historians now consider it possible that these eastern incomers became part of the "proto-Celtic" aristocracy. Almost one in four of the Hallstatt graves have been linked to a warrior aristocracy which possibly included the equestrian incomers. Bronze grave goods were frequently found in the richer graves, while those of aristocratic women contained bronze decorative objects, jewelry, and domestic items.

One distinctive characteristic of Hallstatt burials was the frequent presence of four-wheeled wagons on which the dead were placed. Similar wagons were found in early Celtic grave sites from Bohemia to Burgundy, and once again, they have become linked with the eastern equestrian warriors.

The Hallstatt graves represent a cross-section of society at a time when the ability to produce iron objects was transforming the civilizations of central Europe. They suggest a well-organized, socially stratified people, and the graves of workers and artisans

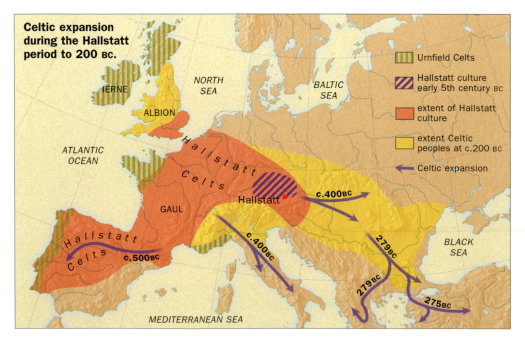

Celtic expansion during the Hallstatt period to 200 BC.

NORTH SEA

BALTIC SEA

IERNE

ALBION

ATLANTIC OCEAN

Hallstatt Celts

GAUL

Hallstatt

Hallstatt Celts

c.500BC

c.400BC

c.400BC

279BC

279BC

BLACK SEA

279BC

275BC

MEDITERRANEAN SEA

- Urnfield Celts
- Hallstatt culture early 5th century BC
- extent of Hallstatt culture
- extent Celtic peoples at c.200 BC
- Celtic expansion

provided as much information for archaeologists as did those of the warrior elite. The most recent graves at Hallstatt date from the early fifth century BC, and they provide evidence of a decline in wealth in the region. It appears that after 600 BC alternative sources were found for salt production, and Hallstatt was overtaken by other, more dynamic communities.

Iron-working and the assimilation of equestrian warriors from the East provided catalysts for further social and political change. The Hallstatt period is usually described as lasting from about 700 until 500 BC. It was followed by the later La Tène culture (*see pages 20–21*).

Since the discovery of the Hallstatt graves in 1824, numerous similar grave sites have been identified dating from the seventh century BC onward. These were scattered throughout central Europe, in Austria, southern Germany and in the western Czech Republic. This region has subsequently been identified as the original Celtic homeland. During the sixth century BC the nucleus of early Celtic power appears to have moved west into the Rhine basin, becoming centered in Switzerland, south-western Germany, and eastern France. This transition also marked the eclipse of the Hallstatt culture by that of La Tène. The Celts were now firmly established as one of Europe's most dynamic civilizations.

Above: A four-wheeled wagon from the early Hallstatt period, recovered from a grave site in Austria.

The Celtic Identity

Who were the Celts? From the first recorded links between the Mediterranean world and Celtic civilization the Celts have exuded an element of mystery. The term "Celtic" itself has obscure origins, and several theories have been proposed about where it came from. Apart from the archaeological evidence, everything we know about the Celts came from the Greeks and Romans. Known as the "Keltoi" or "Galatai" by the Greeks, and "Celtae" or "Galli" by the Romans, we don't even know what they called themselves. To this day, the Celts retain their mystery.

Right: The face and reverse side of a Celtic copy of a Greek sater of Philip II of Macedon, 3rd century BC. Around this time Celts from the Balkans to Belgium began minting Greek-style gold and silver coins.

The first historical mention of the Celts came from Homer, who mentioned them in a passage in the *Odyssey*, written in the ninth or eighth century BC.

We reached the deep-flowing ocean where the Cimmerians (Celts) have their land and their town. This people is hidden under clouds, in mists that the sun's bright rays have never pierced…

Homer heard of the Celts (or Cimmerians) from explorers, and placed the Celtic homeland somewhere to the north and west of Greece. There is some literary evidence that several Greeks ventured into the land of these mysterious barbarians. The eighth or seventh century BC Greek poet Hesiod described rivers and mountains in the Celtic homeland, and Herodotus in his *Histories* of 435 BC provided the first mention of the Celts as a distinct people. His description was clearly based on the writings and maps drawn up by the Greek geographer Hecataeus.

Homer, Hesiod, and Herodotus were among the first writers to give the Celtic peoples an identity.

According to Herodotus, the Celts lived in the territory between the source of the Danube in modern southern Germany and the Pillars of Hercules, or Gibraltar. Modern archaeological evidence supports these boundaries. The Celts have also been linked with the Hyperboreans, a mythical people who inhabited the lands to the north of Greece. As more links were forged between the cultures of the Mediterranean world and the Celtic world, more information became available to Greek and then Roman historians. Herodotus claimed:

The river Iser [Rhône] rises among the Celts and the town of Pyrene and crosses the whole of Europe… the Celts are beyond the Pillars of Hercules [Gibraltar], next to the Cynetes [Portuguese], who live furthest west of all the peoples of Europe.

Carthaginian mariners came into contact with the Celts during the sixth and fifth centuries BC and the fifth century explorer Hamilco ventured as far north as the *Oestrymnides* (possibly the Orkney Islands). The sea was described as

being windless and full of sea monsters. A century later the Greek explorer Pytheas ventured as far as the Baltic sea, and delineated the western and northern boundaries of the European continent.

About the same period an increasing number

of Greek and Carthaginian merchant explorers encountered the Celtic peoples of the Mediterranean coast on a regular basis. Heododotus recounted the story of the Greek

merchant Colaeus who was driven into the Celtic port of Tartessus, in eastern Spain. He described how the local Celts were engaged in silver mining in the area. Trading links were soon established between the Greeks and the Spanish *Keltoi* (Celts).

Entomologists are still debating the roots of the name *Celt* or *Keltoi*. In his *Gallic Wars*, Julius Caesar claims that the Gauls (French Celts) are called Celts in their own language. In other words, the people called themselves Celtic, and the term was adopted by Mediterranean historians to describe the same people. Others have suggested the term came from the Indo-European word *quel*, meaning elevated (similar to the Latin *celsus*, which has the same meaning). This could refer to the role of the aristocracy in Celtic society, or it could be linked with their geographical location. Another suggestion is that the Indo-European term *kel-* (hidden) refers to their geographical isolation from the Mediterranean world.

Above: Celto-Greek dedication of a temple in Vaison, France indicates the cross-cultural references of the southern Celts.

La Tène Culture

During the fifth century BC, the Celts underwent a period of social, cultural, and political change. This era has been identified as the start of the La Tène period, named after the Swiss site that provided archaeologists with their first insight into the cultural wealth of the Celtic world in its heyday. An era of expansion during which Celtic civilization spread across much of Europe, it was also a period of artistic excellence. The La Tène culture marked the highpoint of Celtic civilization, and lasted until its destruction at the hands of the Romans.

Right: The "Prunay vase" (c.400–350 BC) is embellished with a typical early La Tène period abstract swirling decoration painted onto the ceramic surface.

Like Hallstatt in Austria, the small Swiss village of La Tène gave its name to a cultural period in Celtic history because of objects discovered there in the 19th century. The village lies on the shore of Lake Neuchâtel, and while Hallstatt was known for its grave finds, La Tène was noted as the site that produced thousands of votive offerings. For the most part these were decorative metal objects which were thrown into the lake as offerings to the gods.

During the 19th century the lake was partly drained, revealing the lake bed scattered with votive objects. Evidently La Tène was an important religious site, although there were other locations scattered throughout the Celtic world. Taken in conjunction with the Hallstatt finds, the La Tène objects helped to provide a chronological framework for the development of Iron Age Celtic society.

The La Tène period has been divided into three phases; the first—La Tène I—from the early fifth century BC to about the mid-third century BC. La Tène II succeeded it, and lasted until the late second century BC, with La Tène III continuing until the Roman conquest during the mid-first century BC in Gaul and the mid-first century AD in southern Britain. (Since Scotland and Ireland were never conquered by the Romans, La Tène III continued until the fifth century AD in those regions).

The entire period saw the Celtic world at its height, and La Tène period artifacts have been discovered as far apart as Scotland and Turkey. During this period the La Tène Celts came into contact with the Greeks, Carthaginians, and the Romans.

Coming of age

The period also saw a significant expansion of the Celtic homeland, which originally encompassed parts of the Czech Republic, Hungary, Austria, Switzerland, and southern Germany. By the time of the Roman conquests the Celts had expanded into western Spain, most of France, Holland, the Danube valley, and all of the British Isles, including Ireland. Nevertheless, it would be a mistake to even begin to conceive of the Celtic world as a unified body. Celtic society was a tribal one, and this lack of any permanent central control was a leading factor in the eventual collapse of the Celtic civilization.

Burials remained an important aspect of Celtic society, just as they had been during the Hallstatt period. These burial sites provide archaeologists with a unique insight into Celtic society, where a stratified aristocracy, a warrior cult, social gatherings, and religion all played a significant part. The graves also reveal a wealth of information about everyday life in the La Tène period; iron-working, the decorative arts, cloth manufacture, pottery, and woodwork are all present in funerary remains. But although one period followed the other, the La Tène is distinctive in terms of the artistic legacy left behind by the Celts. La Tène was characterized by its unique artistic style, and stunning decorative items have survived to show the cultural wealth of the La Tène artisans and smiths.

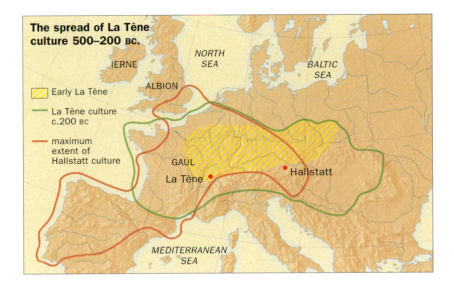

The spread of La Tène culture 500–200 BC.

Early La Tène

La Tène culture c.200 BC

maximum extent of Hallstatt culture

IERNE

NORTH SEA

BALTIC SEA

ALBION

GAUL

La Tène

Hallstatt

MEDITERRANEAN SEA

As such, the La Tène era marked the high point of Celtic civilization, artistically, militarily, socially, and economically. Much of this book will involve an analysis of the La Tène civilization, and its impact on the people who encountered it.

Left: Pair of La Tène shields made from a mix of bronze and iron, 4th century BC, found at Saint-Jean-sur Tourbe, France.

The Archaeological Evidence

While Mediterranean historians and geographers from the sixth century BC onward mentioned the Celts in their histories, these accounts provide little hard evidence about early Celtic society. From the early 19th century, archaeologists have helped to fill in the gaps, and excavations in Celtic fortresses, towns, religious sites, and graveyards have provided valuable information.

Below: Funerary objects recovered from burial sites such as this have provided a wealth of evidence of early Celtic culture. "Hell Stone" Tumulus chambered cairn, near Portesham, Dorset, England.

Since the discovery of the Hallstatt period Celtic cemetery in 1824, burial sites have provided a wealth of knowledge. Sensational new finds are still being made throughout Europe, and fresh investigations are frequently undertaken to discover new information from previously explored sites. In Orkney, off the north of Scotland, archaeologists are currently excavating a Pictish settlement. In southern Germany, the recent excavation of an early Iron Age (Hallstatt period) burial chamber at Hochdorf near Stuttgart is yielding forensic information using technology that was unavailable to earlier generations of archaeologists.

Celtic sites are as varied as they are numerous. At Manching and Heuneberg in southern Germany archaeologists excavated the remains of fortified settlements, while a similar French site at Mont Beuvray revealed a Gallic fort of the late La Tène period. Religious sites have also been discovered, including Roquepertuse and Entremont in the south of France, Snettingham in England and Fellbach-Schmitten in southern Germany.

One of the more gruesome finds was made in a cave in Bohemia. While parts of the cave contained funerary artifacts dating from the Hallstatt period, the rest contained human remains. Over 40 decapitated human bodies had been deposited in the cave together with animal remains. One female skull had even been fashioned into a drinking vessel, presumably for ceremonial use.

At Roquepertuse in southern central France, archaeologists uncovered a Celto-Ligurian sanctuary linked to a nearby hilltop settlement (*oppida*), the capital of the Salluvii tribe. Stone columns had niches carved into them which were filled with human

skulls, and other stones were carved or decorated with depictions of animals, humans, gods, and monsters. The area was also scattered with small statues of gods, which were probably votive

offerings of some sort. The sanctuary was once a long church-like building constructed on a series of raised terraces.

Family sacrifices

Religious ceremonies took place at the site for at least a century. It appears the sanctuary was destroyed by the Romans during the second century BC. Unlike the Bohemian cave, no sacrificial items were found, and archaeologists are still debating the significance of the skulls. Similar finds from other French or Belgian Celtic sites suggest that they may have been linked to some form of hero cult, and were not funerary remains.

The burial mound at Magdalenenberg in the Black Forest region of southern Germany is situated in the center of a region that was exploited by the early Celts for its iron ore. Measuring over 100 yards in diameter it appears to have been constructed about 550 BC, and plundered shortly afterward, probably before 500 BC. Similar burial mounds exist from the north of Scotland to Hungary, and the Magdalenenberg site is little different from the

majority of these mounds, apart from its size.

Archaeological material recovered from the larger of these burial mounds suggests that they were used to house the remains of chieftains and their families. Some of these family members may even have been sacrificed at the same time as the chieftain was interred, as has been suggested in the case of the sixth-century BC burial at Hohmichele in southern Germany.

In several other cases the dead chieftain was interred together with symbols of his wealth and status. At Hochdorf in Germany a tomb dating from about 530 BC was lavishly furnished with a wooden funerary wagon, a cauldron of mead and drinking horns, weaponry, and a beautifully decorated bronze couch, on which the body was laid to rest. Four-wheeled funerary wagons (biers) were a common inclusion in these tombs from the proto-Celtic period until the end of the La Tène culture.

Above: Dun Conor, a Celtic fortress in the west of Ireland, was a stronghold, a royal palace, and a religious center.

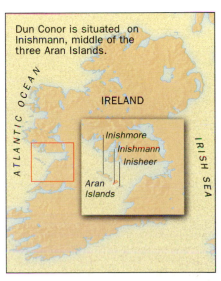

Dun Conor is situated on Inishmann, middle of the three Aran Islands.

ATLANTIC OCEAN

IRELAND

Inishmore
Inishmann
Inisheer

Aran
Islands

IRISH SEA

ATLANTIC OCEAN

Dun Aengus is a Celtic hill fort on the edge of the cliffs of Inishmore, westernmost of the three Aran Islands off the Atlantic coast of Ireland

Clickhimin Broch, one of the many Pictish forts that dot the Shetland and Orkney islands.

NORTH SEA

The skulls of Celtic warriors adorn the columns and lie arranged on the ground of the shrine at Roquepertuse in southern France (*see page 171*).

A Celtiberian four-wheeled funerary wagon, found near Mérida, Spain.

MEDITERRANEAN SEA

Chapter 2

The Celtic Peoples of Europe

About 3000 BC the Stone Age farmers and hunters of central Europe found themselves under threat from a series of warrior tribes. Known as the proto-Celts, over the next thousand years these Indo-European warriors dominated, then amalgamated with the less aggressive aboriginals they encountered. By 1800 BC proto-Celts migrated into what is now western Europe, where the process was repeated. Within two centuries their influence had spread into much of what is now Spain, France, and Germany.

Archaeologists recognize that a distinctive Celtic culture had evolved by 1000 BC; a Bronze Age society known as the "Urnfield" Celts, named after the burial grounds and cremation urns which identified them. By 800 BC these Celts had begun to spread into southern France and Spain. This migration continued into the early fifth century BC, when iron weapons found by archaeologists marked the start of the Iron Age. During the next century Celtic influence expanded throughout Spain, but an Iberian counter-migration into eastern Spain separated these Iberian Celts from the rest of Celtic Europe.

At the same time a second movement, known as the Celtic Hallstatt culture began to spread its influence westward from its original roots in Austria. The Hallstatt culture marks the first period of true Celtic domination in Europe, lasting from the seventh to the early fifth centuries BC. About 500 BC, Celtic peoples reached England, and over the next century their influence expanded into Scotland, Wales, and Ireland. A similar migration spread east along the River Danube, and reached the Black Sea by the late fifth century.

By this time the Iron Age Celtic culture known as La Tène had superseded the earlier Celtic cultural movements. The La Tène (or Gallic) Celts marked the high-water mark of Celtic expansion, although tribes raided northern Greece and Italy intermittently over the next three centuries. The La Tène Celts lacked any centralized control, but rather formed a loose amalgamation of tribes sharing a common culture. This loose-knit confederation continued to dominate most of Europe until the first century BC, when Julius Caesar brought about a collapse of the entire Celtic world.

ADRIATIC SEA

BLACK SEA

AEGEAN SEA

A Celtic horde defeated the Greeks at Themopylae, and then swept on across the Hellespont to populate central Asia Minor in the region of Galatia.

The Gauls

From the start of the La Tène period, the Celts of Iron Age Europe migrated westward into what is now France. This became Gaul, the heart of Celtic Europe. Strong cultural and economic bonds united the Gallic tribes for over five centuries, although they were never a single political entity. However, though capable of resisting the westward incursions of Germanic tribes, the Gauls were unable to repel the power of Rome.

T oward the end of the Hallstatt period, a westward migration of Celts crossed the Rhine. The principal period of Celtic expansion took place during the fifth century BC, when bands of Celts entered Italy, France, and Spain. This expansion was partially caused by fresh waves of European immigrants pressing in from the east and north. The Cimbri (a proto-Celtic culture) and the Teutones migrated toward Celtic homelands from the north, while further to the east other Germanic tribes arrived in central Europe. There is some evidence that many of these Germanic tribes already had some form of cultural contact with the Hallstatt Celts before they reached what is today Germany.

The Cimbri attacked the Celtic Boii tribe in Bohemia, then met the Roman army and defeated it at the Battle of Noreia (113 BC). Further to the west, the Cimbri and the Teutones united to drive the indigent Celtic tribes out of the Rhine and Danube basins, then entered Gaul. They then swung south into Italy, where they were finally defeated by the Romans at Vercellae (101 BC). The effect of these Germanic migrations was that the River Rhine became the effective border between the Celtic and Germanic tribes.

When the Hallstatt period Celts began to migrate westward into Gaul from the fifth century BC, they came as settlers rather than as invaders. Initially the northern and central regions of Gaul were the principal regions of Celtic settlement. The coastal regions to the west and south remained largely unsettled by the Celts, and as late as the first century BC, the Mediterranean coast (Provence) was seen as an essentially non-Gallic region. From the sixth century BC the Phoenicians had established a

Right: The Kilburn Sword, 300–200 BC, found in a burial site in Kilburn, East Yorkshire, England. The polished bronze front plate was decorated in La Tène style "sword" scroll pattern.

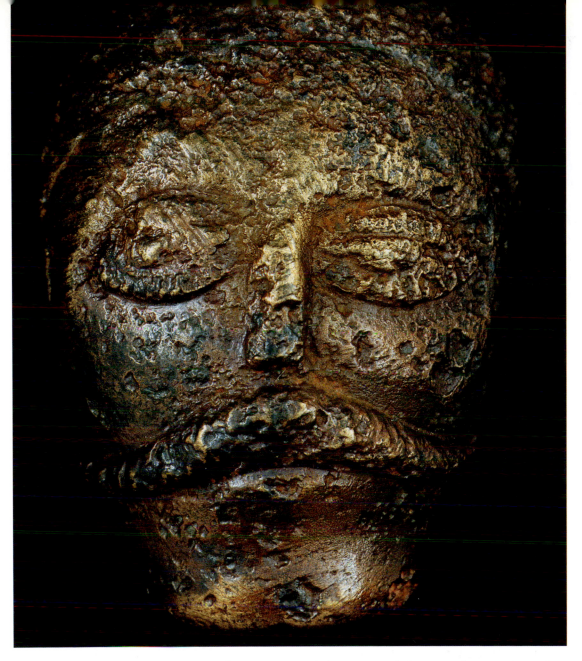

trading colony at Massalia (later Massilia, or Marseilles), and the local Gauls developed closer ties with their Mediterranean neighbors than they did with their Gallic neighbors further inland. Otherwise, the Celts dominated almost all of Gaul, the most notable exception being Armorica (Brittany), which maintained much of its pre-Celtic structure until the Roman invasions of the mid-first century BC.

The Gallic way of life

The typical Gallic tribal area constituted a river valley, with its low pastureland and high grazing slopes for livestock and timber. Small tribal groupings formed alliances with others, creating larger political and social groupings. This was not always a peaceful union. The sprawling tribal territories of the third century BC onward were often created gradually, as a result of conquest or marriage, annexation, or treaty. Although still based along Gaul's river systems, these larger

tribal areas extended to cover large sections of the Gallic countryside.

The rivers themselves provided avenues for communication between these larger tribes (or tribal confederations), as well as formed the core of the tribal homelands. The Aedui occupied the Saône and Loire valleys, the Sequani the Doubs and part of the Saône valleys, the Parisii the Seine valley, and the Lemovices the lands surrounding the Garonne. Smaller tribal divisions remained, and even these political units appear to have been sub-divided into regional tribal units. Gaul was a patchwork of political units, and although Gallic society was a relatively stable one, its lack of political unity allowed the Romans to "divide and conquer." By the time the Gauls succeeded in uniting in the face of the common threat, it was too late to save their civilization.

Gallic Unity

Julius Caesar began his account of the Gallic Wars between Gaul and Rome by describing the political and geographical nature of the Celtic state. When he recounted that Gaul was divided into many parts, he referred to the political patchwork that prevented any concerted military opposition to himself and his legions. Gallic society was administered by a series of local, civic, and tribal councils. These unions were never permanent, and reflect shifts in tribal influence rather than any serious attempt to unify the Celtic world.

Facing below: The typical Gallic tribal area constituted a river valley, with its low pastureland and high grazing slopes for livestock and timber.

During the La Tène period, Gaul was divided into approximately 16 tribal areas. Some of these were not truly Celtic, such as the Ligurian and Saluvii people of northern Italy, or the Veneti or Aquitani on the Atlantic coast, who apparently retained many aspects of their pre-Celtic roots well into the late Iron Age.

Around the start of the fourth century BC the Ligurians entered into an alliance with the neighboring Gallic tribes, forming the Celto-Ligurian league. Perceiving this alliance as a threat, the Romans were prompted into military action to safeguard the northern borders of Roman Italy. Roman influence also spread into Provence as a result of Celto-Ligurian threats to the safety of Massallia. About 125 BC the Romans annexed the Mediterranean coast of Gaul and founded the province of Provence. This in turn would provide a springboard for Caesar's conquest of the rest of Gaul.

Further to the north, a fresh wave of tribal refugees, known as the Belgae, arrived in northern Gaul during the fourth and third centuries BC. They were seeking refuge from the Germanic tribes, and after crossing the Rhine the tribe carved out a new homeland in northwestern Gaul. Caesar reported that they considered themselves to be Teutons rather than Gauls. They also proved to be some of the toughest opponents Rome would encounter in Gaul. The Belgae also established settlements in southeastern Britain, and there is substantial evidence of a busy cross-Channel trade and cultural exchange that predated the Roman conquests of Gaul and Britain.

Tribal organization

Gaul's tribal groups have been described by a succession of Roman historians, who referred to them as *nationes* (nations or peoples), as well as by other less appropriate appellations, such as *civitates* (cities). These in turn were sub-divided into *pagi* (*pagus*, a rural district or portion of a *civitate*), reflecting the smaller tribal units which had amalgamated into larger tribal entities during the course of the fourth and third centuries BC. For example, the Aedui tribe of central Gaul was sub-divided into six *pagi*, the leading one being the Bibracte. These sub-divisions were based around sub-chiefs or lesser tribal rulers, who owed allegiance to the high chiefs.

It appears that these sub-units also

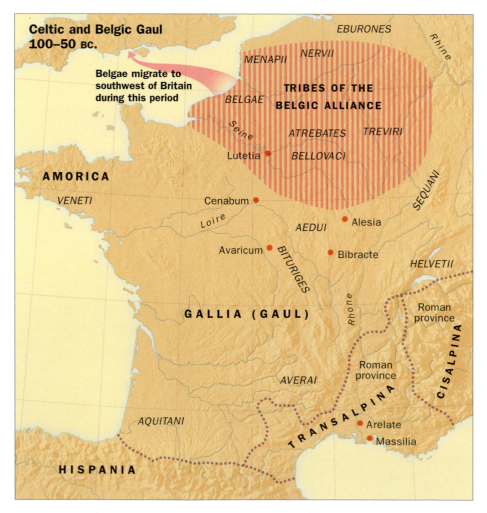

Celtic and Belgic Gaul 100–50 BC.

Belgae migrate to southwest of Britain during this period

EBURONES

MENAPII · NERVII

BELGAE · **TRIBES OF THE BELGIC ALLIANCE**

Seine · ATREBATES · TREVIRI

Lutetia · BELLOVACI

Rhine

SEQUANI

AMORICA

VENETI

Cenabum

Loire

AEDUI · Alesia

Avaricum · BITURIGES · Bibrace

HELVETII

Rhone

Roman province

GALLIA (GAUL)

CISALPINA

Roman province

AVERAI

TRANSALPINA

AQUITANI · Arelate · Massilia

HISPANIA

formed their own military units, and the smaller groups were then united into larger tribal armies. The larger units (*nationes*) usually had their capital in one of the regional *pagi*. Some *pagi* became large towns that still exist today; Paris the capital of the Parisii, Trier the capital of the Treveri, and Chartres of the Carnuti. These also became major trading centers, as well as providing markets for Celtic artisans and metalsmiths. The tribal capitals housed the courts of the high kings or chieftains, such as the king Ambigat of the Bituriges, who was mentioned in Caesar's *Gallic Wars*.

On occasion these tribal chiefs or kings formed alliances among themselves. During the third century BC the Bituriges from central Gaul dominated the neighboring Gallic tribes, uniting them into a larger confederation. A century later the Arverni were the dominant tribe, allying themselves with the Allobroges and the Aedui to form another large tribal confederation. By the time of the Roman invasion of Gaul in 59 BC, the Aedui, the Sequani, and the Arverni had broken another alliance, and were vying with each other for supremacy.

Caesar exploited this with ruthless efficiency. In a last ditch attempt to repel the invaders, the Gauls united under Vercingetorix of the Arverni, but the Gallic leader was outmaneuvered and defeated by Caesar. Following the Gallic defeat at Alesia in 52 BC (*see pages 88–89*), Gaul became a Roman province, and would remain under Roman domination for five centuries. Although the Gauls adapted and even prospered under Rome, the torch of Celtic culture was extinguished. From that point on, the Celtic world was effectively confined to the British Isles.

Right: Gallo-Roman Bronze statue of Greek inspiration depicting a dying Gaul. The lack of political unity among Celtic tribes meant that many would indeed die at Roman hands.

The Bretons

In their invasion of Gaul, the Romans conquered the remote western Breton peninsula, which became Armorica. Its geographical isolation in the province meant that it was never Romanized to the same extent as the other Gallic regions. Following the fall of the Western Roman Empire in the fifth century AD, Armorica provided a haven for Celtic refugees, fleeing the Saxon and Visigothic invaders. By the sixth century AD the region had become Brittany, a Celtic enclave. Traces of this Celtic heritage can still be found today.

Below: Reconstructed Celtic Breton village of c.AD 1000 at Melrand, Brittany, France.

Five Gallic tribes lived in Brittany; the Venetii in the southwest, the Osismii to the north of them, with the Coriosolitae, Redones, and Nametes further to the east. Julius Caesar recorded that the Venetii were a maritime people, whose ships were exceptionally well-built. During the centuries of Roman rule, Armorica was administered in the same way as all the other Gallic provinces of the Roman Empire. The five Celtic tribal areas were divided into *civitates*, local administrative regions, and their capitals became Roman provincial centers: Vorigum (Carhaix) for the Osismii; Fanum Martis (Corseulles) for the Curiosolitae; Condate (Rennes) for the Redones; Namnetes (Nantes) for the Namnetes; and Darioritum (Vannes) for the Venetii. These settlements became bastions of Roman power, where Gallo-Romano chieftains helped Rome administer the region.

In AD 410, when the Romans left Britain, the local Romano-British militia were attacked by successive waves of Saxon barbarians. As the Saxons moved west, Romano-British refugees fled to Armorica in ever-increasing numbers. By 469 when the Emperor Anthemius raised an army to fight the Visigoths in Gaul, part of his force consisted of Britons, presumably recruited

from among these settlers. By this stage the name of the old Roman province had been replaced with that of the resurgent Celtic state, which provided a haven for Gauls and Britons alike.

From the mid-fifth century for two centuries, Brittany attracted a stream of Celtic settlers, and the population of the region swelled. Forests were cleared in the center of the peninsula to provide more arable land for the settlers. Trading links between Armorica and Britain, which had existed for centuries, helped bind southern Britain, Wales, and Brittany into a political and military union.

Slow war of attrition

Brittany was divided into three principal kingdoms; Domnonia, Cornouaille, and Bro Erech. Of these, little is known of the southern region of Cornouaille, but the northern Domnonia retained links with the British kingdom of Dumnonia, located directly across the English Channel. King Cunomorus of Domnonia was described in religious biographies of the period, as was his relationships with his Romano-British allies and his Frankish enemies. Bro Erech (the region of the ancient Venetii tribe) was formed from south-eastern territories captured from the Franks, and it formed a battleground between Celt and Frank for centuries. The history of Celtic Brittany was one of an almost constant struggle for survival. A succession of Frankish (French) invasions from the early sixth century increased the instability.

At the Treaty of Tours (567) the Church recognized that Brittany was a separate entity from the rest of Gaul, which by that stage had become a Frankish State. The Merovingian Franks failed to subdue the Bretons, but religious links were forged between the Frankish and Celtic states. Charlemagne (768–814) established a "Breton March," a form of demilitarized buffer zone after his invasion attempts were thwarted in 786. His successors used it as a base from which to launch a series of invasions that eventually overcame the last Breton resistance by the mid-ninth century AD. From that point on, Brittany became a semi-autonomous region of France, but its Celtic origins continued to influence Breton culture and society. Brittany was the last Celtic foothold

on the mainland of Europe. When its autonomy was lost, the torch of Celtic culture was passed to the nations of the "Celtic fringe."

Above: Remains of Breton farmstead at Melrand, Brittany, C.AD 1000.

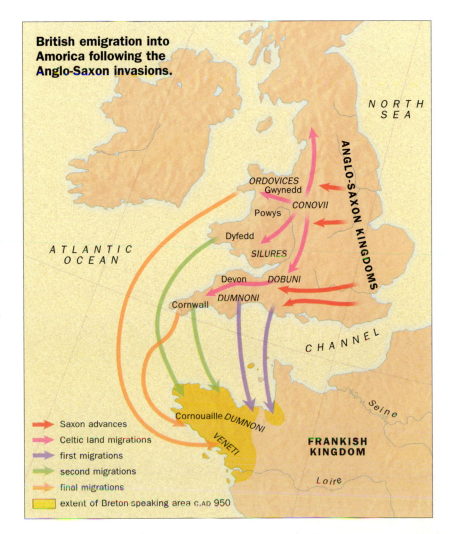

British emigration into Amorica following the Anglo-Saxon invasions.

NORTH SEA

ATLANTIC OCEAN

ORDOVICES
Gwynedd
CONOVII
Powys
Dyfedd
SILURES
Devon DOBUNI
DUMNONI
Cornwall

ANGLO-SAXON KINGDOMS

CHANNEL

Cornouaille DUMNONI
VENETI

FRANKISH KINGDOM

Seine

Loire

→ Saxon advances
→ Celtic land migrations
→ first migrations
→ second migrations
→ final migrations
☐ extent of Breton speaking area c.AD 950

31

The Iberian Celts

The Celts who migrated west and south during the early Iron Age eventually reached the Atlantic Coast of the Iberian Peninsula. Influxes of other tribes severed the link between these Celts and the rest of the Celtic world north of the Pyrenees, but the Iberian Celts maintained their identity. This vibrant Celtiberian culture survived in Spain until the people were finally defeated by the Romans during the second century BC.

Right: Bronze figurine of a woman found in Mérida, Spain, dating from 7th–4th centuries BC.

Around 2500 BC a new cultural group emerged, a culture whom archaeologists called the Beaker people, from the distinctive bell-shaped beakers or drinking vessels found in their collective gravesites. The Beaker people have been labeled as the forerunners of the proto-Celtic civilization known as the Urnfield culture. By the early Bronze Age the descendants of these people returned to the Iberian peninsula, although resistance from the Iberians of the eastern Iberian peninsula drove the Celts away from the Mediterranean coast.

By 550 BC the Iberians occupied half of the peninsula, including much of the Pyrenees, which effectively cut the Celts in Iberia off from their Celtic neighbors in Gaul. The remains of fortified settlements and scattered artifacts have been found in northern Spain dating from the

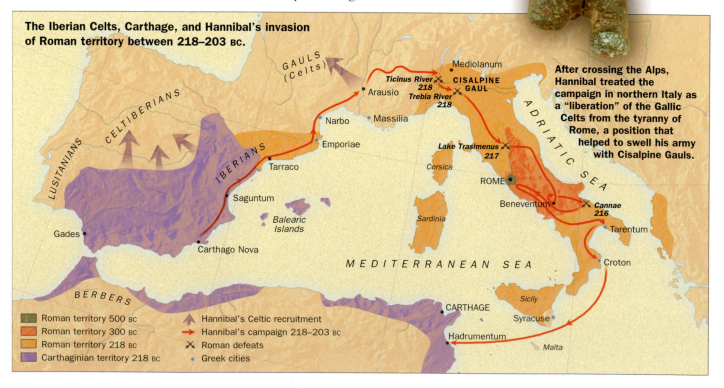

The Iberian Celts, Carthage, and Hannibal's invasion of Roman territory between 218–203 BC.

After crossing the Alps, Hannibal treated the campaign in northern Italy as a "liberation" of the Gallic Celts from the tyranny of Rome, a position that helped to swell his army with Cisalpine Gauls.

GAULS (Celts)

CELTIBERIANS

LUSITANIANS

IBERIANS

Mediolanum

Ticinus River 218 — CISALPINE GAUL

Arausio

Trebia River 218

Narbo — Massilia

Emporiae

Tarraco — Corsica

Saguntum

Balearic Islands

Sardinia

Gades

Carthago Nova

Lake Trasimenus 217

ADRIATIC SEA

ROME

Beneventum — Cannae 216

Tarentum

Croton

MEDITERRANEAN SEA

BERBERS

CARTHAGE

Sicily

Syracuse

Hadrumentum

Malta

- ⬛ Roman territory 500 BC
- ⬛ Roman territory 300 BC
- ⬛ Roman territory 218 BC
- ⬛ Carthaginian territory 218 BC
- ⬆ Hannibal's Celtic recruitment
- ➡ Hannibal's campaign 218–203 BC
- ✕ Roman defeats
- • Greek cities

fifth century BC. These are strikingly similar to La Tène sites in Gaul, indicating a cultural connection to the Celts in southern Gaul.

By the third century BC the Carthaginians had established colonies along the Mediterranean coast of Iberia, and during the Punic Wars (264–218 BC) the Carthaginians hired Celtiberian mercenaries to help them in their struggle against the Roman Republic. However, earlier in the third century BC, the Carthaginians had launched a series of campaigns against the Celtiberians, driving them inland, away from the Mediterranean coast. It was Hannibal who altered Carthaginian policy. He courted the Celts by sending embassies to their settlements and offering financial rewards in exchange for an alliance. By emphasizing that Rome rather than Carthage was the traditional enemy of the Celts, Hannibal succeeded in recruiting large numbers of Celtic warriors into his polyglot army.

When Hannibal crossed the Alps into northern Italy in 218 BC, half of his army was made up of Celts. The Celtiberians and southern Gauls continued to play a significant part in the Punic campaigns until the end of the Second Punic War. While Hannibal was occupied in Italy, other Roman armies campaigned in Iberia, driving the Carthaginians from the region. Following the final defeat of the Carthaginians at the Battle of Zama (203 BC), Rome was free to deal with the Celtiberians. However, a string of military embarrassments forced the Romans to adopt a placatory rather than a confrontational policy with them.

Celtic heritage survives

In 179 BC the Romans offered peace treaties and incentives if the Celts would agree to Roman political control. Many tribes refused, leading to a long campaign of subjugation. Celtiberian resistance was centered around the fortress town of Numantia, and a series of campaigns from 152 to 136 BC ended in either stalemate or Roman defeat. In 134 BC the Roman Senate sent Publius Cornelius Scipio with a fresh army to subdue the stronghold, and Numantia fell in 133 BC, after a bloody siege.

For the next 60 years Rome imposed its stamp on Celtiberian society, destroying the last vestiges of an independent Celtic land. By the time of Julius Caesar, the Celts of Iberia were no longer a political or social force, having become assimilated into the Roman province of Hispania. Despite this, some aspects of Celtic society and identity remained. Following the conquest of Gaul by Caesar in the mid-first century BC, a wave of Aquitanian refugees arrived in the former Celtiberian region of Galicia, in north-western Hispania. Today, this Celtic heritage is still evident in the Basque and Galatian regions of Spain, where the local population consider themselves to be the direct descendants of the Celtiberians.

Left: This bronze four-wheeled chariot and equestrian figure was a votive offering. It was found at Mérida in Spain, and dates from the 7th–4th centuries BC.

The Galatians

During the La Tène period not all of the Celtic migrations took place in a westerly direction. There was another trend of eastward expansion along the valley of the Danube River toward the Black Sea. By the fifth century BC Celtic settlements were established along the eastern Black Sea coast from the Crimean peninsula to Greece, and archaeologists have found some evidence of Celtic settlement in the Ukraine, Poland, and Russia. For the next two centuries, the Celts of Galatia would play a prominent role in Greece and Asia Minor.

Right: Celtic warriors about to descend on the combined Greek forces at the battle of Thermopylae.

Below: On this site in the Pass of Thermopylae in Greece, an army of Celtic invaders defeated an army of Greek defenders in 279 BC.

By the start of the third century BC the Celts had reached the Carpathian Mountains, and Macedonia, Thrace, and Greece were subjected to Celtic raids. Celtic warbands were also employed in the war between Athens and Sparta, and in 274 BC eastern Celtic warriors were reported in Egypt, where they fought as mercenaries. Decades before, in 334 BC, Alexander the Great had made a peace treaty with the Celts who lived along the northern borders of Macedonia, which allowed him to move his army into Asia Minor to fight the Persians without worrying about Celtic raids into Macedonia in his absence.

By the start of the third century BC the Celts had conquered Thrace, forcing thousands of refugees to flee south into Macedonia and Greece. While Gallic incursions into Italy threatened the survival of the Roman city-state, an even more significant Celtic threat was looming over Greece. In 279 BC a large Celtic army finally invaded Macedonia and defeated the Macedonians in two pitched battles. A section of the Celtic force led by King Brennus continued south into Greece where it defeated an army of the combined Greek city states at Thermopylae, then continued on to sack Delphi.

Against Greece and Rome

By the mid-third century Celts had established a state in the central plateau of Asia Minor. From that point on these people were known as Galatians, to distinguish them from the Gauls and Celts further to the west. Their society was a tribal one, with the Tolistoboii, Tectosages, and Trocmi tribes maintaining a social organization similar to that of their fellow Celtic tribesmen in Gaul. The Greeks collectively referred to these tribes as the Commonwealth of Galatia.

In 261 BC the Galatians defeated the Syrians in battle at Ephesus, ensuring Galatian independence for the next few decades. Celtic attempts to carve out their own empire at the expense of the Greek city states in Asia Minor were thwarted when the Galatians were defeated by Pergamon (241 BC). For the next century, Greeks, Syrians, and Galatians would vie with each other for military and political supremacy in Asia Minor.

The Romans became embroiled in Asia Minor during the first decades of the second century BC when the Senate declared war on Antiochus of Syria, who controlled much of Greece and Macedonia. The Syrians and their Galatian allies were defeated at the Battle of Magnesia (191 BC), and within two years a veteran Roman army was sent to invade Galatia. The Romans allied themselves with Pergamon, and between 189 and 187 BC the Galatians were crushed in a series of battles. The Romans gave Galatia to Pergamon as a subject province, although Rome effectively controlled both regions.

For the moment, Asia Minor was under Roman control. While the Romans were distracted by internal disputes the Galatians formed alliances with neighboring provinces such as Bithynia and Pontus to defeat

Pergamon, and by 123 BC a resurgent Galatian confederation had become the dominant power in Asia Minor. The first decades of the first century BC saw the rise of Pontus as a major power in the region. In 88 BC King Mithridates VI of Pontus massacred a gathering of Galatian leaders. The Galatians waged a bitter war for survival against Mithridates, and when the Pontic king declared war on Rome, the Celtic leader Deiotaros allied himself with the Romans. Although Mithridates was defeated, the alliance with Rome would cost the Galatians their freedom. By the mid-first century BC Galatia was a Roman province, and Celtic identity was submerged by the trappings of Roman civilization.

As for the Celts of Thrace and the Danube, they were overcome by the emergent Germano-Slavic society of the Dacians. By 60 BC the last identifiable Celtic tribe in eastern Europe was the Boii of Bohemia, and following their defeat by the Dacians, these people migrated into the territory occupied by the Helvetii in modern Switzerland. This migration would provide an excuse for Julius Caesar to invade Gaul. Celtic culture would eventually be crushed by Roman and German expansion.

Below: Portrait of Mithridates VI based on a contemporary coin. Mithridates treacherously murdered an embassy of Galatian Celts.

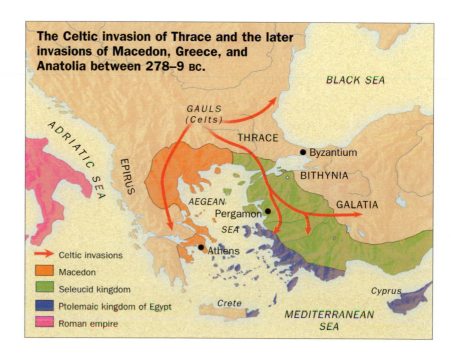

The Celtic invasion of Thrace and the later invasions of Macedon, Greece, and Anatolia between 278–9 BC.

BLACK SEA

GAULS (Celts)

ADRIATIC SEA

EPIRUS

THRACE

Byzantium

BITHYNIA

AEGEAN SEA

Pergamon

GALATIA

Athens

→ Celtic invasions
Macedon
Seleucid kingdom
Ptolemaic kingdom of Egypt
Roman empire

Crete

Cyprus

MEDITERRANEAN SEA

The Italian Celts

The Celtic migrations of the late Hallstatt period saw a southerly movement through the Alpine passes as well as a concurrent expansion across the River Rhine and down the Danube. This brought the Celts into the rich, fertile valley of the River Po, in northern Italy. For the next three centuries the Celts would influence the political development of Italy, and they would prove the fiercest and most persistent opponents of the Roman State.

Right: Paleovenetian votive plaque depicting a (probably Etruscan) warrior with shield and helmet dating from the 4th century BC, a time when the Celtic Venetii were penetrating into Etruscan territories.

About 475 BC the Celts defeated an Etruscan army in the Po valley, and by the end of the century most of the valley and the Italian peninsula north of the Apennine Mountains was in Celtic hands. In 396 BC Melpum, the last Etruscan stronghold north of the Apennines fell to the Celtic invaders. According to the Roman historian Pliny, this initial conquest and settlement of the Po valley was conducted by a confederation of the Boii, Insubres, and Senones tribes. The Celts now threatened the peninsula to the south.

The Etruscan city of Clusium in modern Tuscany was invaded by the Senones, led by their chieftain, Brennus. The Etruscans were allied to the Romans, and asked Rome for help in

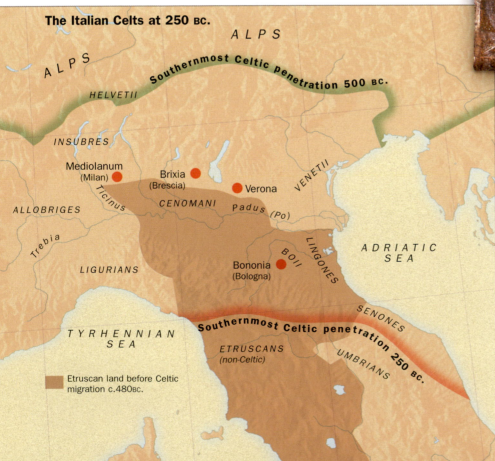

The Italian Celts at 250 BC.

ALPS

ALPS

Southernmost Celtic penetration 500 BC.

HELVETII

INSUBRES

Mediolanum (Milan)

Brixia (Brescia)

Verona

Ticinus

CENOMANI

Padus (Po)

VENETII

ALLOBRIGES

Trebia

BOII

LINGONES

ADRIATIC SEA

LIGURIANS

Bononia (Bologna)

SENONES

Southernmost Celtic penetration 250 BC.

TYRHENNIAN SEA

ETRUSCANS (non-Celtic)

UMBRIANS

Etruscan land before Celtic migration c.480BC.

repulsing the invaders. Brennus correctly saw the Romans as a more significant threat to the Senones than the Etruscans, and he duly bypassed Clusium and marched on Rome. At Allia (390 BC) Brennus defeated the Roman army, then sacked Rome. Only the Capitol was spared, its fortress-like walls proving too difficult for the Gauls to storm.

The Senones occupied the ruins of Rome for several months until the Senators besieged inside the Capitol paid them to withdraw. According to Roman historians, when the Romans complained that the ransom of 100 pounds of gold was being weighed on unbalanced Celtic scales, Brennus threw his sword on the weights, exclaiming *"Vae victis!"* (woe to the vanquished). The Romans paid their ransom of 100 Celtic pounds as well as the weight of a Celtic longsword.

Rome secures its frontiers

Rome's humiliation played a significant part in Romano-Celtic relations from that point on, and the Romans remained fearful of the Celts until the conquest of Gaul in the mid-first century BC. Gallic raids into the Latin state continued until 349 BC, when the Romans were able to defeat the Gauls, forcing the Senones to sign a peace treaty that temporarily safeguarded Rome from further attack.

By this time the Senones had settled near Picenum on the Adriatic coast, while their fellow Gallic allies remained north of the Apennines. The Romans saw this southern spur of Celtic land as a direct threat to the safety of Rome, especially when the Senones allied themselves with Rome's Italian enemies. In 298 BC a joint Celtic-Samnite army was victorious at Camerium, only to suffer a defeat at Roman hands two years later. Another allied victory was not decisive enough to prevent a Roman army capturing Picenum and burning the territory of the Senones. This proved a costly victory, as it led to the remaining Celtic tribes of the Po valley entering the fray as allies of the Etruscans.

A Roman victory over the Etruscans in 283 BC led to the complete conquest of Etruscan lands, which pushed the surrounding Celts into agreeing to a peace treaty. This time the Romans had the advantage. They controlled all of the Italian peninsula south of the Apennine mountains, including the territory of the Senones. For the next few decades they built forts to protect their northern borders, and expelled all the Celts.

In 225 BC, with the Romans poised to conquer the Po valley, the Celts sought help from their northern cousins. The combined Celtic force launched a preemptive strike across the Appenines and defeated the Romans at Clusium, but was then itself destroyed in battle at Telamon (224 BC). The Po valley lay at the mercy of the Romans. Aided by Gallic allies, the Celts resisted for another two years, but by 222 BC the Romans were firmly in control of all of Italy south of the Alps.

The situation changed following the outbreak of the Second Punic War between Rome and Carthage. In 218 BC Hannibal crossed the Alps at the head of a Carthaginian army containing thousands of Celtic mercenaries (*see page 32*). His spectacular victories gave him control of Italy, although he failed to capture Rome itself. Following the Carthaginian collapse in 203 BC, it took Rome a decade to reassert control over the Gauls of the Po valley. By 191 BC the local Boii people were vanquished, and the region became known as Cisalpine Gaul, Rome's northernmost province of the time.

Below: This Celtic silver shield boss found at Manerbio, northern Italy, has 11 Gallic warrior heads arrayed around the circumference.

The spread of Celtic artistic influence.

sphere of influence of Hallstatt and La Tène Celtic art

Shetland Islands

Orkney Islands

Western Isles

ATLANTIC OCEAN

GAELS

PICTS

BRITONS

London

NORTH SEA

Gundestrup

BALTIC SEA

Eigenbilzen

BELGAE

Weisskirchen

Rhine

Somme-Bionne

Basse Yutz

Pfalzfeld

Waldalgesheim

Schwarzenbach

Main

Parsberg

Manching

Amfreville

Paris

Seine

Besseringen

Rodenbach

Holzgerlingen

Danube

Hallstatt

Bouray

Vix

Heidelberg

Trichtingen

Loire

Saône

La Tène

Strett...

GAULS

Lake Geneva

CELTO-LIGURIANS

Po

Aurillac

Rhône

Noves

Fenouillet

Roquepertuse

Entremont

Bononia (Bologna)

Rom...

CELTIBERIANS

Corsica

Sardinia

Balearic Islands

MEDITERRANEAN SEA

Chapter 3
Early Celtic Art

Celtic art has become popular in recent years. Celtic tattoos are common, while Celtic artwork can be seen selling a wide range of products, much of which has little other connection to the Celtic world. The geometric patterns, swirls, intricate interweaving, and stylized faces of the later period of Celtic art have become instantly recognizable around the world.

Earlier examples—although as equally distinctive as the later styles—are less well known. The renaissance of Celtic art in Ireland and Britain owed its cultural roots to the art of the La Tène period, before the Roman invasion of the Celtic world. This in turn owed its development to artistic styles developed in the pre-Celtic Europe of the Bronze Age, or even earlier. Few artistic movements were ever created in a vacuum, and Celtic art is no exception. It owes its distinctive appearance to several influences, including the older indigenous artistry mentioned above but also to the artwork that the Celts came into contact with through trade. Celtic trading links with the Mediterranean cultures of Greece and the Etruscans had a demonstrable influence on the development of Celtic art, while some art historians have even traced a minor influence from oriental artistic styles prevalent in Persia and the Russian steppes.

Much of the artwork left behind by the Celts comes from burial sites; the prized possessions of the Celtic elite which were buried with them, designed to help the dead on their journey to the afterlife. The advent of the Iron Age did little to alter the nature of these grave goods, as the majority continued to be made from bronze. Iron was used for the production of arms and armor, domestic items, and tools. Celtic metalworkers produced some of the most exquisite bronze decorative objects of the ancient period. This outpouring of creative talent reached a peak during the late La Tène period, and the work of these artisans tells us almost all we know of Celtic culture and society before the coming of the Romans. Celtic art, like Celtic belief, mirrored the natural world. This embrace of nature and its translation into works of art ensured that the objects produced by early Celtic craftsmen would remain some of the most esthetically pleasing metal objects ever created.

Brno-Malomerice

DANUBIAN CELTS

Danube

ADRIATIC SEA

BLACK SEA

AEGEAN SEA

GALATIAN CELTS

Sicily

Rhodes

Cyprus

Crete

The Origins of Celtic Art

Patterns evident in late Bronze Age metalwork of the Urnfield period were repeated during the Hallstatt Celtic period of the early Iron Age, and their origins can be traced back even to Neolithic times. Typical forms of proto-Celtic decoration include geometric patterns and animal motifs, and these remained in constant use throughout the Iron Age that followed. Examples can be found on bronze swords, horse furnishings, and on votive offerings.

Below: The Trundholm Sun Car was deposited in a Danish peat bog in about the 12th century BC. The representation of the sun was popular in early Celtic art.

Some graves of the Urnfield period foreshadow the lavishly supplied burial chambers and graves of the true Celtic periods. Bronze items found in graves dating from 1300–1000 BC are decorated with geometric patterns, such as a breastplate left as a funerary offering at Fillinges in southeastern France. A similar example found at Marmesse in north-eastern France has decorative circles crudely resembling the contours of the male chest, and is decorated with a linear trim of two rows of small raised circles, each delineated by outer bands of even smaller dots.

A common ornamental theme in Bronze Age Europe was the seasonal cycle, a major influence on an agrarian society. Another was the animals and birds which surrounded these pre-Celtic people, particularly domestic livestock. Examples from Urnfield period sites in Hungary include horses, pigs, sheep, and dogs. Wild animals were also depicted, particularly boars and bears. About 1500 BC these Urnfield craftsmen began to experiment with depictions of mythical beasts, human beings, and hybrid creatures which were partly human, partly animal. This was a period when a small degree of interaction was taking place

between the Bronze Age cultures of central Europe and those of the Mediterranean basin.

Artistic models encountered to the south and east of Europe may have influenced this new realism or surrealism. A noticeable feature was the depiction of bird-men, birds with human faces. It is unclear whether this had any religious significance, but it predates a trend found in later Celtic art, where the transformation of man into animal or vice versa appears to have been a recurrent theme.

Elusive meaning

A bronze object discovered in a bog at Trundholm in Denmark dates from about 1200 BC, and was possibly a votive offering. It consists of a "sun car"; a six-wheeled cart carrying a gilded disk, which most probably represents the sun. The sun itself is decorated with geometric swirls, while a lifelike standing pony or small horse surmounts the front of the cart. Although the exact meaning of this piece is unclear, evidence from stone circles and burial chambers provides clear proof of the importance of the sun in Bronze Age European society. This decoration of bronze and even gold objects with geometric patterns is evident in other less spectacular examples of Bronze

Age metalwork. Linear patterns, concentric circles, and triangular designs appear to have been the most common. This curvilinear ornamentation is also encountered in later Celtic art.

Two of the most spectacular pieces of artwork dating from the Urnfield period are bronze vessels shaped to resemble ducks or geese. They were found in the Carpathian mountains, and have been dated to between 1200 and 800 BC. One is evidently a depiction of a mythical bird, since it combines horns and a beak. The other is a reasonably accurate representation of a duck with a graceful neck and beak. It stands on its own webbed feet.

Widespread iron-working began around 700 BC, and the blurred line between the end of the Bronze Age and the start of the Iron Age mean that there is really a period of transition from the Urnfield culture to the Hallstatt culture. The line between the two cultures was drawn where it was for the convenience of museum curators and archaeologists. The continuity of the art of the proto-Celtic and early Celtic periods is a clear indication that this is a purely arbitrary dividing line.

The Hallstatt Period

The Hallstatt culture was named after the western Austrian town where 19th-century archaeologists discovered an extensive burial site. The period marks the start of Iron Age culture in Europe and the official beginning of the Celtic civilization. The Hallstatt period is deemed to have lasted from approximately 700 until 500 BC, and ended with the period of extensive westward migration brought about by pressure from waves of Germanic settlers. The period set the scene for the artistic explosion that was to follow.

Below: Several bronze and ceramic Hallstatt finds were decorated with representations of human figures, which possibly had a votive significance.

In the case of artistic objects, use of iron as a material was rare, because ironworkers usually produced functional items rather than decorative ones. In terms of funerary objects, iron was confined to the aristocratic elite of Celtic society, while bronze decorative items were still widely produced for most levels of the social order. Artists of the Hallstatt period developed motifs first used by metalworkers of the Urnfield period that predated them.

Objects recovered from Hallstatt graves include stylized animals and birds, and possibly reflect the religious significance of cattle, bulls, and birds in later Celtic society and mythology. These symbols from the natural world that surrounded the early Celts remained in use well into the early historic period (after AD 500). Other Hallstatt sculptures comprise of equestrian figures, cauldrons decorated with domestic animals, and wild and domestic beasts. One of the most dramatic of these is a bronze bull found in the Blansko cave in the Czech Republic, part of a sacrificial vessel.

One of the most spectacular grave finds of the Hallstatt period was that made during the excavation of an early Celtic burial at Eberdingen-Hochdorf in Germany in the late 1970s. The burial chamber contained a bronze couch dated to about 530 BC, and the body of a well-dressed warrior was laid out on top of it. Its back was decorated with depictions of warriors and wagons, while the whole couch was supported on eight castor wheels, shaped like female figures. The primitive style of these depictions is deceptive, since the overall effect is one of great detail and esthetic perfection.

A similar crude human figure was found a few miles away in the late sixth- or early fifth-century burial at Hirshlanden near Leonberg. The stone figure stands about five feet high and, although naked, the subject was clearly a warrior. He is shown wearing a metal torc around his neck, a helmet on his head similar to that found in the Eberdingen-Hochdorf grave site, and he is armed with a short sword or dagger.

Long-distance trade

Art historians have traced several outside influences on early Celtic art. One is from the southeast, as characterized by the peculiar "Strettweg" wagon found near Steiermark in Austria. While it was found in a burial chamber of the Hallstatt period, it could date from the Urnfield period, making it a contemporary of the Trundholm "sun wagon" (*see previous page*).

A bronze offering dish is decorated with a series of paired metal spirals. The dish is balanced on the head of a female figure, who in turn is surrounded by a host of warriors and deer. The whole piece is mounted on a small four-wheeled cart, and stands approximately nine inches high.

"Cult wagons" of this type have been linked to Thessaly in Greece, and it has even been suggested that the piece has Greek origins, although the figures are similar to the primitive Celtic depictions described above. A Greek connection has also been suggested for some of the collection of Hallstatt era objects found in a burial site in Vix in southern France. A wagon was used to support the body of a woman, who wore a gold torc bearing Greek-style designs. Trading links existed between the Hallstatt Celts and the Greeks, so it is possible the object provides evidence of a Celtic market for Greek decorative objects.

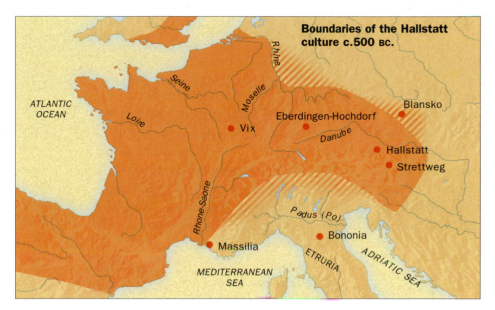

Left: The lower portion of the "Strettweg wagon" from Steirmark in Austria depicts warriors and deer, surrounding a nude female figure who supports the baseplate for a bronze offering dish. Probably 6th century BC, it could be earlier.

The Gundestrup Cauldron

In 1891 a large decorated Celtic cauldron was discovered in the Raevemosen Bog at Gundestrup in Jutland, a province in northern Denmark. It was clearly a ceremonial vessel, and it had been dismantled into its component parts before being deposited in the bog. It is almost certain that it was placed there as a religious votive offering. Beyond that, historians have debated the significance and origin of the cauldron ever since.

Below: The Gundestrup cauldron was deliberately dismantled, then placed in a Danish peatbog as a votive offering. The joints holding the seven panels to the lower bowl can be clearly seen.

The Gundestrup cauldron was made from gilded silver, and consists of 13 separate plates sitting around a rounded lower bowl. Each of the plates carries a bas-relief (*repoussé*) portrayal of a religious scene. The iconography of the plates and the inner bowl is remarkable, and suggests a variety of influences, although the majority of the images have Celtic associations.

Current research suggests that the cauldron was produced outside the Celtic world, possibly in Thrace, although this supposition is still hotly contested. Part of the confusion lies in the generic Indo-European nature of some of the iconography used to decorate the object. Jutland was also a Germanic area rather than a Celtic one, and it has been suggested that the piece was originally plundered from the Celts by the Germanic Cimbri people, who subsequently offered the cauldron up as a votive gift. What is most remarkable is the detail it provides about early Celtic society and belief, bringing together strands of Celtic mythology and religious practice that supports archaeological information gathered from throughout the Celtic world.

The cauldron was almost certainly a prized

religious object, and was probably used by the Celts for ritual purposes, such as the holding of sacrificial blood or even a small offering. The cauldron measures approximately 30 inches in diameter, and it is constructed using partially gilded silver. It has been dated to the first century BC, before the conquest of Gaul by the Romans and the collapse of the La Tène period culture.

Uncertain meanings

The outer surface of the plates surrounding the lower dished bowl carry the images of what could be deities or mythical animals. The inside of the cauldron depicts a religious scene, possibly representing some sacrificial ritual. It shows a long procession of priests, nobles, and other people, accompanied by musicians, while a figure is lowered into a cauldron by a god or priest figure.

The inner base of the bowl is decorated with a scene showing a man brandishing a sword, standing over a sacrificed bull. A dog, a lizard, and other animals complete the scene. Even more enigmatic are the side pieces, produced by a different artist than the base. A seated god (probably Cernunnos, known as "the horned one"), a boy on a dolphin, a bearded god holding a wheel, and a series of mythical animals augment the faces of other deities.

The god Cernunnos surveys the proceedings, depicted sitting cross-legged with a ram-headed snake in one hand as a symbol of worldly prosperity and power, and a Celtic neck ring (torc) in his other hand. The god is also shown wearing a similar torc around his neck. Torcs of gold, silver, or bronze were common items of jewelry in the Celtic world, and usually seem to have been worn by people of high social status. Many depictions of Celtic deities include torcs, and in almost every representation of Cernunnos the god is shown wearing one. The god is also shown wearing an antler head-dress, similar to one found at Hooks Cross in Hertfordshire in England, among fourth century AD Romano-British artifacts. It is considered likely that Celtic priests wore these forms of headgear as part of a ritual that helped "unite" them with the natural world.

Mythical and exotic animals include elephants, a cat, deer, griffins, and a tiger. These differ from many other mythical animals represented in Celtic art, and may indicate an eastern influence, although Celtic coins found elsewhere have carried images of elephants, and griffins have also been depicted in Celtic metalwork. Cattle were ritually slaughtered on a regular basis in the Celtic world. The sacrifice of bulls is depicted in two places on the cauldron, including the base. Whatever its function and its origin, the Gundestrup cauldron remains one of the most beautiful artifacts connected with the Celtic world.

Art of the Early La Tène

The La Tène period is seen as the high period of pre-Roman Celtic culture, and La Tène period artifacts are found throughout much of Europe. To most art historians, "Celtic art" is synonymous with this period, which lasted from the fifth century BC until the Roman conquest of Gaul. La Tène art has been categorized into four distinct styles: Early; Waldalgesheim; Plastic; and Sword. These were not sequential phases but rather they represent artistic themes.

The geographical roots of the "early" style have been traced to the middle Rhine region of Germany. It is characterized by abstract curving and repetitive patterns, usually of natural floral designs. Formal Greek and Etruscan examples were modified into a more distinctive flowing design. The influence of the Hallstatt period on this "Early" style was in the use of geometric ornaments and animal motifs, which were adapted into these repetitive patterns.

While some of these geometric patterns were drawn freehand, others were produced using compasses. An actual pair of La Tène period compasses, which were probably used by artists, were discovered in Celles in western France. It seems as though these Celtic artists were combining the beauty of the natural world around them with their own sense of geometric order. The plants and animals in their metalwork were only partially realistic, since their stems or limbs were stretched and intertwined. The natural subject matter was adapted to conform to the order imposed by the human artist.

In some cases animal or human faces were intertwined with these designs, such as the gold drinking horns from a grave site at Weisskirchen in Germany, which ended in ram and ewe heads. A Celtic human face was added to an imported Etruscan vessel as a handle, but it combined human and animal qualities. Celtic art of this period was symbolic and symmetrical rather than realistic. Greek, Etruscan, and even Oriental (Persian) influences have all been suggested in early Celtic art, indicating that these Celtic artists sought inspiration from the objects brought from the Celtic world's trading neighbors as well as from the natural world surrounding them. A gold bracelet found at Rodenbach in Germany was probably influenced by contemporary "oriental" artwork, while other objects found in the same fifth century BC grave site were Etruscan and Greek in origin.

Below: Pair of linchpins for a wagon, 3rd century BC, found in Yorkshire, England. Vehicles of any kind would have been extremely valuable and therefore decorated as befittted their importance. These end pieces display the swirling forms of early La Tène style.

The Eifel and Hundsrück regions to the west of the River Rhine contained a large number of graves, and many of these held rich gold and bronze jewelry, equestrian equipment, drinking and eating items, and weapons. Most of these objects exhibited this new free-flowing style. While some of the objects still exhibited a degree of symmetry and uniformity, many of them combined this with less constrained forms of decoration. Neck torcs were commonly produced in this free Waldalgesheim form. Running tendrils and swirls of decoration were commonplace on these objects, and by the third century BC similar patterns appeared in Celtic sites in northern Italy and western France.

These Waldalgesheim patterns were not limited to jewelry. A bronze "jockey cap" helmet from Amfreville in France was decorated with a series of relief patterns hammered onto the helmet from the back (the *repoussé* method). The base was decorated with an ironwork frieze, while a Greek-style recurring wave adorned the central band. Although some styles had regional roots, influences for Celtic craftsmen came from a variety of sources, and different styles could be used concurrently.

Left: The Basse-Yutz Flagon c.400 BC, shows clear Etruscan influences in the handle and spout design.

Below: A bronze bead from the La Tène II period (3rd to 2nd centuries BC), found in what are now the suburbs of Paris.

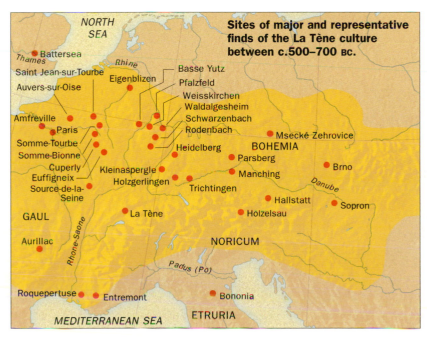

Sites of major and representative finds of the La Tène culture between c.500–700 BC.

NORTH SEA
Thames
Battersea
Rhine
Saint Jean-sur-Tourbe
Eigenblizen
Basse Yutz
Auvers-sur-Oise
Pfalzfeld
Weisskirchen
Waldalgesheim
Amfreville
Schwarzenbach
Rodenbach
Paris
Msecké Zehrovice
Somme-Tourbe
Heidelberg
BOHEMIA
Somme-Bionne
Parsberg
Cuperly
Kleinaspergle
Brno
Euffigneix
Manching
Source-de-la-Seine
Holzgerlingen
Trichtingen
Danube
GAUL
La Tène
Hallstatt
Holzelsau
Sopron
Aurillac
NORICUM
Rhône-Saône
Padus (Po)
Roquepertuse
Entremont
Bononia
MEDITERRANEAN SEA
ETRURIA

A more free-flow form

The grave of a Celtic princess was discovered at Waldalgesheim in Germany, and finds from the site mark a departure in Celtic style. The principal feature of this style is the replacement of symmetrical geometric patterns with an unrestrained flowing form of decoration. Similar lavish female graves dating from the fourth century BC have also been found in the same area, which has been identified as a cradle of Celtic art.

The Evolution of La Tène

As art of the La Tène period developed, artists experimented with new styles, including the use of three-dimensional representations. While art historians claim that Celtic metalwork reached a cultural peak during the second century BC, many of these styles were mirrored or embellished in later British Celtic art. The La Tène artists developed a series of styles which have come to personify Celtic artistry, including the development of free-flowing intricate patterns and human and animal forms in heavy relief.

Below: This bronze mirror frame found in Desborough in Northamptonshire, England uses a symmetrical tripartite design, over a basket-weave base. It dates from the 1st century AD.

Facing: The Battersea Shield, found in the River Thames in London, probably belonged to a prestigious ancient British chieftain, and dates from the 1st century BC.

The early artistic styles of the La Tène period were largely two-dimensional, emphasizing either realistic or stylized relief decoration on three-dimensional objects. Around the third century BC a new style emerged, and like the early and Waldalgesheim styles it was seldom used in conjunction with other forms. The "plastic" style was one where the artist or metalworker conceived of the decoration in three rather than in two dimensions. The relief work on these plastic metal pieces is so substantial that it often appears to be free-standing.

One of the most representational plastic-style pieces was found in Aurillac, near the French town of Tarn. This gold amulet consists of two intertwined bands covered in decorative beading. These beads are in high relief, and are intertwined with representations of nuts, berries, and twigs, albeit in distinctly abstract forms. Similar designs incorporated human or animal faces, and even combined these with functional pieces of metalwork, such as cauldrons and shield bosses.

A fourth identifiable artistic style has been labeled "Sword," because most of its examples come from the decoration of weapons, scabbards, or armor. Consequently, it has been suggested that the sword style was created for, and exclusively used by, armorers and swordsmiths. This was a means of decoration used on a range of purely functional objects, so the

exuberance of the plastic style would have been inappropriate on arms and armor. Instead, the sword style was a form of incised decoration on the existing surface of metal (mostly iron) objects.

It has been claimed that the style originated in what is now Hungary around the fourth century BC, although examples have been found in both eastern and western Europe. Many of the surviving examples were votive offerings, cast into the waters of lakes or rivers as part of a religious ceremony. Much of this "sword" decoration was in the "Waldalgesheim" style; free-flowing patterns and sworls, incorporating the occasional representation of humans or animals. Pairs of dragons appear to have been favored by these swordsmiths, and examples of dragons have been found as far apart as Britain and Hungary.

The art of sculpture

Apart from metal artifacts, Celtic artists excelled in the production of sculpture. These have been found in stone, metal, and wood forms, and examples range from crude stone-carving to highly detailed bronze works of art. Stone sculpture was not particularly common during the La Tène period, and most examples were produced either in southern Germany or in southern France. Those in Provence are particularly striking, since they form part of the landscape of religious sanctuaries such as Roquepertuse or Entremont. Those in Germany are more enigmatic. A four-sided column at Hunsrück is based on the form of a stylized human head, while another from Holzgerlingen at Württemberg represents a larger than life warrior or chieftain. These may have been produced for religious reasons, but their meaning is now lost.

Wooden examples are even rarer, and obviously few have survived. Votive objects were used during periods of threat to the tribe who deposited them. It therefore comes as no surprise that many of these from southern Gaul date to the period of the Roman conquest. At Source-en-Roche in France, several thousand wooden votive statues were deposited around the same time.

Gaul c.60 BC, just before the campaigns of Julius Caesar, showing the Romanized provinces of Cisalpine Gaul and Transalpine Gaul, non-Celtic Aquitania, Celtic Gaul, and the Belgae tribes.

Right: For the Celts, rivers, lakes, trees, and even rocks held religious significance, and the evidence suggests that Celtic sanctuaries were often located in hidden groves in the middle of woodland. The Celtic word *nemeton* (or oak) probably refers to these sacred groves, and numerous place names can be identified throughout the Celtic world.

BRITANNIA

TRINOVANTES

BELGAE   REGNI   CANTII

Portus Itius

MARE BRITANNICUM
(ENGLISH CHANNEL)

MENAPII   NERVII   EBURONES

MORINI   NERVII   ADUATUCI

AMBIANI   ATREBATES   CONDRUSI

Sambre

BELGAE   TREVERI

Samarobriva
(Amiens)

CALETES   BELLOVACI   REMI   MEDIOMETRICI   Moselle

Somme   Meuse

UNELLI   Rotomagos
(Rouen)   Durocortorum
(Reims)

BAIOCASSES   VELIOCASSES   Seine   SUESSIONES   Marne

LEXOVII   PARISII   Lutetia
(Paris)   LEUCI

OSISMI   AULERCI
EBUROVICES   PARISII MELDI   SEQUANI

CURIOSOLITAE   AULERCI
DIABLINTES   SENONES

REDONES   AULERCI
CENOMANI   CARNUTES   LINGONES

VENETI   Sarthe   Loire   Cenabum
(Orléans)
Main oppidum of Carnutes
and druidical center   MANDUBII   Alesia
(Alise Ste.-Reine)

NAMNETES   ANDEGAVI   CARNUTES   SENONES   AEDUI   SEQUANI

Condevincum
(Nantes)   CARNUTES   BITURIGES   Loire   Bibracte
(Mont Beuvray)   Cabillonum
(Châlon-sur-Saône)

TURONES   BITURIGES   Avaricum
(Bourges)

GALLIA
(CELTIC GAUL)   Cher   AEDUI   Saône

MARE OCEANUM
(ATLANTIC OCEAN)   PICTONES   Limonum
(Poitiers)   AMBARRI

SEGUSIAVI   Lugdunum
(Lyons)

LEMOVICES

BAY
OF
BISCAY   Charente   SANTONES   AVERNI

BITURIGES
VIVISCI   PETROCORII   Dordogne   TRANSALPINE GAUL

BOII   Garonne   CADURCI   Lot   Rhône

TARBELLI   Adour   AUSCI   RUTENI   Arelate
(Arles)

AQUITANIA   Tolosa
(Toulouse)

HISPANIA   Narbo
(Narbonne)

CHAPTER 4

Celtic Belief

The popular conception of Celtic religion is that it was dominated by druids and human sacrifice. Both played a substantial part in Celtic belief, but their importance has been exaggerated, largely by the Romans. The Romans had an almost paranoid distrust of the Celts, partly due to the near-constant threat they posed to Rome for over two centuries, until the end of the Punic Wars. The Celts were demonized, and the apparent excesses of their religion were amplified for their sensational propaganda value.

Certainly druids played a significant role in Celtic society. As well as supervising religious ceremonies, they also served as archivists, diplomats, and arbiters. Among the Celts, druids were prized for their knowledge and even their healing skills rather than their ability to perform blood-curdling ritual sacrifice.

Roman historians grossly over-emphasized the incidence of human sacrifice and its importance to Celtic tribes. Animal sacrifice was far more common, as indeed it was in the Roman sphere of influence. Human sacrifice seems to have been reserved for periods when the Celts themselves were threatened by external forces, such as Roman invasion. Far more widespread was the less sensational "sacrifice" of votive offerings; bronze or wooden statues or images that were cast into rivers, lakes, and bogs throughout Celtic Europe.

For the Celts, rivers, lakes, trees, and even rocks could hold special religious significance, and the evidence of their gods were all around them. Roman historians attempted to link the leading Celtic deities to Roman gods in an attempt to help bind the conquered Celtic peoples of Gaul, Spain, and Britain to Roman beliefs. This was only partially successful, and Romano-Celts continued to worship their old gods throughout the Roman period and beyond, until their conversion to Christianity. The Christian religious calendar itself was adapted to conform to the Celtic one, and even today the traces of annual Celtic ceremonies can be found. Much of the Celtic belief system was based on the annual cycle of seasons, harvests, and movements of the sun, since it was an agrarian society.

The Celtic Calendar

Long before the Celts the indigenous peoples of western Europe governed their lives by seasonal changes. They were also aware of the cycles of the moon, sun, and the major celestial bodies. Evidence from stone circles such as Stonehenge suggests that cosmology was widely practiced. The Celts further developed the cosmological discoveries made by earlier peoples.

Facing below: The Standing Stones in Stenness, Orkney. Research has proved that the builders had extensive calendric and astrological knowledge.

The Coligny Calendar is the earliest known Celtic calendar, and dates from the first century BC. Of Gallic origins, it consists of a series of engraved bronze plates, inscribed with Gallo-Celtic inscriptions. Since its discovery in 1897 historians have studied it extensively and, by combining this with other sources, researchers can understand how the Celtic people used their calendar and linked it to religion, farming cycles, and solar or lunar events. The Coligny calendar was based on a 30-year cycle, confirming the observation made by the historian Roman Pliny. Comparisons with other calendar systems from older Indo-European cultures suggest a relationship between the Celtic version and these earlier systems. The Celtic calendar was certainly more advanced and complex than the Roman Julian one that replaced it.

The annual cycle centered around the month of midsummer (Samon) and that of winter (Giamon). This divided the year into a light period (after midsummer) and a black period (after midwinter). Months were also labeled as either good (Mat) or bad (Anm). Each month consisted of 29 or 30 nights—the Celts measured by nights rather than days as we do today. Pliny suggests that the beginning or end of a month followed the lunar cycle (either a full moon or no moon). The months themselves followed a 62-month (or five-year) cycle rather than a 12-month one, which was repeated six times in the cycle of the calendar.

Cycle of life and death

The yearly cycle was a crucial point of reference for an agrarian community, and festivals marked the transition from one season to the next. Samhain (linked with death, and not to be confused with Samon) is the period now celebrated as Halloween. Beltane (now Mayday) represented youth and love. Midsummer and midwinter also formed crucial phases of the calendar, and marked the start of the light or dark

Right: The Celtic New Year is still marked in Burghead in Scotland by means of their annual Tar Barrel burning ceremony. The celebration has Celtic roots.

phases of the annual cycle.

Early Irish literature provides details of the four main seasonal festivals in the Celtic year, marking important points in the annual agrarian cycle or to simply mark the passage of the four seasons. Samhain was seen as a time when spirits roamed among the living, giving rise to the Halloween mythos of today, while Beltane marked the beginning of summer, when livestock was released to pasture. Light or fire has been associated with this festival, and a ninth-century Irish chronicler recorded that during Beltane cattle were driven between two bonfires to symbolically ward off disease.

Spring was marked by the festival of Imbolc (February 1st) and marked the start of the lambing season, while Lughnasadh was an autumnal harvest festival celebrated on August 1st, and was celebrated by gaming and feasting. Imbolc is still marked by a Celtic New Year ceremony in Burghead in northeast Scotland, while Harvest Festival and Halloween have Celtic roots.

The Coligny calendar provides a timetable for religious festivals which suggests that the festivals celebrated by the Irish in the Dark Ages had also been marked by the Gauls in the first century BC. Following the Roman conquest of Gaul in the mid-first century BC, the Roman calendar was adopted, although it was sometimes adapted to incorporate local festivals. A similar abandonment of the Celtic calendar took place in Roman Britain. Another Romano-Celtic development was the adoption of Roman astrological symbols in preference to the older Celtic ones.

Above: A Gallo-Roman zodiac carved on wood and ivory from the 2nd century AD and found in the Vosges region of France.

Death and the Afterlife

Although much of Celtic belief is difficult to substantiate due to the lack of written records, archaeology provides us with a wealth of information regarding the Celtic attitude toward death, burial, and the afterlife. Caesar wrote on the subject of the Gallic perception of life after death, and this unique Celtic perception of the afterlife was still being described by Irish chroniclers six centuries later, at the very end of the Celtic era.

Below:

Reconstruction of a La Tène period chariot burial from the Marne region of France. A Celtic chieftan lies with his weapons, utensils, and framed by two wagon wheels. Another burial had been made above the first, shown on the top shelf.

Archaeological evidence shows that from the early Iron Age in the seventh century BC Celts were buried with some of their worldly possessions. Burial practices have long been used to date or identify ancient civilizations. The Urnfield Culture of central Europe dating from the early first millennium BC has been described as proto-Celtic, and the culture's name was derived from their burial practice of cremating their dead in urn burial grounds.

During the period of the Hallstatt Culture (c.1200–475 BC), burial practices reverted to the body being placed in a grave together with possessions, and wagons seem to have been commonly used in burials, reflecting an earlier nomadic and eastern tradition. The discovery of this form of burial in northern Austria and Bavaria have led to the identification of this Hallstatt Celtic culture with that geographical area, but these wagon graves also provided valuable information about the society the deceased once lived in. In most cases the body was laid out on a four-wheeled wagon, surrounded by personal effects. This was then enclosed in either a sunken wooden burial chamber or a mound.

The La Tène culture that succeeded the Hallstatt period saw a change in the grave goods buried alongside the dead. Instead of wagons, two-horse chariots were used, while increasingly ornate jewelry became a common burial item. Warrior graves could be identified by the deposition of arms and armor (spears, shields, helmets, and swords), while other graves emphasized drinking horns, cauldrons, and platters. Irish chroniclers mention a Celtic tradition of banqueting in the next world, and the presence of drinking and eating utensils in graves may represent the continuance of this tradition from the Iron Age to the Dark Age.

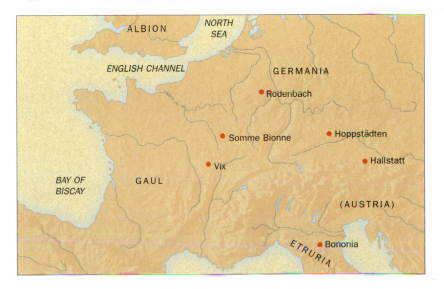

Women as well as men were buried surrounded by these items, and a Hallstatt grave at Vix in eastern France dating from the sixth century BC is one of the earliest examples of a burial containing feasting items. It also shows that women were capable of reaching a high status in Celtic culture, as reflected in the comments of Roman observers such as Tacitus writing late in the first century AD. Some burial items also contained symbolic references to death and the afterlife, such as the gold amulet recovered from a grave in Rodenbach in Germany dating from the late fifth century BC. Its decorations have been interpreted as representing death and resurrection.

Extremes of Celtic religion

Other more bizarre traditions concerning death and the afterlife surrounded the period before the Roman invasion of Gaul. The head was seen as the repository of the soul, so the severed heads of warriors were sometimes displayed in Celtic shrines, or buried in special grave sites. This practice may have led Roman observers to conclude that human sacrifice had taken place—it certainly provided grounds for widespread propaganda that justified the continued annexation of Gaul.

While sacrifice and ritual killing are discussed elsewhere, the La Tène culture produced examples of group or family burial that might have included human sacrifice. Archaeologists have speculated that although a family grave at Hoppstädten in western Germany may have represented a family unit whose members succumbed to disease at the same time, it could also indicate that the rest of the family were killed and buried alongside the head of the family when he died, a practice known as *suttee*. Caesar describes the practice in the mid-first century BC, but said it was becoming obsolete. This practice further suggests a strong belief in the afterlife.

Above: A warrior's funeral from the 5th century BC. As four men lower the war chariot into the pit, one druid sings over the body while another pours a libation.

Sacrifice

For many, Celtic religion has been closely identified with human sacrifice. This is largely due to Greek and Roman writers who seemed to revel in describing this aspect of Celtic ritual in detail. In recent years archaeological discoveries have substantiated this evidence of human and animal sacrifice. While Celts certainly engaged in ritual murder, these ceremonies can now be placed in their true perspective as an integral part of the Celtic system of belief.

Below: Roman historians described a Celtic sacrificial ceremony involving the burning of victims inside a wicker cage in the shape of a man. It is more likely that wicker images were burned, and were part of a sacrificial practice, especially in times of need.

S acrifice is the gift of something of value (not always another human being) to the Gods, either by killing the victim as part of a ritual, or by irretrievably disposing of it. Caesar, Strabo, and Diodorus described Gallo-Celtic sacrificial ritual in the first century BC, and emphasized the role played by druids in the process. Caesar suggested that the selection of sacrificial victims was far from random: "They believe that the immortal Gods delight more in the slaughter of those taken in theft or brigandage or some crime, but when the supply of that kind runs short, they resort to the sacrifice of the innocent."

Sacrifice was also a response to the threat of war, pestilence, or drought to a Celtic community: "those suffering from sickness or amid the danger of conflict either kill human beings as sacrificial victims or pledge to do so."

The skeleton of a man was found behind the rampart of the Celtic British hillfort at South Cadbury in Somerset, and from his posture it is likely he had been bound then killed as a sacrificial offering. While the Cadbury victim was possibly an enemy warrior, during the Boudicca revolt in Britain women and children were also sacrificed in druidic ceremonies. Warfare and sacrifice seemed to be closely interwoven. The Gauls were known to practice head worship—cutting off the heads of enemies killed in battle and preserving them. Although not a form of sacrifice, this "head-hunting" formed part of Celtic warfare, and has been associated with Celtic ritual. Diodorus expanded on the manner these sacrifices took:

"In times of great worry they [the druids] put to death a human being, and plunge a dagger into him… and when the victim has fallen they read the future from the way he fell, or from the twitching of his limbs or the flow of his blood."

Tacitus recalled that: "…it was their religion to drench their altars with the blood of prisoners, and consult their Gods by means of human entrails."

Cauldron of Death

A similar form of sacrifice, described by Roman historian Strabo, was the suspension of a victim over a cauldron, at which point the throat of the victim would be cut, allowing the blood to drain into the cauldron. This is borne out by the Gundestrup cauldron (*see pages 44–45*) in which to one side of a panel there stands a larger figure holding another smaller figure over a cauldron.

Caesar reported that due to a strong belief in the afterlife, the Celts had little fear of death. The soul did not die, but simply passed into another body. His description of wickerwork sacrifices is an aspect of Celtic sacrifice that has been colored by popular imagination: "Some tribes build enormous images with limbs of interwoven branches which they then fill with live men.

The images are then set alight and the men die in a sea of flame." It is now considered likely that these accounts were incorrect, possibly influenced by the writings of the earlier historian, Posidonius: only wicker or straw images of human forms were burned (as they still are in Britain on Guy Fawkes night).

A Celtic community could also make a valuable offering to the Gods by sacrificing prized domestic animals rather than wild ones, and dogs and horses were often included in burial rituals. A byproduct of this was the production of votive offerings of animals; a less drastic form of sacrifice. Countless examples of votive carvings of domestic animals have been found throughout the Celtic world. But sacrifices, despite the lurid tales shown in horror films, were rarely as prolific or commonplace as non-Celtic historians might lead us to believe.

The Bog People

For the past 180 years, the remains of human beings have been recovered from the waterlogged marshes and peat bogs of northwestern Europe. Many of these were well preserved, despite lying submerged in the bog since the Iron Age.

Above: The preserved head of a bogman who was strangled before being ritually placed in a peat bog near Tollund, Denmark.

Not all these preserved bodies were necessarily those of sacrificial victims—criminals may have been executed, then their bodies deposited in bogs. The Roman historian Tacitus recorded that in Germany "the coward, shirker, and the unnaturally vicious are drowned in miry swamps under a cover of wattled hurdles."

In 1984 peat cutters working in Lindow Moss in Cheshire, England, uncovered a human body. After foul play was ruled out, archaeologists were called in to examine the

corpse. The Lindow Man was in his mid-20s when he died, had a mustache, and was well-nourished and groomed. He had met a grizzly end, sustaining heavy blows to the back of the head (which would have knocked him unconscious) before being garrotted by a sinew cord fastened around his neck.

His throat was then cut open, and the body deposited face down in the bog. Carbon dating suggests that he was executed during the first century AD, around the time of the Roman invasion of Britain. His death was almost certainly a ritual killing, since he had been stripped naked except for a fur amulet, and his body had been painted. His last meal consisted of bread containing cereal seeds and mistletoe pollen. The pollen has led to speculation that his death involved a druidic ceremony, since mistletoe has been associated with druid ceremonies. From his appearance it seems he was of a high social standing. This ritual murder involving "three kinds of death" has a parallel in an early Irish Celtic myth of a king sacrificed by a three-stage killing.

Cruel death

Although Denmark lay beyond the Celtic territories in Europe, the indigent Danes shared a common material culture. Several ancient bog bodies have been recovered in Denmark and all have contributed to our understanding of Celtic bog sacrifice or punishment. In 1839 the remains of a large, fully-dressed woman of about 50 was recovered in Juthe Fen in Jutland, and the evidence suggests she was still alive when she was buried.

Wooden hooks had been driven through her knees and elbows, pinning her to the bog surface. Large branches were then laid over her body, pushing her under the surface of the mire. The 19th-century antiquarians who first examined the remains record that her face bore a horrific expression. The execution took place during the Iron Age, and historians have speculated that she could have been a sorceress.

A second female body was discovered at Windeby in Schleswig-Holstein, in northern Germany. The corpse was that of an adolescent, of between 12 and 14 years of age. Her death was clearly a ritual act, as part of her head had been shaved, and she was blindfolded before being executed. Her body was pinned under the surface of the marsh by birch branches and a large stone. It is unclear whether she was executed as a criminal or was a sacrificial victim, but archaeologists speculate that the latter was more likely. Tacitus also records that death by drowning was a punishment for adultery.

The body of an Iron Age man was discovered at Tollund in Denmark, and the corpse bore the signs of a ritual execution similar to that inflicted on the

Lindow man. The Tollund Man was naked except for a leather belt and a cap, and had been garrotted by a sinew rope. Like the Lindow man, his last meal was a form of seed bread, consumed just before his death. The similarities strongly suggest that this form of ritual execution was common throughout the Celtic world and its fringes. Two other European bog men were discovered, one of whom had been garrotted (Borre Fen Man) and the other had his throat slit (Grauballe Man), both forms of execution inflicted on the Lindow Man. Water bore a ritual significance for the Celts, and therefore bog sacrifices may have formed part of some long-forgotten religious ceremony.

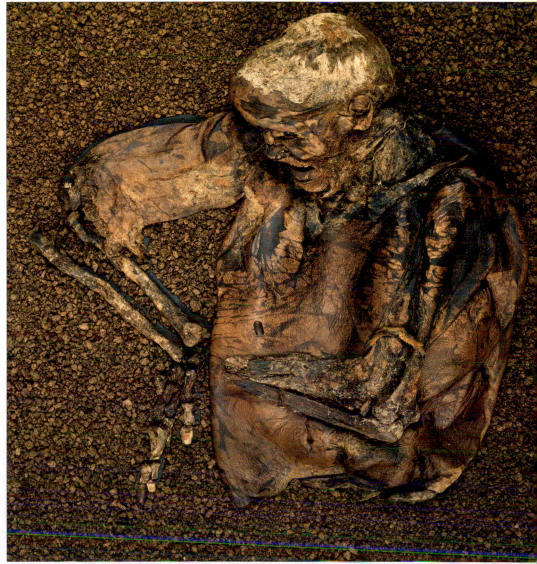

Below: Lindow Man suffered "three deaths" before being deposited in a bog in Cheshire, England some two thousand years ago.

Sacred Landscape

Roman chroniclers report that Celtic worship often took place in the open air, in places regarded as having a sacred nature. These included oak groves, springs, lakes, islands, ponds, or rivers. Archaeological evidence for their existence is scant, save a handful of votive offerings or other religious items. The Celts also made use of religious structures such as shrines or temples, and the remains of many of these can be identified today.

Below: The Hostage's Mound at Tara Hill, County Meath, Ireland. Tradition has it that the Fal stone, associated with the crowning of Irish kings, stood on this burial mound.

The Roman chronicler Lucan reported the finding of a sacred grove by Caesar's army in southern Gaul during the mid-first century BC.

"A grove there was, untouched by men's hands from ancient times, whose interlacing boughs enclosed a space of darkness and cold shade, and banished the sunlight from above. No rural Pan dwelt here… but gods were worshiped there with savage rites, the altars were heaped with hideous offerings, and every tree was sprinkled with human gore. On these boughs birds feared to perch; in those coverts wild beasts would not lie down; no wind ever bore down upon that wood, nor thunderbolt hurtled from black clouds; the trees, even when they spread their leaves to no rustle, rustled among themselves. Water also fell there in abundance from dark springs. The images of the gods, grim and rude, were uncouth blocks, formed of felled tree trunks."

The Nemetons

Evidence suggests that Celtic religious sanctuaries were often located in hidden groves in the middle of woodland. The Celtic word *nemeton* probably refers to these sacred groves, and numerous place names can be identified throughout Celtic Gaul and Britain. Tacitus records the presence of sacred groves in Anglesey in Wales, while Strabo reported similar locations in Asia Minor (now Turkey). The Galatians in Asia Minor met at a place called

©CPAT: CS90-43-323

Drunemeton, which translates as "sacred oak grove," a place for religious worship and for meetings of tribal councils.

These woodland locations are almost impossible to identify by archaeological methods, although the wooden images of gods described by Lucan have occasionally survived, such as the crudely carved figure of a woman found at Ballachulish in Scotland in 1880. Apart from oak, trees considered of religious significance to the Celts included beech, alder, elm, and yew. Even today, certain trees are seen to have spiritual properties, and "rag trees" where people tie scraps of clothing to branches can be found as far apart as Cyprus, Spain, France, Ireland, and Scotland.

By the late Iron Age, some Celts began to erect permanent structures, designed in part to resemble the older natural sacred groves. These artificial groves were probably simple temple structures, such as the first century BC structure at Narvan, County Armagh in Ireland. From the early Bronze Age, wooden circles were used. One of these sacred timber structures has been reconstructed near Welshpool in Wales (Sarn-y-Bryn-Caled), and surrounds a pit that contained cremated human remains. Some archaeologists have argued that sites such as these developed into the later temple structures

In Ireland, Tara has long been associated with the crowning of the High Kings of Ireland throughout the Celtic period, and it has also been described in Irish annals as a religious site. Similarly, areas that provided defensive works for the Celts also contain evidence of religious use, such as the Irish coastal fort of Dun Aengus on Inishmore, County Galway, or the La Tène period hilltop fort at Závist in Bohemia. In this latter fortification, a shrine was placed on the highest portion of the hill. A substantial wall probably enclosed a religious structure similar to that at Narvan. Fortifications (*oppidum*) at Roquepertuse in southern France and Liptovska Mara in Bohemia both incorporated shrines and religious porticoes into the main structure; the French version was adorned with human skulls (*see page 171*). While these temples were evidently important, and associated with centers of political and military power, the Celts still retained an affinity with the natural landscape, and also worshiped in other, more remote sacred locations.

Above: Reconstruction of the sacred timber circle at Sarn-y-Bryn-Caled, near Welshpool, Wales.

Sacred Waters

The presence of sacred lakes are mentioned by the Roman historian Strabo, and archaeological evidence suggests that religious ceremonies took place by lakes and ponds during the La Tène Period. Prehistoric Europeans deposited votive offerings in lakes, and many of these locations remained in religious use until the late Iron Age. Water had a particularly strong symbolic influence on Celtic belief, and certain bodies of water seem to have held a particular religious significance.

Facing: Doon Holy Well in County Donegal, Ireland was sacred to the Celts. Modern Irish Catholics still leave Christian votive offerings at the site.

Below: Water sacred to the goddess Sulis springs from the ground at the Roman baths of Aquae Sulis, in the modern town of Bath, England.

In 1857 the level of Lake Neuchâtel dropped, and beside the Iron Age settlement at La Tène (which gave rise to the name for that period of Celtic culture) a system of wooden bridges and piers was discovered. Beneath them lay over 3,000 metal votive offerings, most of which dated from the peak of the La Tène period (between the third and first centuries BC).

The Welsh lake Llyn Cerrig Bach in Anglesey (an island mentioned by Tacitus as having special religious significance for the ancient British) was a similar site used for the deposition of votive offerings. Most date from the first century AD, when Anglesey became the last bastion of Druidic power in southern Britain, and took the form of metal objects of various forms, from small sculptures to weapons, domestic objects, chariot fittings, and cauldrons. The majority of these were bronze. Anglesey was overrun by the Romans in AD 61. At Narvan Fort in Ulster, human, animal, metal and ceramic offerings were deposited in an artificial pool near the fort from the ninth century BC, and the site later became associated with a Celtic temple structure.

In Gaul, the source of the River Seine was

seen as an area of particular spiritual power, and excavations at Fontes Sequana near Dijon have produced over 200 wooden (mostly oak) carved votive offerings dating from the mid-first century AD. Many of these pieces were full statues, some shaped in the form of people with physical deformities. The spring that gave rise to the river was regarded as having healing properties, and most probably became a source of pilgrimage to those seeking a cure from their afflictions. Sequana is a name associated with a physician goddess, and a bronze statue of her was found in a shrine close to the spring.

Celtic deity becomes Roman

Bath in England was also regarded as a place possessing powers that healed the sick, and "taking the waters" there for healing purposes remained popular until the late 19th century. The Waters of Sulis (*Aquae Sulis* to the Romans) was a spot where hot springs pumped up heated mineral-rich water. The goddess Sulis was venerated by the Ancient Britons in a similar fashion as Sequana, and votive offerings have been found in the area, although much of this pre-Roman activity was covered by subsequent Roman and post-Roman construction. Worship of Sulis continued into the Roman period, where Sulis Minerva was seen as a healing goddess.

Strabo's reference to Celtic sacred lakes comes from his description of the votive treasure of the Volcae Tectosages, pillaged by the Romans at the south-eastern Gallic settlement of Tolosa (Toulouse) in 106 BC. Much of this votive treasure consisted of gold and silver, a portion of which reputedly comprised of fine Greek metalwork looted from Delphi. Strabo mentions that although much of the treasure was recovered from "a temple much honored throughout the countryside," more treasure was beyond reach, cast into the lakes surrounding the religious and political center.

For the Gallic and British Celts, the practice of casting votive offerings into water did not die out following the arrival of the Romans, and Irish examples can be found well into the sixth century AD. Gregory of Tours writing at the end of the sixth century recorded that peasants still cast animals, food, and drink into nearby lakes as votive offerings, suggesting an unbroken tradition

stretching back for many centuries. Following the collapse of the Roman Empire these older beliefs briefly reasserted themselves before being submerged by the rising tide of Christianity in the Celtic world.

Below: The Roman baths at Aquae Sulis, c.AD 200, with the Temple of Minerva Sulis in the foreground.

Gods and Divinities

Because the Celts left no pre-Christian written legacy, our knowledge of their gods is based on Greco-Roman writings, whose evidence points to the Celts worshipping literally hundreds of gods and goddesses. The discovery of likenesses and votive offerings sheds further light on this pantheon. Recently historians have tried to determine the hierarchy of Celtic divinities, and to link gods with particular religious beliefs.

H istorians have managed to identify a collection of gods who were venerated throughout the Celtic world. Others had a regional following, while still more were linked to particular tribes or sacred locations. Each god or goddess had a devoted following, and the interrelation between them is still difficult to determine. Often when historians describe Celtic religion they are speaking of Celtic mythology, as recorded in the Irish annals. This is an offshoot of a far older and more complex system of devotion. A combination of this later evidence, contemporary non-Celtic observers, and the remains of religious artifacts and shrines combine to establish a somewhat rudimentary understanding of the Celtic religion.

We have already observed that the Celtic system of belief was polytheistic, and even by temporarily setting aside regional deities, we are still left with over 100 gods and goddesses who

Right: Depiction of the Celtic god Cernunnos, in a detail from the Gundestrup cauldron. He is shown holding a snake and a sacred torc.

were venerated throughout the Celtic world. Roman and Greek historians tried to link Celtic deities with their own, creating a further degree of confusion. Although both the Roman and the Celtic religions followed Indo-European polytheistic forms, they were very different. Caesar recorded that the Celts believed their gods to be their ancestors, yet they were usually unwilling to view their deities as having a human form.

The key gods

An exception was Cernunnos, identified as the Dagda (Good God) of Irish mythology, who was often depicted in human form, but wearing stag antlers. This leading Celtic god was often portrayed with animals, and historians have tried to identify him as "Lord of the Animals," but he is also seen as a sort of creator and taker of life. Another version shows him with a symbolic phallus (a creator of life). As a taker of life, he is often portrayed wielding a club, and the Cerna Abbas Gint hill-carving in Dorset in England has often been identified with this aspect of Cernunnos. Incidentally, the Romans identified him with their own Hercules.

The Celtic mother-goddess was Danu, who created a river (often identified with the Danube) as a form of divine water gift. In Irish mythology it watered the sacred oak tree from which all subsequent Celtic gods and goddesses (the children of Danu) were derived. Danu has also been linked with the Irish goddess Anu, who was the "mother of the Irish gods." Venus was probably the closest Roman equivalent. Modern new-age practitioners might call her the "earth-mother."

Ogmios (also Ogmia or Ogma) was the god of learning. He was portrayed with sun rays extending in a halo around his head (like later Christian depictions), and is also attributed as the god of eloquence. In Irish myth Ogma was the son of Dagda, and has been linked to the Roman god Heracles. Lugus (or Lugh) was another deity worshiped throughout the Celtic world, and has been associated with harvest, and the festival of Lughnasadh. In Irish mythology he is seen as a warrior god, identified with light, and the god of crafts, skills, and invention.

The Romans equated him to Mercury.

Brigandu (also Brigantia or Brigit) was the goddess of fertility, who the Romans linked to Minerva. A British god, Brigandu was unknown on the mainland of Europe. It has also been suggested that she was another personification of Danu, and linked to the festival of Imbolc. Camulos was the Celtic war god, and naturally the Romans linked him to Mars. In Irish annals he is known as Cumal, which was the old Irish term for "warrior."

Left: Bronze figure of the Goddess of Caldevigo, 5th century BC, Paleovenetian.

A Multi-Faceted Religion

We have already seen that while some Celtic deities were worshiped throughout the Celtic world, others only appealed to certain regions. The Celts worshiped places as well as gods, seeing supernatural elements in everything around them; animals and trees, hills and rivers. While the main group of Celtic deities could be identified as having Roman counterparts, other aspects were unique, and ultimately influenced that nascent monotheistic religion, Christianity.

Below: Stone sculpture of a two-headed god c.4th century BC, found at Roquepertuse in France.

The regional aspect of Celtic worship was significant, because of the 400 named Celtic gods, only 100 are mentioned more than once, and many were therefore worshiped in a small and clearly defined area. For example, the Gallic goddess Sequana was worshiped in what is now the French province of Burgundy, but was largely unknown elsewhere. She has been identified with only one shrine, as has Sulis from western England. Some gods clearly had regional variations, based on the same identifiable figure. Others were delineated by tribal or geographical boundaries, such as Lenus, the god of the Treveri (centered around the modern German town of Trier). Another was the god worshiped by the Remi in northern Gaul, in the region around modern-day Reims, who was portrayed as a triple-faced bearded god, although his purpose or name has not yet been identified.

One peculiar aspect of the Celtic deities is that many were portrayed as triune or triple-faced divinities, having three forms or faces, and even three names. Consequently many representations of Celtic gods are depicted with three heads or faces. Examples include a janiform bust found in the Celtic sanctuary of

Roqepertuse in France, and dating from the third century BC, and similar examples from Leichlingen in Germany (fourth century BC) and Reims in France (second century BC).

Three was viewed as a sacred number, as it was by other Indo-European religions, but beyond that, the exact significance of these heads has been lost. Three divisions (earth, fire, and water; body, soul, and spirit; heaven, sea, and underworld) have been a constant in religious belief for as long as can be determined. The Holy Trinity is an obvious Christian parallel.

A belief in the afterworld

Spiritual power could be found in the everyday landscape, flora, and fauna surrounding the Celts. The god Vosegus occupied the Vosges mountains in central Gaul, while others are reflected in the names of springs, rivers, woods, or even marshes. These topographical spirits were often associated with the fertility of the land, and the annual farming cycle. They were worshiped during times of planting, harvest, or drought, and the Celtic farmers who relied on the goodwill of the deities gave votive offerings to them on a regular basis. It is likely, although as yet unproven, that many of Gaul's votive centers were linked to the worship of particular deities. This also applied to areas where human sacrifice was practiced.

Celtic religion was based on a moral system of right and wrong, or good and evil. Certain Christian notions such as predestination or universal sin were unknown to the Ancient Celts, and each individual was responsible for his or her own fate, albeit influenced by the gods. While the druids officiated worship and sacrifice, they were also the spiritual advisers to the community, not simply the interpreters of a fixed set of religious values. From Irish sources it is clear that the Celtic religious ideal was to live in harmony with their surroundings, to accept their own virtues and faults, and to accept that birth and death were part of a divine plan for mankind. Moral weakness, lack of courage, and evil actions were seen as sins that could earn divine retribution, while truth was portrayed as a virtue.

One problem with any interpretation of Celtic belief is that it is either portrayed through the eyes of Roman or Greek outsiders,

or through the works of the much later Irish chroniclers. Later still, Christian influences distorted the Celtic religious system, and adapted old Celtic beliefs into the Christian doctrine as a means of encouraging the conversion of those who adhered to the old ways. Following the widespread adoption of Christianity the remaining Celtic peoples of Europe abandoned their polytheistic practices, but by examining the roots of many early Christian practices we can find the last vestiges of the old Celtic religion as it was once practiced throughout the pre-Christian (and pre-Roman) Celtic world.

Above: In this statue of an unknown Celtic deity, carved from chalkstone, representations of three other Celtic gods appear carved on this reverse side. Dated c.AD 30–40, it was found at Saintes, Charente-Maritimes, France.

The Celtic British Isles showing territories of the Celtic tribes at about AD 44, and the basic structure of Roman Britannia to AD 120.

■ major Roman center or fort
○ Roman or tribal civic center
▬ major roads
— minor roads
PICTS Celtic tribe
••• site of Antonine Wall AD 142
••• site of Hadrian's Wall AD 117

ORCADES INSULAE
(Orkney Islands)

CORNAVII
CAERENI
CARNONACAE
SMERTAE
LUGI
CREONES
DECANTAE
VACOMAGI
CALEDONII
TAEXALI
EPIDII
C A L E D O N I A
VENICONES
DUMNONII
VOTADINI
SELGOVAE
Veluniate
(Carriden)

OCEANUS GERMANICUS
(North Sea)

NOVANTAE

Onnum
(Halton)
Segedunum (Wallsend)
Luguvalium
(Carlisle)
CARVETII
Pons Aelius (Newcastle)

DARINI

PICTS

DUMNONII

ULSTER

MONAVIA
(Isle of Man)

Cataractonium
(Catterick Bridge)

CONNAUGHT

MEATH

(Lancaster)

PARISI

B R I G A N T E S

Eburacum
(York)

H I B E R N I A

GAELS

CAUCI

OCEANUS HIBERNICUS
(Irish Sea)

Namucium
(Manchester)

LEINSTER

MONA
(Anglesey)

Deva
(Chester)

CORITANI

Lindum
(Lincoln)

GANGANI

MENAPII

Segontium
(Caernarvon)

DECEANGLI

GWYNEDD
ORDOVICES

(Littlechester)

Branodunum
(Brancaster)

MUNSTER

Ratae
(Leicester)

CORITANI

Venta Icenorum
(Caistor St. Edmund)

BRIGANTES

Viroconium
(Wroxeter)

CORNOVII

Venonis

I C E N I

IVERNI

POWYS

B R I T A N N I A

Bravonium
(Leintwardine)

CATUVELLAUNI

TRINOVANTES

DEMETAE

SILURES

Glevum
(Gloucester)

DOBUNI

Corinium
(Cirencester)

Fosse Way

Watling Street

Ermine Street

Camulodunum
(Colchester)

DYVET

Venta Silurum

Aquae Sulis
(Bath)

Londinium

Durobrivae
(Rochester)

Rutupiae
(Richborough)

OCEANUS
ATLANTICUS

A T R E B A T E S

Calleva Atrebatum
(Silchester)

Durovernum
(Canterbury)

CANTII

B E L G A E

Venta Belgarum
(Winchester)

Lemanis
(Lympne)

Dubris
(Dover)

DUMNONII

Isca
Dumnoniorum
(Exeter)

DUROTRIGES

R E G N I

Noviomagus
(Chichester)

Portus Itiu

Durnovaria
(Dorchester)

VECTIS INS (Isle of Wight)

Sorviodunum
(Salisbury)

MARE BRITANNICUM
(English Channel)

Chapter 5

The Celts of the British Isles

Many of the cultural and technological movements that spread through the Celtic world of the Iron Age were slow to reach the British Isles, isolated from the rest of Europe by the Channel. So too were the Romans, who brought Celtic civilization to its knees. Following the Roman invasion of Britain in the mid-first century AD, independent Celtic states continued to flourish in the furthest corners of the island, territories the invaders deemed not worth conquering. The Britons of what would become England and Wales

By the time of the Roman invasion of Britain, Celtic society had enjoyed hundreds of years of sophisticated tool-making. Intricate implements were cast from iron using stone molds like this one.

Roman soldiers newly arrived in Britain may have been surprised to find Belgic and Gallic coinage in use, but the flourishing cross-Channel trade meant the regular exchange of goods and money. This coin, minted in northern Gaul, displays a Greek theme, with its ornate head of the god Apollo.

MENAPII

ATREBATES

submitted to Roman rule and even prospered as part of a Romano-British society. But traces of their vibrant Celtic past remained—in Cornwall, Scotland, and Ireland, the Romans never seriously attempted conquest, and life continued as before.

Although the British Isles were inhabited by Celts, there seems to have been no clearly defined common language. Instead, while the tribes in southern Britain spoke a language related to the Gallic tongue of the continent, further north a different dialect prevailed. Similarly, in what are now Scotland and Ireland, a further linguistic division hindered any attempt at unifying these Celtic islands on the fringes of Europe. Otherwise, both Ireland and the mainland of Britain consisted of a patchwork of small tribal political units, with little or no higher level of unity. High-kings had been present in Ireland, but in most cases, larger alliances were purely temporary arrangements, designed to help the confederation of tribes counter an external threat.

Following the subjugation of southern Britain to Roman rule, the Celts within the borders of the Roman province of Britannia became subjects of the emperor. As trade flourished, these Romano-British people benefited from the economic and cultural advantages of being part of the Roman world. In Wales and Cornwall, although subject to Roman influence, the Celtic nature of the local society remained relatively intact due to their location on the periphery of the province. Even further afield, in Ireland and northern Scotland, the Celts who remained free from Roman domination continued to develop and, as the Roman grip on Britannia waned, these peoples became pernicious raiders of Roman Britain. Celtic culture did not end when the Romans conquered southern Britain. In some places, it was simply covered by a thin veneer of Roman civilization.

The Southern Britons

Before the Romans arrived, Britain consisted of a patchwork of tribal areas, each with its own king. There was no political unity, although some of the more powerful leaders could call on the assistance of neighboring tribes in times of crisis. The Romans exploited this fragmentation and it was hard for the Celts to counter the Roman invasion.

Below: The Pimperne House (named after the location of an important find) at Buster, Hampshire, England is a reconstruction of a British Celtic roundhouse.

By AD 43, the Britons and the Romans knew a lot about each other. Caesar made two armed reconaissances of southeastern Britain in 55 and 54 BC. Military and political distractions in the Roman world prevented any further invasion for a century, but the Romans and Romano-Gauls on the mainland of Europe traded with the Celts of southern Britain. In addition, the Romans sought informants and spies in Britain, and strove to destabilize the region by forming alliances with British chieftains. The fragmented tribal nature of Celtic Britain encouraged the Roman policy of divide and rule that had served Caesar so well during the conquest of Gaul.

In the southeastern corner of Britain a succession of Belgic tribes had established themselves, at the expense of other Celtic tribes who were displaced further north. These people were Gauls, driven across the Channel by a combination of a population increase in northern Gaul, and by pressure from the Germans to the east. By the mid-first century BC the territory of the Belgic tribes in Britain stretched from the coast in Kent as far west as the headwaters of the River Thames in the Cotswolds.

Apart from the tribe labeled the Belgae, other Belgic tribes have been identified as the Atrbates to the south of the Thames and the dominant Catuvellauni tribe located to the south of the Wash. Some British tribes already maintained links with the Romans in

Gaul, such as the Iceni, the Cantii, and the Trinovantes, all located within sailing distance of the Romano-Gallic Channel ports. Following the defeat of the unified British resistance at Colchester, their tribal chiefs lined up to become client states of Rome.

Limited links

Further afield, the British tribes were far less willing to submit. The Parisi, the Silures, and the Brigantes located in the center of Britain had little or no contact with the Roman world before the Roman invasion, and they strove to maintain their independence at any cost. Further to the west, in what is now Wales, the tribes in the region endeavored to ally with any other Celtic tribe that was opposed to Roman rule. This resistance continued undiminished until the destruction of Celtic (and druidic) power in Anglesey in AD 61.

Of the 20 main tribal groupings that existed south of the Solway Firth in the first century AD, no clearly defined patterns of allegiance can be determined, save the cultural links of the Belgic tribes and the economic links of those on the eastern coast. Military leaders such as Queen Boudicca united tribes during times of crisis, but these unions were temporary. This endemic lack of unity ultimately brought about the end of Celtic civilization.

Trade flourished during the pre-Roman Celtic period in Britain. Native coinage was first introduced by the Belgae, and by the mid-first century AD it was produced in several locations in southern Britain. Objects from throughout Europe have been discovered in Celtic sites in the region during this period. There is even evidence of a small but vibrant wine trade between southern Britain and the Mediterranean. The name of the modern port of Dover is derived from the Celtic word for *dovr* or *dwfr* meaning "water," and there is ample evidence that the harbor was used for trade between the Belgic territories on both sides of the Channel. Southern Britain was an energetic, bustling society immediately before the arrival of the Romans in Kent. It was nevertheless unable to channel this energy to protect itself.

Above: This coin bearing the name of Tincomarus, a British king of about the late 1st century BC, carries this depiction of a sacred horse on its reverse side.

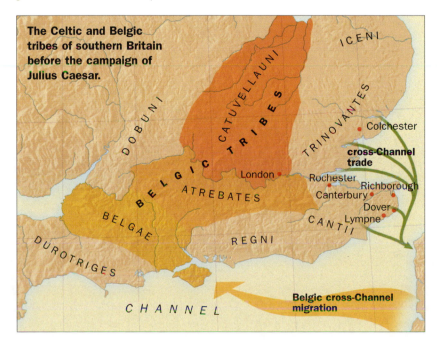

The Celtic and Belgic tribes of southern Britain before the campaign of Julius Caesar.

ICENI

DOBUNI

CATUVELLAUNI

BELGIC TRIBES

TRINOVANTES

Colchester

cross-Channel trade

London

Rochester

Richborough

ATREBATES

Canterbury

Dover

BELGAE

CANTII

Lympne

DUROTRIGES

REGNI

CHANNEL

Belgic cross-Channel migration

The Irish

While the British Isles—the far north excepted—fell to Rome, Ireland was never conquered. Roman historian Tacitus recounts in his biography of Agricola that the Roman general stood on the western coast of Scotland and stared across the Irish Sea at the Emerald Isle. Although he considered conquering it, he never tried, probably because Ireland was seen to lack anything that Rome needed. Together with northern Scotland it would remain an unconquered Celtic bastion at the extremities of the Roman world.

Below: Model of a ship, from Broughter, County Kerry, Ireland. This is a contemporary representation of the craft used by Irish raiders to attack the coast of Roman Britain.

During the Bronze Age, Ireland was occupied by the Erainn people (or the Iverni as Ptolemy labeled them). Later Irish chroniclers claim these people were divided into four tribes, corresponding to the provinces (or "fifths") of Ulster, Leinster, Munster, and Connaught. These early Irish were probably the proto-Celtic cultures who inhabited the rest of western Europe. Irish Celtic mythology describes the period as one where a high king ruled Ireland, with the entire country being governed as a unified whole.

It is mere speculation whether this was the case, or whether the Irish political geography reflected the disunity that came later. By the first century AD Munster had become the dominant province in the island, and the chieftain or king there exerted an influence over much of the southern portion of Ireland. His court was located at Tara, in County Meath, a location that housed a hill fort settlement (*oppidum*) and a meeting area (later called the Rath of the Synods).

Apart from the occasional scrap of archaeological evidence or the mythological tales of later Irish chroniclers, little is known of Irish society and culture of the La Tène period or earlier. The first hard evidence emerges at around the same time as the Roman withdrawal from Britain, around the start of the fifth century AD. By this time, the Irish possessed a similar tribal structure and social organization to that which had existed in Gaul almost 500 years earlier.

Ireland was a patchwork of small tribal kingdoms, each independent of the rest.

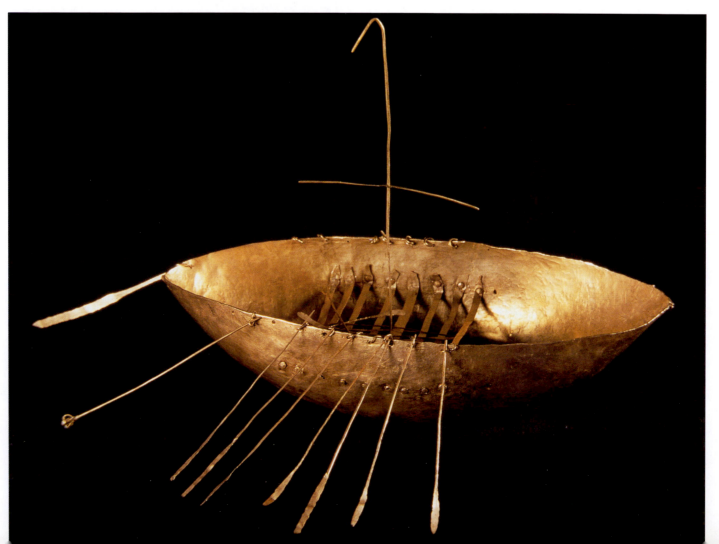

There was no trace of a high king, or a unified state. The only unifying factors in the island were language, religious practices, and social structure.

Nurturing Christianity

At the time the Romans left Britain, the king of Munster was reputedly Niall Noígiallach, whose residence was at Tara. After conquering the central province of Meath, and the region of Ulster in northern Ireland, Irish annals suggest that he divided his territory in Ireland between his sons. His eldest son, Leary Uí Néill (O'Neall), ruled the south from Tara, while his brothers occupied the northern portion, basing themselves in Derry and Donegal.

During the reign of Leary, St. Patrick came to Ireland and began the process of converting the Irish to Christianity. From Tara, St. Patrick continued north to Armagh, where he established his great religious sanctuary. By his actions, Patrick was proclaimed the primary saint of Ireland, protected by the Uí Néills. This protection would have been important at a time when the lack of political unity outside their territories would have made traveling hazardous.

During the last years of the Roman occupation of Britain, Irish raiders began encroaching on the western shores of Britain. They had also established footholds on the mainland of Britain, along the shores of the Severn estuary and the southern coast of Wales, where the kingdom became an Irish colony. A series of devastating raids by the Norsemen, based in Norway, brought any tenuous stability to an end. Coastal raids were followed by attacks on towns and religious centers, and by AD 870 the Norse began to establish permanent settlements in Ireland.

The area around Dublin became a Scandinavian province for over two centuries. While the Norse in Ireland developed trading links, they provided little else for the Irish. This era of Norse rule came to an end in 1018, when an Irish army defeated the Norsemen at the Battle of Clontarf, near Dublin. Although the Norse were evicted from the island, they were only the first in a series of peoples who tried to colonize Ireland, the most persistent of whom were the English. Ireland remained a Celtic country, but it had become inextricably involved in the political dynamics of the rest of the British Isles.

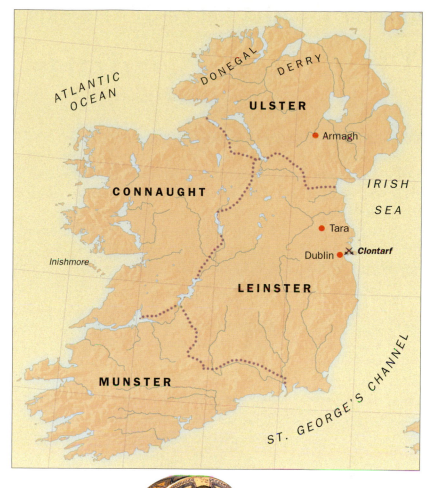

Left: St Cuiléin's bell, from Glankeen, County Tipperary, dates from about 650–750, but the ornate extra work dates from the early 12th century.

73

The Caledonians and Picts

In remote, unconquered northern Britain, Roman conquest was resisted by the Caledonians. They proved a sufficient thorn in the side of the Romans that Hadrian's Wall was built to keep them at bay. Two centuries later the same people were referred to as the Picts, or "painted people." This mysterious group has left behind little trace, but their legacy survives in hundreds of enigmatic stone monoliths and carvings.

Right: Meigle Stone II, one of a series of striking Pictish carved reliefs from the early 8th century, depicting a hunting scene.

Humans have lived in Scotland since at least 7500 BC, and by 4000 BC people had become Neolithic farmers, and also the builders of substantial burial mounds (*see pages 12–13*). Circles of standing stones such as the Ring of Brodgar in Orkney stand as mute testimony to the achievements of these early Scots. There is evidence that the continental cultural exchanges that characterized the Bronze Age had become far less commonplace by Celtic times. Instead,

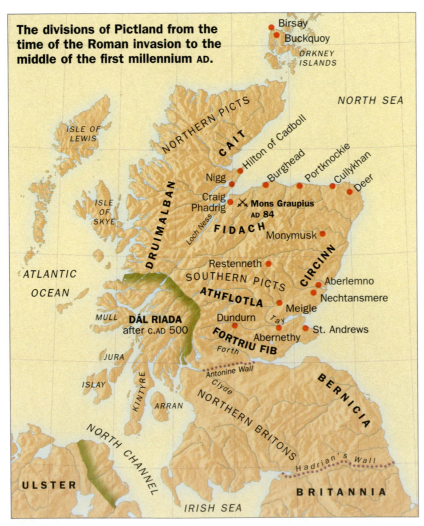

The divisions of Pictland from the time of the Roman invasion to the middle of the first millennium AD.

Birsay
Buckquoy
ORKNEY ISLANDS
ISLE OF LEWIS
NORTHERN PICTS
CAIT
NORTH SEA
Hilton of Cadboll
Nigg
Burghead
Portknockie
Cullykhan
Deer
Craig Phadrig
Loch Ness
✕ Mons Graupius AD 84
FIDACH
Monymusk
ISLE OF SKYE
DRUIMALBAN
ATLANTIC OCEAN
Restenneth
SOUTHERN PICTS
CIRCINN
Aberlemno
ATHFLOTLA
Meigle
Nechtansmere
MULL
DÁL RIADA after c.AD 500
Dundurn
Tay
St. Andrews
FORTRIU FIB
Abernethy
Forth
JURA
ISLAY
Antonine Wall
Clyde
BERNICIA
KINTYRE
ARRAN
NORTHERN BRITONS
NORTH CHANNEL
ULSTER
Hadrian's Wall
BRITANNIA
IRISH SEA

Scotland at the start of the Iron Age was more insular, reflecting similar fragmenting traits in Ireland and southern Britain. The Celts in Scotland were not migratory tribes from other regions. Instead, they were the direct descendants of the Bronze Age people who preceded them.

During the first century AD, Scotland was a Celtic tribal region, its land divided into 16 tribal divisions. Four of these peoples lay south of the Forth-Clyde line, in what is now southern Scotland. Of the remaining northern tribes, the Caledones inhabited the Great Glen, a glacial rift incorporating Loch Ness. To their north lay the territories of the Creones, Decantae, Carnonacae, Lugi, Smertae, and Cornavii (*see map page 68*). In northeast Scotland were the Vacomagi, Taexali and Venicones, while the Epidii inhabited modern Argyll.

The Greek geographer Ptolemy, writing in the second century AD, recorded these tribal names, and if other smaller groups existed, their details went unrecorded. By the time of the first Roman contact with the Scottish Celts in the late first century AD, the northern tribes were collectively known as the Caledones (or Caledonians). The Roman historian Tacitus reported that these northern peoples had "red hair and massive limbs," drawing a distinction between them and their southern neighbors. There is also evidence that these tribes had united into a larger Caledonian confederation.

Agricola advanced into Scotland in AD 79, and in AD 84 he defeated the Caledonians at the Battle of Mons Graupius. Despite his victory, Agricola withdrew his forces into southern Scotland. Although later Roman punitive expeditions were conducted into Caledonian territory, there was never any further attempt to occupy it. By the third century AD, references to Caledonians had been replaced by ones to the more mysterious Picts (painted people).

Shrouded in myth

The Picts are some of the most misunderstood peoples of the Celtic world. As late as the 12th century, an Icelandic historian wrote that they were a race of pygmies. A reference from AD 313 speaks of the Picts and Caledonians as separate people, but it probably meant the "Caledonians and other Picts." It appears that the Picts were the same Celtic people who inhabited northern Scotland, only they were given a new collective name.

During the fourth century AD the Picts reputedly allied themselves with the Dál Riadan Scots to attack settlements in southern Scotland and beyond Hadrian's Wall. Repeated Pictish and Scottish raids continued until the final withdrawal of the Romans in the early fifth century AD. From that point on until the union of the Picts and Scots four centuries later, evidence comes from archaeology and from other non-Pictish sources, such as the Irish annals.

Pictland consisted of all of what is now Scotland north of the Forth and Clyde, apart from the southwestern portion which formed Dál Riada. This region was divided into northern and southern portions, which in turn may have been further subdivided into smaller provinces: Cait, Fidach, and Druimalban in the north and Fortriu, Fib, Athflota, and Circinn to the south. The first historically identifiable Pictish king was Bridei mac Maelcon, who was converted to Christianity by St. Columba about AD 570. From then on, Celtic missionaries recorded the details of the Pictish monarchs and their almost incessant warfare against their neighbors or rebellious subjects. For a century the Picts raided to the south and west, and in AD 685 they defeated the Anglo-Saxons of Northumbria at the Battle of Nechtansmere, which ensured that the Saxon military and cultural assimilation of the Britons was limited to the territories to the south of Pictland.

Below: Built by the proto-Pictish Broch People, Mousa Broch in Shetland served as a fortification throughout the Pictish period. It remained in use until the early middle ages.

The Scots

It is easy to think of the inhabitants of Scotland at the time of the Roman occupation of Britain as "Scots," but a mistake. Roman writers referred to the Irish as the Scotii. In the centuries following the collapse of Roman Britain, these Irish Scotii launched raids against the west coast of the British mainland. In the west coast of what is now Scotland, these raiders were followed by settlers.

A new kingdom was formed by the "Scots" settlers called Dál Riada. It encompassed Ulster in northern Ireland and large portions of the Scottish west coast. By the ninth century AD the Dál Riadan Scots had somehow united with the Picts who occupied the east of Alba (Scotland), to create a new, unified Celtic country in the north of Britain.

A significant body of archaeological and documentary information has provided historians with the opportunity to better understand the Scots of Dál Riada. Irish chroniclers recorded significant events in the development of the colony, while monks from the Celtic monastery at Iona provided even more detailed information from AD 563 onwards. There is also archaeological evidence for earlier contacts between western Scotland and northern Ireland. Both regions share similar Bronze Age features, such as the remains of crannog lake dwellings, fortified villages or raths, burial mounds, and ceramic production.

The first Irish raids against the west coast of Britain date from the first decades of the fifth century AD. Accounts are contradictory, but the favorite version of the founding of Dál Riada comes from an Irish account, which claims that around AD 500 the colony was founded by the Ulster nobleman Fergus Mór, son of Erc. He then divided it into three parts with his brothers Oengus and Loarn. Another suggestion is that the region was already partially settled before AD 500, and the three divisions of Dál Riada reflect a coalition of three distinct settlements (known as Cenel Loairn, Cenel Gabrain and Cenel Oengusa).

Gabran and Comgall were the grandsons of Fergus Mór, and they consolidated the family grip over the colony, adding the island of Arran to Dál Riada during the mid-sixth century AD. Gabran (who died around AD 558) conducted campaigns against the Picts and the Celtic tribes in the Clyde and Forth valleys, but his successor Conall was too occupied by internal trouble to consider war against his neighbors.

Conall (c.AD 558–74) fought rebellions in the Western Isles, and campaigned against the other sub kings of Dál Riada. The colony was reunified by his cousins Eoganan and Aedan mac Gabran, and the arrival of St. Columba added further stability

Below: Mote of Mark, major fortified center of kingdom of Rheged-Cumbria in the 6th century AD, Dumfries & Galloway, Scotland.

to the region. Of the two, Aedan was the most successful, helping the Celts against the Saxons of Northumbria, and campaigning against the Picts.

Picts and Scots unite

A Celtic defeat at the Battle of Degsasten (AD 603) brought an end to Dál Riadan involvement in British resistance to the Saxons, and it appears that for the next generation the Scots avoided external adventures. This period of isolation ended around AD 635, when the Scots king Domnall Brecc fought a string of unsuccessful campaigns in Ulster and Pictland. He died in battle at the hands of the Celts of Strathclyde in AD 645, when it is said that "ravens gnawed his head." His passing marked a change in the internal structure of Dál Riada.

The kingdom was split up into small tribal territories, although a high-king drawn from the descendants of Gabran and Comgall exerted some degree of overall control over the colony. Unity was finally restored by Ferchar the Tall (c.AD 680–96), a ruler of Cenel Loairn. Although the details remain unclear, some form of political or marriage alliance between the Scots and the Picts led to a temporary union between the two nations during the first half of the eighth century AD. The Pictish king Oengus may have conquered the Scots in AD 741, but the colony regained its independence in AD 778.

Dál Riada was effectively controlled by the Picts, then it appears the reverse took place, with the Scots gaining ascendancy over their eastern neighbors. Eventually, the Dál Riadan high king Kenneth mac Alpin united the Picts and the Scots in AD 843. How or why this happened is still unclear. What is certain is that Kenneth mac Alpin was the first king of a unified Scottish nation. Scotland would remain an independent Celtic country until the death of its last Celtic king, Macbeth, in the 11th century.

Left: The Church tower at Abernethy in Angus dates from the 11th century, but was built on the foundations of an earlier settlement established in Pictland by Scots-Irish Celtic missionaries.

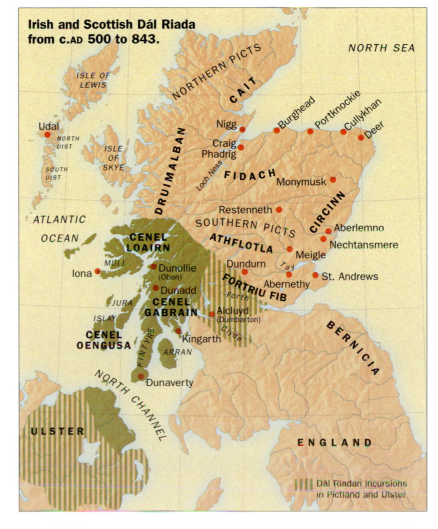

Irish and Scottish Dál Riada from c.AD 500 to 843.

The Welsh

The inaccessibility of the mountainous Welsh lands ensured that the region would remain a bastion of Celtic resistance to the Roman invaders. After the Romans left the British Isles the region's inhabitants were threatened first by fellow Celts from Ireland, and then by the Saxons. The Welsh Celts were eventually subdued by the English in the Middle Ages, but Celtic identity remained strong in the country, and continues to the present day.

A lack of written sources mean that much of the early history of the Britons of Wales is obscure. Archaeological evidence points to trading links existing between Ireland, Wales, and the rest of Britain long before the arrival of the Romans in the first century AD. Four Celtic tribes occupied the area; the Deciangeli in the northeast, the Ordovices in the northwest, the Demetae to the southwest and the Belgae to the southeast. The latter were the same tribe whose territory extended across southern Britain from the River Severn to the Solent.

The island of Anglesey (*Mona*) provided a last refuge for the Celtic druids, and when the Roman governor Suetonius Paulinus captured the island in the mid-first century AD he destroyed the power of the druids, who he saw as the instigators of resistance to the Romans. Later Welsh chronicles suggest that the region prospered under Roman rule, and the withdrawal of the Romans from Britain in the early fifth century AD left the region vulnerable to attack by the Irish. The Romans had allowed the local Celtic rulers to govern their own affairs, and these tribal leaders suddenly found themselves responsible for the defense of independent kingdoms.

Clashes between the Welsh Celts and those in the rest of Britain and Ireland continued over the next few centuries, but increasingly the sub-Roman British were being forced westward by Anglo-Saxon invaders. As Wales played host to streams of Celtic refugees, the local Celtic rulers did whatever they could to halt the Anglo-Saxon advance. When the Saxons reached the River Severn in the late sixth century AD, the Welsh Celts found themselves on the front line.

By this time the old Celtic tribes had matured into a handful of small Celtic states. Dyfed in the southwest was the descendent of the tribal territory of the Demetae, although it was ruled by an Irish dynasty during the late Roman period. The origins of Powys are obscure, but it was based in mountains of north Wales, and maintained a good relationship with the Romans and its sub-Roman neighbors. Gwynedd was based around the territories of the Ordovices, and was named after its ruling dynasty. These rulers were singled out by the historian Gildas as being evil, and were linked to *Maglocunus*, the dragon, which eventually became the national symbol of Wales.

Land of Weahlas

The sixth century AD was seen as a particularly vibrant period for the Welsh, and the era was subsequently known as "the age of saints." The Christian conversion of the Welsh was completed during the sixth century AD, while the first written accounts of Celtic Welsh culture were produced.

By the seventh century AD the Anglo-Saxon

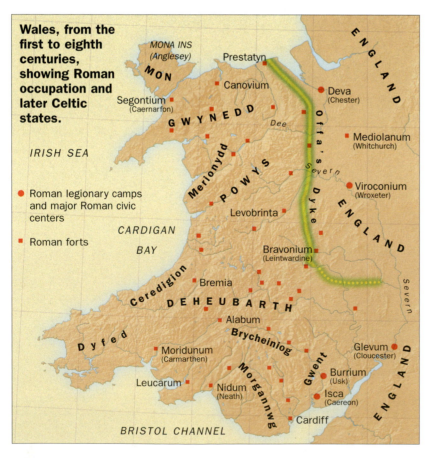

Wales, from the first to eighth centuries, showing Roman occupation and later Celtic states.

MONA INS (Anglesey)
MON
Prestatyn
Canovium
Segontium (Caernarfon)
GWYNEDD
Dee
Deva (Chester)
ENGLAND
Mediolanum (Whitchurch)
IRISH SEA
Merionydd
POWYS
Severn
Offa's Dyke
Viroconium (Wroxeter)
ENGLAND
Levobrinta
● Roman legionary camps and major Roman civic centers
CARDIGAN BAY
Ceredigion
■ Roman forts
Bravonium (Leintwardine)
Bremia
DEHEUBARTH
Alabum
Brycheiniog
Severn
Dyfed
Moridunum (Carmarthen)
Glevum (Gloucester)
Leucarum
Nidum (Neath)
Morgannwg
Gwent
Burrium (Usk)
Isca (Caereon)
Cardiff
ENGLAND
BRISTOL CHANNEL

Left and Below: Din Lligwy, Celtic village from the Late Roman era, Anglesey.

English had established their western border at the foot of the Welsh mountains, enclosing the remaining Celts in the Welsh peninsula, which they called the land of the *weahlas*, or foreigners. The Celts themselves called the country *Cymru* —land of the comrades. During the following century the English king Offa (AD 747–96) built a dyke that joined the Rivers Severn and Dee, creating a boundary between Wales and English Mercia. For the next five centuries, the Welsh struggled to retain their political independence in the face of English and Norse incursions.

After the Norman conquest of England in 1066 the Normans created a military buffer zone along the Welsh border. By the end of the 13th century, the English were simply too powerful for the Welsh to stop. Edward I of England (1272–1307) not only invaded and occupied Wales, but also built huge castles to maintain English control. Although Wales would maintain its cultural identity, apart from brief periods of revolt the region would remain firmly controlled by the English. Despite this, the Welsh retained a good measure of autonomy, and today Wales (Cymru) is a truly Celtic country, whose cultural and linguistic roots are treasured.

The Cornish

The only region of what is now England to avoid Roman occupation, Cornwall was left with its Celtic identity intact. The peninsula even thrived by exporting Cornish tin throughout the Roman Empire, as it had done centuries earlier with other Mediterranean peoples such as the Phoenicians. Following the Roman withdrawal from Britain and the subsequent invasions by Angles and Saxons, Cornwall's geographical isolation allowed it to retain a fragile autonomy.

Land's End—Celtic Cornwall remained isolated from Roman and then Anglo-Saxon influence, and still retains aspects of this independence today.

Before the Roman invasion of Britain in the mid-first century AD, Cornwall was the tribal homeland of the Cornovii, and the region was largely unaffected by the Roman occupation of Britain. Trade between the Cornovii and Romans flourished, with the Roman city of Exeter becoming the trading center for exported Cornish tin and imported Gallic produce. When the Romans left Britain at the start of the fifth century AD, Cornwall (or *Kernow*) maintained its prosperity, and trade continued with the sub-Roman Kingdom of Dumnonia to the east, and that of Cornouaille in Brittany. This all changed with the coming of the Saxons.

As the Anglo-Saxons moved westward through Britain and established the Kingdom of Wessex, the Kingdom of Dumnonia (now the counties of Dorset and Devon) provided a bulwark from the Saxons for over a century. In 577 the Saxons drove a wedge between Dumnonia and the remainder of Celtic Britain when they captured the valley of the River Severn. Dumnonia finally fell to the Anglo-Saxon armies advancing from Wessex during the first decade of the eighth century. King Geraint, the last British King of Dumnonia was killed in battle, and by 710 the Saxons had reached the old Roman city of Exeter.

By the time the invaders had finished consolidating their hold on their new territories, the Britons had reorganized their defenses around Exeter. In 721 the Britons defeated a Saxon invading army at Camelford, on the River Camel. This decisive battle effectively prevented any further Anglo-Saxon incursions into Devon and Cornwall for another century.

Cornwall was seen as a distinct political entity in Britain by the late eighth century, as Bishop Kentsec of the Celtic Church is recorded as being granted the title of Bishop of *Kernow*, the Celtic name for the region. (*Kern* was a term given to Celtic warriors). To the Anglo-Saxons or *English*, the inhabitants of Kernow were known as the *Kearn Weahlas*, or Kern foreigners. The term Cornwall was derived from this (but note the similarity to *Cornouaille*, accross the Channel in Brittany).

Throughout the early Medieval period, the Cornish were also known as the West Welsh. At the start of the ninth century *Kernow* extended beyond the modern county boundary of Cornwall which starts at the River Tamar, and stretched through much of former Dumnonia to Exeter. The city was probably seen as a frontier fortress between the English and the Britons.

The Celtic peninsula

In 814 a revitalized Anglo-Saxon kingdom renewed the offensive. Led by King Egbert of Wessex, the border raids started again and, in 825, he won a significant victory over the Cornish. Although it has never been proven, it has been suggested that the Cornish were driven back to the line of the Tamar, and the Celtic area from modern Plymouth to Exeter was occupied by the English.

The Cornish were driven to desperate measures to ensure their own survival. In 838 they made an alliance with the Norsemen, and a combined Celtic-Norse army fought King Egbert's Anglo-Saxons at Hingston in Devon. Although the allies were defeated, Egbert died the following year, and the English were unable to take advantage of their victory. Internecine fighting among the English prevented any renewed offensive against Cornwall for almost a century.

Finally in 927 the Anglo-Saxon high-king Athelstan marked his victory over the Celts of Northumbria and Cumbria by holding a ceremony, where the remaining Celtic rulers of southern Britain paid homage to him. These Celtic rulers included King Hywel of the West Welsh. Three years later Athelstan invaded *Kernow*, although it is likely that he simply re-established the frontier along the Tamar by driving the Celts out of Devon to the east. The English crown claimed overlordship of Cornwall, as King Edmund (939–46) styled himself King of the British Province (Cornwall). Nevertheless, the Cornish territories were only incorporated into Anglo-Saxon England on paper, and the region maintained its own laws, Church, and social hierarchy. It was only after the Norman conquest of 1066 that Cornwall was forced to become an integral part of the English state. To the Cornish, the notion of a separate identity continues to this day.

Left: Celtic bronze mirror found in a grave at Trelan Bahow, St. Keverne, Cornwall, dating from the 1st century BC.

BRISTOL CHANNEL

Old Burrow

Barnstaple

Tiverton

Bury Barton

North Tawton

Cullompton

Ochementone (Okehampton)

D U M N O N I A

Isca (Exeter)

Ide

Tintagel

✕ **Camelford 721**

Nanstallon

K E R N O W   (C O R N W A L L)

Totenais (Totnes)

Cornish territory to 825

Cross-Channel trade with Cornouaille in Brittany

81

Expansion of Republican Rome from 200 BC to the eve of Julius Caesar's conquest of Gaul in 58 BC, and the frontiers at the end of the Gallic Wars in 43 BC.

NORTH SEA

BALTIC SEA

ALBION
(BRITANNIA)

ATLANTIC OCEAN

GERMANIA

BELGICA

GALLIA

AQUITANIA

GALLIA
NARBONENSIS

CISALPINE GAUL

Mediolanum
(Milan)

Aquileia

ILLYRICUM

DALMATIA

Narbo

Massilia

TARRACONENSIS

Tarraco

Salonae

ADRIATIC SEA

LUSITANIA

CORSICA

ITALIA

Rome

Emerita Augusta

BAETICA

SARDINIA

Brundisium

Corduba

BALEARICS

Gades
(Cadiz)

MEDITERRANEAN

SICILY

MAURETANIA

Carthage

SEA

Syracuse

AFRICA

MALTA

Left: Before Julius Caesar, Rome's greatest general was Gaius Marius, who reformed the Roman citizens' army and made it into the professional force that would soon conquer the Western world. The forced-march tactics he developed and the roads he built later helped Julius Caesar's campaigns in Gaul. But it was Caesar who honed the Roman legionaries that, because they carried everything needed on their backs, were known as "Marius's Mules."

▨ Roman territory c.200 BC

▨ Roman territory c.100 BC

▨ disputed territory at 58 BC

▨ Roman territory after conquests of Julius Caesar c.43 BC

● provincial Roman capital

Chapter 6
The Roman Conquests

At the start of the second century BC, the Roman Republic controlled Spain, Greece, North Africa, and much of Italy and the rest of the Mediterranean basin. Within 50 years the Celtic regions of northern Italy and southern Gaul would be added to the inventory, turning the Mediterranean into a Roman lake. These provinces would also serve as a springboard for Rome's conquest of the Celtic world.

Pressured by migrating Germans from the east, the Gauls of the late La Tène period were forced to give up their territories to the east of the River Rhine. As the Dacians overran the last Celtic outposts along the Danube and in Bohemia, the Romans consolidated their control over the southern Gauls. The alliances forged between Rome and these southern tribes, and the problems caused by the migrating Germans proffered the excuse Julius Caesar needed to launch a campaign of conquest in Gaul. The tool at his disposal was ideally suited to the task. Following the military reforms of Gaius Marius, the Roman legionary was the best trained and most versatile soldier in the ancient world. With commanders such as Caesar, victory was all but assured.

In a well-orchestrated campaign, Caesar systematically destroyed Celtic resistance in Gaul, and even launched punitive expeditions against Germania to safeguard the Rhine frontier. In battle after battle, Gallic bravado and impetuosity led to defeat at the hands of the well-trained and superbly disciplined Roman legions. By 52 BC Gallic resistance had been crushed following the bloody siege of Alesia, and Vercingetorix, the Gauls' last hope, was a prisoner in Rome. From that point on, Gaul was a Roman province. Only the Celts of Britain remained free from Roman domination.

A century later the Roman legionaries landed in southern Britain and brushed aside the British forces opposing them. With the south of Britain in Rome's hands, a series of governors extended Roman rule in the province, despite a bloody rebellion led by the warrior queen Boudicca in AD 60. The last resistance in Wales was crushed in a bloodbath on the Celtic holy sanctuary of Anglesey. Over the next decades the Romans advanced as far as the north of Scotland, but were unable to subdue the few remaining free Celts in the remote mountains of the highlands. Instead, they built a wall to protect the northern border of their Roman province of Britannia. Ireland and (to a lesser extent) Scotland were left to their own devices; the last truly independent outposts of the Celtic world.

The Cimbri Migration

During the last decades of the second century BC a seemingly aimless Germanic migration led to conflict between Germans, Gauls, and Romans. The German Cimbri and their Celtic allies defeated a series of Roman armies, before being forced down into Italy by the northern Gauls. The Roman legions of Gaius Marius defeated the migrating tribes and, in saving Rome, laid foundations for Roman intervention in Celtic affairs.

In 113 BC reports reached Republican Rome of the fullscale migration of a barbarian horde headed toward Italy from Bohemia. According to Roman historian Plutarch the horde comprised two Germanic tribes—the Cimbri and the Teutones—possessing a military strength of 300,000 men. Most accounts record that the two tribes had amalgamated for convenience, and were referred to generically as the Cimbri.

Although the Celtic Boii in Bohemia

persuaded these intruders to kep moving, conflict with other tribes was inevitable. Somewhere in the vicinity of Belgrade they came into contact with the Scordisci, a tribe of Danubian Celts. The Celts defeated the Germans and forced them to divert to the west, into Noreia (modern Austria). When the Cimbri encroached on the territory of the Taurisci Celts, who were Roman allies, the Senate began to take notice of the migration. The Taurisci invoked the terms of their protection treaty and called on the Senate for help.

Carbo, one of the two Roman consuls for the year, set out and brought the Germans to battle at Noreia (113 BC), where he was soundly defeated for his pains. Carbo committed suicide and the remnants of his army straggled back into Italy. Italy lay at the mercy of the two German tribes, but inexplicably they turned away and spent the next three years in the northern Alpine foothills of Austria and southern Germany.

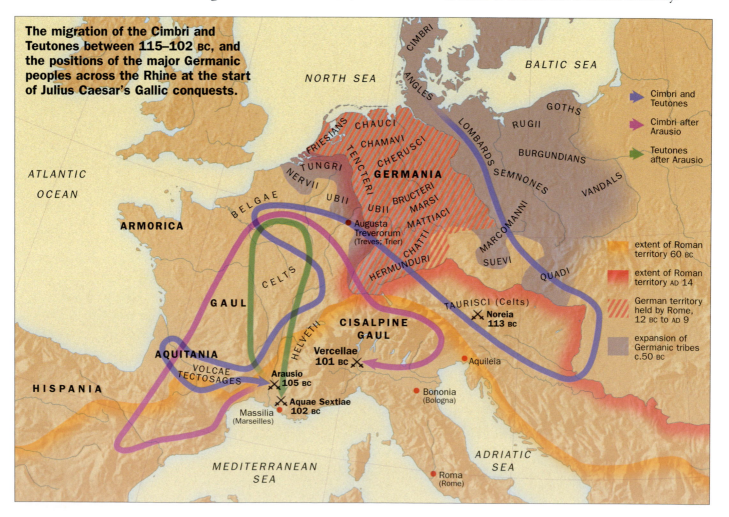

The migration of the Cimbri and Teutones between 115–102 BC, and the positions of the major Germanic peoples across the Rhine at the start of Julius Caesar's Gallic conquests.

When they reached the Rhône valley, the Cimbri were joined by a number of Gauls, including the Helvetii and the Tigurini. In 109 BC the Roman consul Marcus Julius Silanus marched into the Rhône valley to bring the Cimbri to battle, but once again the barbarians were victorious. When news of the Roman defeat spread, other Gauls joined the migration. The Volcae-Tectosages Gauls from around Tolosa (Toulouse) broke their diplomatic ties with Rome, but the Celts were defeated by the Consul Lucius Cassius Longinus in 107 BC.

For Longinus, it was to be a short-lived victory. When he turned and marched against the Tigurini, Longinus was defeated. The new first consul for 106 BC was Quintus Servilius Caepio. An experienced soldier, he was expected to reverse the string of Roman defeats. After recapturing Tolosa (and capturing the fabled Celtic gold of Tolosa), Caepio repeated the mistakes Longinus had made.

Rome acts decisively

The Senate was exasperated. A mob of barbarian Germans and Gauls had defeated every army sent against it by Rome. In 104 BC the veteran soldier Gaius Marius was elected consul for a second term of a year, breaking established Republican protocol. It was an indication of the seriousness with which the Roman Republic viewed the Cimbri threat that it was prepared to create what amounted to a dictatorship.

Marius took the opportunity to overhaul and reorganize the Roman Army, recognizing that the traditions of a once agrarian tribe no longer suited the requirements of a city-state rapidly expanding into an empire. The result was the professional standing army that came to epitomize Roman military might throughout the western world for 500 years.

By 102 BC the Cimbri had returned to southern Gaul, and Marius and his revitalized legionaries marched north to meet them. He found that the Cimbri had split into three groups. The Teutones and Ambrones were moving eastward into Italy along the Mediterranean coast. At Aquae Sextiae, the modern Aix-en-Provence, Marius decisively beat both tribes in a two-day defensive battle (102 BC). The Cimbri entered the Po valley, forcing the Roman garrison there to retreat ahead of them. When Marius arrived, the Romans went over to the attack. At Vercellae (101 BC), the Cimbri warriors were slaughtered, as were their families who accompanied them. The Gallic Tigurini avoided battle, and turned north again to join the Helvetii in the Swiss Alps. Although both Rome and Gaul had been saved, the Roman Senate subsequently considered southern Gaul as a vital protectorate; a buffer state against further barbarian incursion. Fifty years later, this would lead to the Roman conquest of the whole of Gaul.

Above: Romans fighting Gauls—relief from a triumphal arch at Les Antique, St. Remey, Provence. In reality, Celtic and Germanic armies repeatedly defeated the Romans in battle until the military reforms of Gaius Marius.

Caesar's Conquest of Gaul

In 58 BC, Julius Caesar led his Roman legions into Gaul, ostensibly to protect the Celts from external enemies, such as the Germans or the Helvetii. In reality he was launching a full-scale invasion of Celtic Gaul. By adopting a policy of divide and conquer he schemed, allied, and fought his way through the Celtic and neighboring Belgic nations and defeated the disunited Gauls in battle after battle. Within three years he had conquered most of Gaul, and even launched expeditions into Britain. Within six years the conquest was complete.

In 125 BC the Greek colony of Massilia (now Marseilles) had been besieged by the Saluvii Gauls, and it appealed to Rome for help. A Roman army captured the Saluvii capital, then defeated an allied Gallic army comprised of the Saluvii and the neighboring Allobroges. Another tribe, the Arverni, joined in and were also defeated.

Rome duly annexed the coastal territories of the Saluvii, the Allobroges, and Massilia and turned the region into the province of Gallia Narbonensis, named after its capital at Narbonensis (modern Narbonne). Together with Gallia Cisalpina (conquered in the early second century BC), the two previously Gallic provinces were given the collective name of Gallia Transalpina. This region was destined to be Caesar's base for his conquest of the rest of Gaul.

His opportunity came in 58 BC. A decade before, in 70 BC a Germanic people called the Suevi had crossed the Rhine and settled in Alsace, in northeast Gaul. Ten years later their king, Ariovistus, defeated a Gallic army sent to drive the Suevi back into Germany. At the same time the Dacians subdued the Danube Celts, including the Boii, then made an alliance with the Suevi. Faced with this joint threat from north and east, the Celtic Helvetii people (of modern Switzerland) migrated toward the relative safety of southeast Gaul.

Superior tactics

Caesar refused to give them permission to cross the territory of the Allobroges to safety, and portrayed the migration to the Senate as a serious threat to Gallia Transalpina. He reinforced his troops in the region, then when the Helvetii entered the Gallic lands of the Sequani, he moved up the Rhône to attack them. At the Battle of Bibracte (58 BC) his four legions

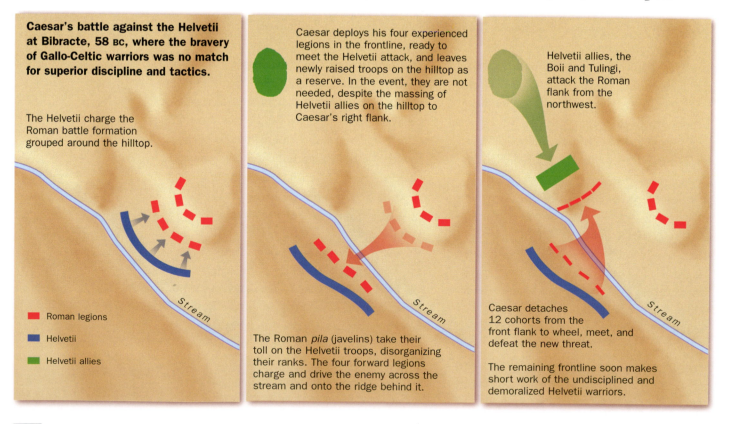

Caesar's battle against the Helvetii at Bibracte, 58 BC, where the bravery of Gallo-Celtic warriors was no match for superior discipline and tactics.

The Helvetii charge the Roman battle formation grouped around the hilltop.

- 🟥 Roman legions
- 🟦 Helvetii
- 🟩 Helvetii allies

Stream

Caesar deploys his four experienced legions in the frontline, ready to meet the Helvetii attack, and leaves newly raised troops on the hilltop as a reserve. In the event, they are not needed, despite the massing of Helvetii allies on the hilltop to Caesar's right flank.

The Roman *pila* (javelins) take their toll on the Helvetii troops, disorganizing their ranks. The four forward legions charge and drive the enemy across the stream and onto the ridge behind it.

Helvetii allies, the Boii and Tulingi, attack the Roman flank from the northwest.

Caesar detaches 12 cohorts from the front flank to wheel, meet, and defeat the new threat.

The remaining frontline soon makes short work of the undisciplined and demoralized Helvetii warriors.

defeated the greater number of Helvetii and their Celtic allies, and drove them back into the Swiss Alps. He used the support of pro-Roman Gallic chiefs such as Divitiacus of the Aedui to force the Senate to nominate him Protector of the Gauls.

Caesar now had the excuse to move even further north and attack Ariovistus of the Suevi. Caesar already occupied the lands of the Sequani, and was allied to the Aedui further east. With his lines of communication secured by garrisons, he advanced into Alsace, where he defeated the Suevi. After spending the winter in eastern Gaul, Caesar heard of disunity in the tribal ranks of the Belgae, his neighbors to the northwest. There were 11 distinct tribal subdivisions of the Belgae. Caesar attacked them in 57 BC, destroying each tribal host individually before they could combine forces.

His most serious opponents were the Nervii and the Aduatuci, who almost checked Caesar on the Sambre before he defeated them. During the same year, Publius Licinius Crassus, Caesar's lieutenant, subdued the various small tribes who inhabited modern Normandy and Brittany. In the following year (56 BC) a revolt by the maritime Veneti people of Brittany prompted Caesar to build a fleet, which he manned with crewmen from Gallia Transalpina and Roman legionaries.

While the Veneti relied on large sailing craft, Caesar used a force built around war galleys. During a sea battle fought in Morbihan Bay in Brittany, his galleys attacked the becalmed Veneti and destroyed them. With control of the sea, Caesar was free to launch a reconnaissance against the Belgae tribes in southeast Britain.

Alesia: The Final Battle

If Caesar's Gallic campaigns were marked by innovative tactics, Celtic disunity was also a major factor in Roman success… until Vercingetorix. This unusual prince of the Averni led the Gallic tribes in rebellion, and his guerrilla tactics almost ejected the Romans from Gaul. The first mistake Vercingetorix made—closing his army in the fortress of Alesia—was also his last, and the outcome of the siege would determine the fate of Gaul.

Below: Statue in honor of Vercingetorix by Aimé Millet (1819–91).

It is likely that Caesar first contemplated launching an expedition against Britain while he was campaigning in Brittany. An initial expedition in 55 BC was met with fierce opposition from the Cantii tribe in Kent, and storms disrupted Roman communications with Gaul. The expedition was recalled. In the following year the Romans returned and fought their way through the Cantii heartland to reach the River Thames. Caesar fought a British coalition of tribes led by Cassivelaunus of the Catuvellauni and defeated them before returning to Gaul.

Caesar's return was in part prompted by logistical problems of cross-Channel supply and also by a growing revolt among the Gauls. Unrest was stirring among the Senones, the Carnutes, and the Eburones. During the first phase of his campaign, Caesar was able to play on the lack of unity between the various Celtic tribes. But as Gallic resistance hardened, this became increasingly difficult.

In 52 BC, Celtic resistance centered around Vercingetorix, a prince of the Averni. The Carnutes led the call for rebellion against Rome. Vercingetorix called for a concerted strategy, aimed at severing Caesar's lines of supply. The first signs of revolt came in the form of attacks on Roman outposts and patrols. With his supply lines threatened, Caesar had to prove he still held the upper hand. He thwarted a Gallic invasion of Gallia Transalpina, then helped defend his Aedui allies. Vercingetorix responded by instituting a scorched-earth policy, and called on his fellow Gallic rebels to support him by destroying their vulnerable strongholds.

End of Gallic resistance

Vercingetorix was a realist among Celts—he recognized that his people were no match for the sleek Roman fighting machine in open battle. He favored a guerilla policy, abandoning fixed positions and fullscale battles. This ran contrary to everything the Celtic warrior

French museum model of the Roman lines of circumvallation built around Alesia in 52 BC.

believed in, but was a vital change in strategy. The scorched earth policy failed when the Bituriges tribe refused to destroy their principal Oppidum to prevent the Romans occupying it.

Roman engineering overcame Gallic resistance, and the city fell, with the loss of 40,000 inhabitants. Next, Caesar besieged the rebel hilltop stronghold of Gergovia (near modern Clermont-Ferrand), only to be driven off by the defenders. This was Caesar's first setback, and he planned a general withdrawal into Transalpine Gaul to reorganize his forces. But now, Vercingetorix made a fatal error. While his army was harassing the retreating Romans, he allowed his cavalry to become involved in a large engagement, where they were defeated by Caesar's German mercenary cavalry. This time it was the turn of the Gauls to retreat, and Caesar pursued them northward.

Vercingetorix rallied his forces at the hilltop fortress of Alesia, the capital of the Mandubii. When Caesar arrived he laid siegeworks around the hilltop; lines of circumvallation, with two lines of defenses, facing outward as well as inward. A "minefield" of sharpened stakes, caltrops, and ditches reinforced these defensive lines. After a month, Vercingetorix sent the women and children away from the fortress, but Caesar refused them passage through the Roman lines. They were left to perish between the two forces. A long-awaited Gallic relief army finally arrived, and concerted Gallic attacks were launched on both sides of the Roman siege lines. Caesar's defenses resisted three furious assaults before the relief army withdrew.

With his men starving, Vercingetorix rode to Caesar's camp and surrendered, bringing to an end the last concerted resistance to Roman rule in Gaul. Over the following year Caesar consolidated Roman control, subduing all the remaining Gallic tribes and capturing their capitals. With Celtic resistance crushed in Gaul, only the British Isles remained as a bastion of Celtic civilization.

Above: A coin of Vercingetorix. Several types of coin were minted. The drawing below depicts another, with Vercingetorix's hair arranged in traditionally jagged Gallic spikes.

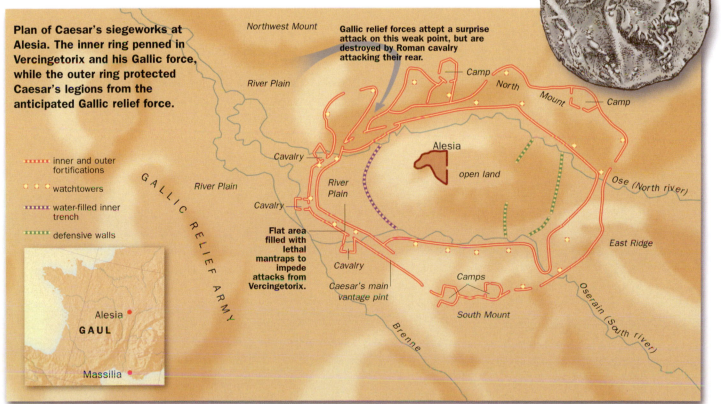

Plan of Caesar's siegeworks at Alesia. The inner ring penned in Vercingetorix and his Gallic force, while the outer ring protected Caesar's legions from the anticipated Gallic relief force.

Northwest Mount

Gallic relief forces attept a surprise attack on this weak point, but are destroyed by Roman cavalry attacking their rear.

River Plain

Camp

North Mount

Camp

Cavalry

Alesia

open land

Ose (North river)

GALLIC RELIEF ARMY

River Plain

River Plain

Cavalry

East Ridge

:::::: inner and outer fortifications

• • • watchtowers

:::::: water-filled inner trench

:::::: defensive walls

Flat area filled with lethal mantraps to impede attacks from Vercingetorix.

Cavalry

Caesar's main vantage pint

Camps

South Mount

Brenne

Oserain (South river)

Alesia •
GAUL

Massilia •

Conquest of Britain

In AD 43 a Roman army landed in Kent and carved out a beachhead. What probably started as an opportunistic military enterprise soon became a lengthy campaign of conquest. Despite fierce Celtic opposition the Romans spread out across southern Britain, expanding and consolidating their control over the island. This was the beginning of nearly four centuries of Roman occupation that would put an end to the Celtic way of life in all but the remotest corners of the British Isles.

King Verica of the Atrebates appealed to Rome in AD 43 for help in a war against the neighboring Catuvellauni tribe. The Roman Emperor Claudius realized that this offered an opportunity for military glory, and duly assembled a force of four legions and supporting troops in northwest Gaul. These legions were *II Augusta*, *XIV Gemina*, and *XX Valeria* from Germany, and *IX Hispania* from

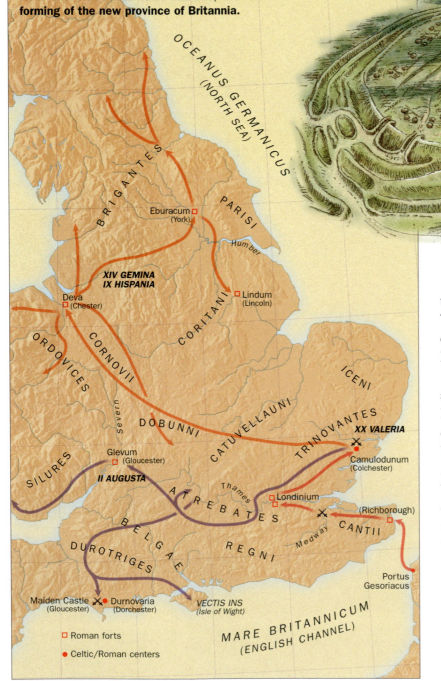

The initial routes of the Roman expeditionary force to Albion under Aulus Plautius, and the forming of the new province of Britannia.

OCEANUS GERMANICUS (NORTH SEA)

BRIGANTES

PARISI

Eburacum (York)

Humber

XIV GEMINA
IX HISPANIA

Deva (Chester)

CORITANI

Lindum (Lincoln)

ORDOVICES

CORNOVII

Severn

ICENI

DOBUNNI

CATUVELLAUNI

TRINOVANTES

XX VALERIA

Glevum (Gloucester)

SILURES

II AUGUSTA

ATREBATES

Thames

Camulodunum (Colchester)

Londinium

(Richborough)

BELGAE

REGNI

Medway

CANTII

DUROTRIGES

Maiden Castle (Gloucester)

Durnovaria (Dorchester)

VECTIS INS (Isle of Wight)

Portus Gesoriacus

MARE BRITANNICUM (ENGLISH CHANNEL)

□ Roman forts
● Celtic/Roman centers

Reconstruction of the ancient British hillfort at Maiden Castle in Dorset, c.1st century AD.

the Dacian border, plus Batavian, Dacian, Thracian, and German auxiliaries, including cavalry. The veteran Roman general Aulus Plautius commanded the expeditionary force.

The Roman navy transported Plautius's force across the Channel to land at what is now Richborough, in Kent. There was little Celtic opposition and, after establishing a fortified beachhead and supply base, Plautius marched northwest through the territory of the Cantii. The tribe and their Belgic allies made a stand on the line of the Medway, but were brushed aside. The Romans continued their advance to the Thames, where a second Celtic force was defeated. According to Roman historians, in both battles Plautius used his auxiliary troops to lead the assault, keeping his veteran legionaries back as a reserve.

From a fortified camp on the south bank of the Thames, the Roman forces forded or used boats to cross the river, and on the site of what is now London established another fortified camp on the north bank (probably in the vicinity of the site of the Tower of London). Here, they waited for reinforcements and supplies. In August Emperor Claudius visited his army, escorted by the Praetorian Guard. Under his nominal command the army advanced on the fortified town of Camulodonum (Colchester), the capital of the Cunobelinus of the Catuvellauni. The capital fell, and within its walls Claudius received the formal surrender of a series of British tribal chieftains.

Divide and conquer

In early AD 44 the Romans divided into three columns. While the *XX Valeria* remained in Colchester, *II Augusta* moved west to occupy the lands of the people who had called Rome for help, their erstwhile allies the Atrebates. *XIV Gemina* and *IX Hispania* marched together northwest into the territory of the Cornovii. In the course of the next few years the legions conquered the Dobunni and Durotriges tribes, captured over 20 towns and large settlements, and conquered the Isle of Wight.

Their most spectacular achievement was the capture of the massive Iron Age Celtic hillfort at Maiden Castle in Dorset. Archaeologists have uncovered evidence of the Roman siege, including catapult bolts and the remains of siegeworks. By AD 47 the Romans had conquered the south of Britain as far west as the River Severn, and as far north as the River Humber.

Over the next 12 years the Romans consolidated their hold on Britain, and extended their borders. Campaigns against the Silures led to the subjugation of what is now the south of Wales, while similar campaigns in the north pushed the Brigantes back from the Humber to the Solway Firth. Another campaign against the Ordovices in the north of Wales and along the Mersey was waged in the face of desperate British resistance. A series of intermittent campaigns in central Wales failed to dislodge the Celts from their mountain

bastions, so in AD 59 the Roman governor Suetonius Paulinus led two legions into north Wales in the largest show of force seen since the initial invasion of Britain.

His two-year campaign culminated in the reduction of a series of Celtic fortified positions, ending with the holy island of Mona (Anglesey). An amphibious assault across the Menai Straits met with bitter resistance, but eventually the defenders were crushed, the Druids massacred and the sacred Celtic sanctuaries destroyed. When the fighting was over in Wales it seemed as if resistance in Britain was finally crushed. The Romans were unprepared for the revolt that would soon come.

Below: Carved tombstone of the 1st century AD from Colchester, showing a Roman cavalryman riding down a naked Celtic warrior.

Boudicca's Revolt

A heavy-handed Roman policy toward the British tribes led to a revolt that brought Roman Britain to its knees. The Celts were led by the warrior queen Boudicca, and before the revolt was crushed, her followers had sacked some of the leading Romano-British cities in the island and defeated the Romans in battle. To this day, Boudicca is remembered as one of the great historical figures of Celtic Britain.

Below: The Celtic Queen Boudicca was commemorated as a patriotic heroine in this 19th-century depiction in London.

The Iceni were a Belgic tribe who occupied parts of east Britain (now forming the counties of Norfolk and Suffolk). Following the initial Roman invasion of Britain in AD 43, King Antedios of the Iceni made an alliance with the Romans, thereby ensuring that his lands would be spared from destruction. In spreading out throughout Britannia, the conquering legions left Colchester thinly garrisoned by AD 49. The Romans disarmed the Iceni, a precautionary move that caused resentment among the tribal warriors.

King Antedios, regarded by tribal hotheads as a Roman puppet, was ousted in a coup. Although Prasutagus—Antedios's replacement—renewed the treaty of alliance with the Romans, his political stance was far less pro-Roman than his predecessor. Following Prasutagus's death in AD 60 the Roman governor, Suetonius Paulinus, became concerned that the Iceni would break the treaty. The governor's solution was to annex Iceni lands, and he sent in colonial administrators to enforce Roman rule.

The heavy-handed action of these Roman agents enraged the Iceni, and the political atmosphere became volatile. The excuse for a fullscale revolt came when Boudicca, the widow of Prasutagus, was whipped as a punishment for criticizing the Roman administration.

Queen Boudicca rapidly became the instigator of a widespread revolt against Roman rule. A later Roman historian, Dio Cassius, described her:

> *"...tall, terrible to behold and gifted with a powerful voice. Bright red hair flowed to her knees, and she wore an ornate gold torc, a multi-colored robe, and a thick cloak pinned by a brooch. She carried a long spear, and inspired fear in all who beheld her."*

She has long been associated with a chariot, and her bronze likeness portrayed on a war chariot remains one of the most popular statues in London.

Celtic atrocities

The Trinovantes (from modern Essex) joined the Iceni, and together the tribes moved south against Colchester. As the Roman governor and all the legions were in the west and north of the province, there was nothing to stop Boudicca. Colchester was essentially a Roman city, colonized by former soldiers and their families. While a small group took refuge in

the Temple of Claudius, the remainder of the Roman population of around 3,000 was massacred.

The temple was then surrounded and burned to the ground. A relief force of 2,000 legionaries and cavalrymen from *IX Hispania* marched to quell the revolt, but were ambushed to the northeast of Colchester. Only the cavalry escaped alive. As settlements were sacked and burned, Roman civilians fled by sea to Gaul or escaped southward, and accounts of Celtic atrocities spread, causing widespread panic in the province.

When word of the revolt reached Suetonius Paulinus in Wales he gathered together a force of 10,000 legionaries and about 4,500 auxiliary troops, including cavalry from *XIV Gemina*, and elements of *II Augusta* and *IX Hispania*. After a series of forced marches down the Roman road known as Watling Street, Paulinus reached Londinium before Boudicca, but decided to withdraw north. According to Tacitus: "He decided to save the whole situation by the sacrifice of a single city." Boudicca then fell on the city and massacred the population wholesale, before marching northwest to sack Verulamium (although this time, forewarned. the population had fled to safety).

Again Paulinus moved to counter Boudicca, and found her army lining the River Anker, near the modern town of Lichfield. Although outnumbered several times over, Paulinus used the ground to his advantage. He halted the initial British charge, then forced them back to become trapped by their encampment and baggage. Unable to maneuver, the Britons were hacked to pieces. The revolt collapsed, and Boudicca took her own life.

However, the rebellion had alarmed Rome, and fresh reinforcements were shipped into the province from the German frontier. While the legionaries exacted revenge by ravaging tribal homelands of the rebellious tribes, steps were taken to ensure such a rebellion could not happen again by strengthening fortresses and towns. Despite his victory, Suetonius Paulinus was recalled to Rome.

His successor, Petronius Turpilianus, was less vindictive than had been Paulinus, and over the next few years he ensured maintenance of Roman control of the province without resorting to the heavy-handed policies that had led to the revolt in the first place. From that point on, southern Britain became a largely peaceable province of the Roman Empire, where the old tribal loyalties of old were gradually replaced by the ties of burgeoning commerce.

Above: Having to use both hands to carry his shield and spears, the British warrior rode to battle by bracing his legs firmly against the wicker sides of the chariot. His driver rode on the bracing pole between the horses. When battle was joined, the warrior lept from the chariot to fight on foot, while the driver maneuvered at a safe distance, waiting to pick him up.

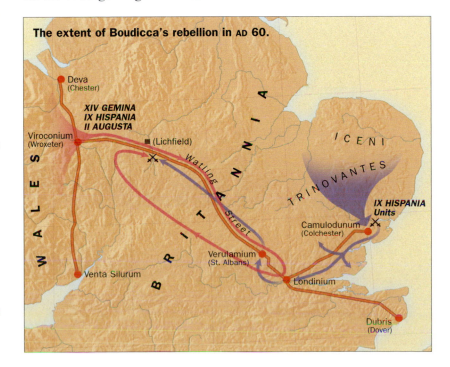

The extent of Boudicca's rebellion in AD 60.

93

The Romans in Scotland

Roman historian Tacitus said that the Caledonians were the last free Celtic people in the Roman Empire—behind them, there was nothing but sea. In AD 84 Agricola led a Roman army north. Despite defeating the Caledonians, Agricola and his successors were unable to subdue these proud northern people. The Roman solution was to construct a series of fortified walls, stretching across Britain.

Below: The Roman engineers who built Hadrian's Wall took advantage of natural topographical features to strengthen the line of fortifications.

After the crushing of Boudicca's revolt, Petronius Turpilianus consolidated Rome's hold over its most isolated province. However, his successor, Julius Agricola, undertook a policy of expansion in Roman Britain. Between AD 71–74 he subdued the Brigantes in the north of England. He then penetrated beyond their tribal boundaries as far as the rivers Forth and Clyde; the lands of the Votadani, Selgovae, Novantae, and Damnonii.

In AD 80–81 he ventured into the foothills of the Scottish Highlands and established a legionary fortress at Inchtuthill, on the Tay.

The Roman province of Britannia now extended into southern Scotland. Inchtuthill marked the limit of any direct advance into the highlands, and while a series of blocking forts were built to prevent Caledonian raids into the Roman territories to the south, Agricola continued his campaign into northeastern Scotland. His aim was to bring the last Celtic army in Britain to battle. In AD 84 he advanced north from Inchtuthill to the mouth of the Don (at modern Aberdeen).

Having established a supply base, Agricola pushed on to the northwest, where he encountered a Caledonian army led by Calgacus at Mons Graupius (probably the mountain of Bennachie, near Inverurie). As usual, the Celts were outmatched, and Agricola won a decisive

victory. But Mons Graupius also marked the northernmost limit of Roman penetration in Britain, because Agricola now withdrew to Inchtuthill. They may have been defeated, but the Caledonians had not been subdued.

About AD 100, the Romans withdrew from their forts on Tayside and pulled back to the area between the Firth of Forth and the Firth of Clyde. The Romans encouraged the tribes to act as buffer states between their garrisons and the Caledonians further north. Since these border tribes were linked to the Romans by trade, it was thought that they would be reluctant to support any attack on Britannia. However, a rebellion in northern Britain in 117 prompted Emperor Hadrian to visit Britannia to see the situation for himself.

The great wall

He withdrew troops from northern Britain, and established a new fortified line stretching from Wallsend on the River Tyne to Bowness on the Solway Firth. Hadrian's Wall was a colossal engineering project, but when completed the line blocked any attempt by the northern Celts to raid into Britannia to the south. Today, the remains of the wall serve as a reminder of the engineering skill and military might of Rome.

Within 20 years policy changed, and again Romans reoccupied southern Scotland. This time, the legions established a new fortified line from the Forth to the Clyde. This turf-and-wood defense became known as the Antonine Wall, after Antonius Pius. The region remained volatile, and a series of incursions over the Antonine Wall and rebellions in southern Scotland were a continual drain on Roman manpower and resources.

Early in the third century the emperor Septmus Severus arrived in Scotland to lead a campaign against the Caledonians. By this time the Roman garrisons had been withdrawn to the south again, leaving the area to the south of the Antonine Wall to be defended by pro-Roman tribes. Although a success, Severus's campaigns in Scotland failed to bring the Caledonians to battle. Denied the victory accorded to Agricola, the emperor returned home.

Hadrian's Wall was an engineering marvel, but it also required a substantial garrison. During the third and fourth centuries AD, the Romans came to rely on troops recruited in northern Britannia. Inevitably, these soldiers established links with their fellow Celts to the north. As internal strife within the Roman Empire led to a gradual weakening of the frontier defenses, incursions by Picts, Scots, Irish, and Saxons became commonplace. By the end of the fourth century, there was little to stop the Celts of northern Britain from striking into the heart of the crumbling Roman province.

Above: Reconstruction of Hadrian's Wall looking west near Chesters, showing mile castle number 26 in the foreground. Two turrets and a further mile castle can be seen in the background, just before the land drops into the North Tyne valley where Cilurnum (Chesters) cavalry fort was situated.

Hadrian's Wall, forts, military camps, and roads.

Chapter 7

The Druids

The great subjugator of the Gauls, Julius Caesar, described this powerful and mysterious priesthood as a hierarchical, pan-tribal organization. Recruits from all over the Celtic world underwent a rigorous 20-year training, where they had to learn the unwritten knowledge of the religious order. By the end of this process the apprentices were welcomed into a secret order that held enormous influence over Celtic society. Druids administered religious sacrifices and ceremonies, but they also served as advisers to kings and tribal leaders, as arbiters in disputes, as justices, and as diplomats. They were also believed to have supernatural abilities, such as knowing the will of the gods. By acting as the link between monarchs and deities, druids held a uniquely powerful position in society.

While it is relatively simple to disregard Roman accounts of the druids as sorcerers, there is evidence that there was a belief in magic and witchcraft during the Celtic period. The ability to heal the sick, predict the future, and to determine the will of the gods through the

reading of omens were the three cornerstones of druidic power. While this influence was brought to an end in Gaul and much of Britain by Roman invasion, the druids continued to dominate Celtic society in Ireland until the coming of Christianity. While female priestesses certainly existed in Celtic religion, they never acquired a social standing on a par with the druids, who were ranked alongside the most noble of the warrior aristocrats of Celtic society. Although much of our knowledge about the druids comes from Roman or Christian sources, this offers us a glimpse at the unique role played by druids in the Celtic world.

A druid prepares to throttle a sacrificial victim. It is likely that human sacrifices replaced the more usual animal offerings only as a last resort in the case of the most desperate threats to a Celtic community.

Power of the Druids

In his "History of the Gallic Wars," Caesar presented a concise and usually favorable account of his own military activities. He also touched on several aspects of the Celtic civilization he was trying to destroy. Inevitably, he included a description of the Gallic druids, and the part they played in Gallic society. It is the most comprehensive account still in existence of the role played by druids in the Celtic world.

Caesar wrote: *"Throughout Gaul there are two classes of men of some dignity and importance... one of the two classes is that of the druids, the other that of the knights. The druids are concerned with the worship of the gods, look after public and private sacrifice, and expound religious matters. A large number of young men flock to them for training and hold them in high honor. For they*

have the right to decide nearly all public and private disputes, and they also pass judgment and decide rewards and penalties in criminal and murder cases, and in disputes concerning legalities and boundaries. When a private person or a tribe disobeys their ruling, they ban them from attending sacrifices. This is their harshest penalty. Men placed under this ban are treated as impious wretches, all avoid them, fleeing their company and conversation, lest their contact bring misfortune upon them; they are denied legal rights and can hold no official dignity.

"It is thought that this system of training was invented in Britain and taken over from there to Gaul, and at the present time diligent students of the matter mostly travel there to study it.

"The druids are wont to be absent from war, nor do they pay taxes like the others… it is said that they commit to memory immense amounts of poetry. And so some of them continue their studies for 20 years. They consider it improper to entrust their studies to writing… I think they established this practice for two reasons, because they were unwilling, first, that their system of training should be bruited abroad among the common people, and second, that the student should rely on the written word and neglect the exercise of his memory…. They are chief anxious to have men believe the following: that souls do not suffer death, but after death pass from one body to another; and they regard this as the strongest incentive for valor, since the fear of death is disregarded. They have also much knowledge of the stars and their motion, of the size of the world and of the earth, of natural philosophy, and of the powers and spheres of action of the immortal gods, which they discuss and hand down to their young students."

Caesar's key to power

To modern ears, Caesar's account seems well reasoned, even-handed, even favorable toward the druids. It should be remembered that in general, Rome during its territorial expansion showed great tolerance to local religious customs, rites, and even different deities. The two major exceptions were the druids and—in the early imperial period—the Jews. So why were Caesar's actions so at variance with the tone of his words?

In a word: politics. Caesar quickly recognized that druids held a pivotal place in Celtic society. Not only were they the leading administrators of their tribal societies, they also acted as the interpreters of religion, as historians, as diplomats, as spokesmen, and as the arbiters of justice. Druids held a social position on par with the leading members of the Celtic warrior aristocracy. As such, druids had great influence over their tribal leaders, chieftans, and kings.

To Caesar it was clear—break the power of these priests and he would destroy the core of Celtic civilization and deprive the Gauls of their will, even ability, to resist. This perception led to the systematic persecution of the druids by the Romans in both Gaul and Britain.

Above: This Iron Age crown and skull, found at Deal, England, date from c.150 BC. The crown's similarity to ones worn by some priests in Roman Britain, has led experts to conjecture that this may be a druidic head-dress.

Facing: The island of Anglesey abounded with sacred sites, and became a last bastion of druidic power in Britain.

Witchcraft and Sorcery

Druids have long been associated with mystical ritual. Some Roman historians even claimed that they were sorcerers, representing a strong Roman tendency to cast druids in a harsh light. What little evidence there is suggests that although druids were no sorcerers, the Celts did believe in witchcraft, and in the power of druids to summon mystical healing forces through a combination of herbal medicine and ritual.

Later writers allude to the fact that the druids practiced magic. The Egyptian historian Hippolytus writing in the late second century AD referred to the druids as "magicians." Similarly the Greco-Roman writer Diogenes Laertius in the third century AD spoke of their "riddles and dark sayings." Of course, these historians never encountered a Celt, let alone a druid. They were passing on the rumors that had accumulated over the centuries, developed around a morbid interest in the secretive nature of the druidic order.

To Romans, Celtic religion was a practice that ran contrary to their religious belief. These mystical aspects were fascinating, but did not reflect true belief, in much the same way as doctors today sometimes look disparagingly at the practices of alternative medicine. During Caesar's invasion of Gaul, the Romans who encountered evidence of human sacrifice and blood rituals saw the druids as an evil force. And seen in this light, they were thought easily capable of sinister practices such as sorcery.

The extremely superstitious Romans were no strangers to magic. They offered up prayers to their gods for divine intervention on a regular basis and looked for omens and portents in almost every natural occurrence. The desire to portray the druids as evil sorcerers suited Caesar's policies, and had an impact on all subsequent representations of druids, and of Rome's dealings with them. However, there is no hard evidence that the druids ever participated in witchcraft, sorcery, or magic, other than invoking the mysticism associated with religious rituals.

Alternatively, there is another reference to sorcery in Celtic society. An inscribed lead sheet dating from the late La Tène period was found in a tomb in southern France. The tablet was written in Gallic using Latin script, and was found broken into two pieces, covering a pot containing female remains. It describes the existence of two "women endowed with magic,"

Right: This Gallo-Roman forest god from Mont St. Jean, France, signifies the importance the Celts placed on the spirituality of the natural world.

and how one had attempted to harm the other through the use of magic. The second woman used wise women to counter these evil spells. This is similar to the curse tablets (*defixiones*) which existed in Roman society at the same time.

Ritual and healing

European societies believed in witches until the late 17th century, and accounts of witchcraft can be found in Celtic society just as in contemporary Rome or Greece. There is circumstantial archaeological evidence for witchcraft in Roman Britain, since a few burials of older women during the third and fourth centuries AD have produced evidence of ritual decapitation, and the removal of lower jaws. It has been suggested that this indicates a desire to deprive the dead of speech, and so prevent the casting of spells from the afterlife.

The Greek historian Pliny in his *Natural History* wrote:

"The druids of Gaul have recorded that [the selago plant] should be kept on the person to ward off all fatalities, and that the smoke of it is good for all diseases of the eyes."

To the druids, selago was a plant with magical qualities. Pliny also recounts the importance that mistletoe had for the druids, along with the ritual manner in which both plants were gathered, and used for medicinal purposes. This is hardly the basis for sorcery, but represents an awareness of the healing properties of nature. It has been argued that the ceremony involving cutting mistletoe was important because it reinforced the superiority of the druids over others in society. If anyone could cut mistletoe and heal themselves, then there would be little need for druids.

Above: Mistletoe growing on poplars near Valencay, France. The white berries of the parasitic mistletoe are poisonous, and only druids would have touched them.

Prophecy and Divination

According to classical Roman historians, one of the principal roles of the druids was to know the will of the gods, and therefore predict the future. This was usually done through the medium of omens, whose accurate interpretation was one of the druidic preserves. The druids sometimes acted as prophets for their people, and evidence of this role is provided by both archaeology and Celtic literature.

Below: The ritual slaughter of animals for the purposes of divination was a common practice by druids. Detail from the Gundestrup cauldron.

In his *Library of History*, the Roman historian Diodorus Siculus wrote: "The Gauls likewise make use of diviners, accounting them worthy of high approbation, and these men foretell the future by means of the flight and cries of birds and the slaughter of sacred animals, and they have all the multitude subservient to them."

The ability to foretell the future was a skill that ensured the respect of tribal chieftains and kings, and a place for the druids in the planning of almost every event, be it military, social, or political. This was achieved in a variety of ways, the most popular of which involved the observation of omens or naturally occurring phenomena. This included the behavior of animals or birds, such as the study of birds in flight.

This is not peculiar to druids. Many of these methods of divining omens from the gods were used by Roman priests in religious ceremonies. Until the beginning of Roman Christianity, Rome's priests took auguries from the entrails of freshly slaughtered "sacred" animals. To Romans, a sudden flight of birds from the right (*dexter*) was auspicious, whereas the same from the left (*sinister*) was unlucky. The importance of this kind of divination was widely acknowledged throughout Europe and the Mediterranean.

What was less acceptable was the use of

Left: Found in Westmorland, these spoons of c.50 BC to AD 100, are suspected of having a religious significance. A liquid, perhaps water, ale, or blood, might have been allowed to drip through the hole in one spoon onto the other spoon during attempts to see into the future.

humans in sacrifice. There are numerous examples of references to human sacrifices in classical writings, and archaeological evidence supports this. One method was to execute a bound prisoner and watch the way in which he died, the way he fell, the amount of blood he lost and so on. These practices appalled the Romans (other than the very Roman fight to the death in gladiatorial combat, itself probably derived from earlier religious rites), and Julius Caesar used the evidence of human sacrifice to encourage the destruction of religious sanctuaries and sacred groves which they would normally prefer to leave alone.

Telling of omens

Druidical ability to foretell the future was recorded by Cicero, who wrote that the pro-Roman druid Divitiacus could predict events through the reading of omens through augury and by inference. Later Roman and Greek historians continued to report that the druids practiced divination. In his second century AD work *Oratorio*, Dio Chrysostom referred to the druids' ability to use oracles, and a century later the writer Hippolytus referred to the druids as prophets. He expanded on this claim, stating that they used cyphers and numbers to determine future events, which may form a

reference to the importance placed on the calendar in Celtic religion.

The Celts saw evidence of their gods all around them: in the streams, forests, and animals of the natural world. It is hardly surprising that these same natural elements were seen as providing omens that could determine the will of the gods. Certain animals and birds were especially favored by the gods, and both doves and ravens had "voices," and so omens involving these birds were regarded as particularly powerful. Similarly, certain sacred places were honored by the druids since they provided a source of divine inspiration.

Sometimes this ability to act as seers went beyond reading omens. In Irish Celtic literature a series of druids are recorded who acted as prophets for their royal masters. Cathbadh, the druid of King Conchobar of Ulster is reputed to have advised the king and acted as a soothsayer. Other late Celtic prophets, such as the Scottish Brahn Seer, continued this belief into medieval times. For the Celts, the gods provided clues to their will, and the druids were able to interpret these messages. The power of this belief is reflected in the continued appearance of soothsayers and messengers of god throughout history.

Women and the Priesthood

Women could attain powerful status in Celtic society. Unlike other contemporary civilizations, women could and did hold high social and political positions. Obvious examples include Boudicca, Queen of the Iceni, Cartimandua, Queen of the Brigantes, and the semi-legendary Irish Queen Medb (Maev) of Connacht. Although women do not appear to have been allowed to join the order of druids, several examples of female prophets and lower priestesses exist.

Below: In this carved stone votive offering found at Alesia, a priestess is shown offering a token to a Celtic deity.

The Roman historian Strabo writing in the late first century BC recounts the role played by women among the Cimbri (*see pages 84–85*). Priestesses were also described by Caesar and Tacitus in their histories. Strabo reported that: "…women would enter the camp sword in hand, and go up to prisoners, crown them, and lead them up to a bronze vessel… one woman would mount a step, and leaning over the cauldron, would cut the throat of the prisoner who was held over the vessel's rim. Others then cut open the body, and after inspecting the entrails would foretell victory for their tribe."

This is similar to accounts of the ritual human sacrifice of prisoners of war by druids. A wooden figurine of a Celtic woman was discovered in a spring at Chamalières, in central France. Clearly a votive offering, like the thousands of other wooden statues and figurines recovered from the site, the woman is shown wearing a torc (signifying aristocratic status), and a drape covering her head. The figurine has been interpreted as that of a priestess, as the draping of a cloth over the head has been linked to druid sacrificial rituals.

Rites and ruthlessness

Strabo also described an account of a Celtic religious ceremony recorded by his fellow historian Posidonius. A colony of female priestesses inhabited an island near the mouth of the Loire, on the west coast of Gaul. Men were never allowed on the island, which was seen as a sacred place to the Gauls, although the priestesses were free to come and go as they pleased. According to Strabo: "…it is their custom once a year to remove the roof from their temple and to roof it again the same day before sunset, each woman carrying part of the burden; but the woman whose load falls from her is torn to pieces by the others, who then carry the pieces around the temple crying 'euoi,' and continue until their madness passes."

This reference to a female religious community reflects other accounts from classical sources. In the first century AD the Roman Pomponius Mela described an island called Sena, part of the archipelago known as Cassiterides (now the Scilly Isles). The island was the home of a Gallic oracle, serviced by nine virgin priestesses. These women could control the elements, predict the future, and heal the sick.

In the Welsh Celtic heroic poem *Preiddu Annwyfn* which survives in an early medieval form, King Arthur is described arriving in Wales to steal the holy cauldron of Annwn (the underworld). It was guarded by nine virgin priestesses, just like the oracle on Sena mentioned centuries earlier.

A series of later Roman accounts describe encounters between leading Roman historical figures and Gallic priestesses, who foretold their futures. While he was still a mere soldier, Diocletian encountered a Celtic priestess who told him he would become emperor after he slew "the boar" (*Aper*). He duly became emperor after killing the Aper, interpreted as the Prefect of the Praetorian Guard. The emperor Aurelian consulted a Gallic priestess, who assured him that although his descendants would become emperors after him, they would not be considered more illustrious than the descendants of Claudius. Another emperor, Severus, was warned by a Celtic priestess not to trust his soldiers. She turned out to be right—they eventually murdered him. Although female priests and seers lacked the respect granted their male druidic counterparts, they played a significant role in the Celtic system of belief.

Right: Stone bas-relief depiction of a female deity or a priestess recovered from Alesia.

Druids in Celtic Myth

Although the power of the druids was destroyed by the Romans in Gaul and most of Britain, it remained part of Celtic society in Ireland. Irish mythology provides a rich source of information about druids, their power, and their abilities. Although only myths, many of these accounts are based on true observations of Celtic society. As such, they provide a link with the Celtic past that cannot be ignored.

Evidence for druidic activity in pre-Christian Ireland comes from two sources; accounts of the lives of Christian saints such as St. Patrick, and from Irish mythological texts, such as the *Annals of Ulster*. Both sources were compiled after the arrival of Christianity in Ireland, written at some time between the seventh and eleventh centuries AD. In one important respect, the writers of these accounts some hundreds of years after Julius Caesar had something in common with him. The Christian monks who recorded these tales had a vested interest in portraying these pagan religious figures in a poor light. It is likely that—like the earlier classical accounts of the druids—these early Irish accounts contained some accurate aspects, but the accounts need to be viewed with caution.

To the Celts in Ireland, learned men were divided into three overlapping groups; bards, seers, (*filidh*) and druids. The druids are shown to have wielded significant power in their community, influencing both secular and religious affairs with equal ease. They are portrayed as advisers to the Irish kings, like the relationship between the druid Cathbadh and Conchobar of Ulster (*see page 102*). As advisers in spiritual as well as temporal matters, they relied on divination to assist their monarch in his decision-making.

The link between druid and king was therefore a strong one, and the king risked his special relationship with the gods if he ignored his druid's advice. Of the three groups of

Below: The oak tree was held sacred by the druids, and oak groves formed a central part in both druidic practices and in Celtic myth.

learned men, the druids were by far the most powerful. Bards kept alive the tribe's oral traditions, and entertained the court with tales of past bravery. Seers had some of the powers of druids, such as divination, but lacked the divine power of their druidic betters. Significantly, the seers continued to thrive under the Christian system, replacing the druids as prophets to the Irish kings, although they remained careful to place this advice in a suitably Christian context. Bards, too, continued to thrive after the advent of Christianity, no doubt because their more secular function as historian-entertainers retained its importance in parallel with the clerical Christian story-telling. The tradition of kings or lords appointing bards in Wales continued well into the medieval era.

A pre-Celtic order

According to the *Book of Invasions*, the first colonists in Ireland brought three druids with them, named Intelligence, Knowledge and Enquiry. They were followed by the *Tuatha Dé Danann* (People of the goddess Danu), who tried unsuccessfully to keep the Gaels (Celts) out of Ireland. These accounts indicate that the druids were perceived to have existed in Ireland before the Celtic migrations of the Iron Age.

The Celts brought their own druids, one of whom reputedly established his dominance over the indigenous druids in Ireland. In the *Táin Bó Cuailnge* (Cattle Raid of Cooley), the great Irish warrior hero Cú Chulainn (*see page 175*) won a string of victories for Conchobar of Ulster (and his druid Cathbad) before succumbing to the magic of the sorceress Queen Medb of Connacht and her own druids. This link between kings, druids, magic, and the spirit world remained a recurring theme in early Irish mythology.

There was also a link between druids and kingship. Kings were seen as sacred, chosen by the gods, and their accession was marked by

extensive rituals, supervised by the druids. These rites included sacrificial ceremonies and

divination; attempts to determine the divine destiny of the new king.

This close relationship ended with the coming of Christianity, and at this point the Irish writings lapse into Christian moralizing. Kings who retained their druids and pagan beliefs are reputed to have met their fate, and St. Patrick portrays the druids he encountered as hostile and reactionary. Given that Christianity brought an end to their unique power in Ireland, their antipathy toward the saint is understandable.

Above: In Wales, the bardic element of Druidic tradition survived through history and today forms an important part of Eisteddfod ceremony. Here a bard is honored by being offered a drink from a drinking horn.

Chapter 8

The Celtic Warrior

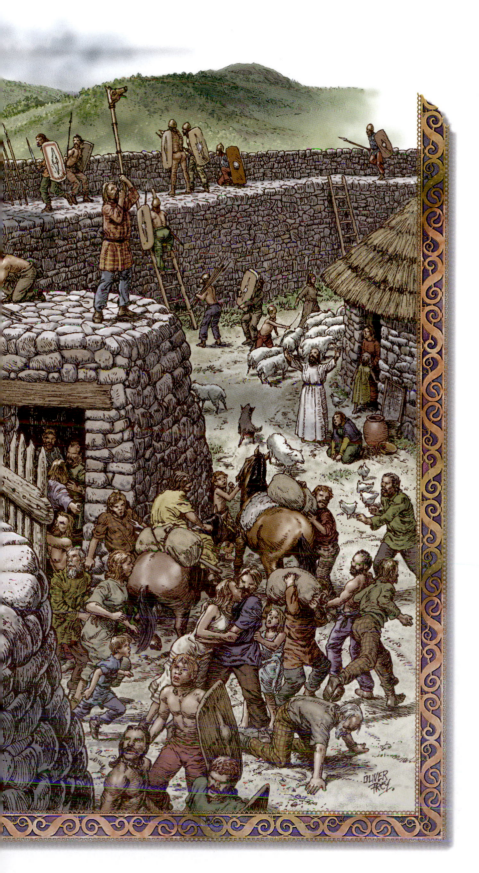

L ed by an elite warrior aristocracy, warfare played a central part in a Celtic society that was organized around tribal groupings. As chapter six shows, this warrior society and its loosely grouped, semi-anarchical group of tribes lacked the political unity that would allow them to oppose the Romans. This failing was reflected in Celtic military operations—continuously individual tribes (occasionally a tribal confederation) went to war without the support of other neigboring tribes, and usually without any proper central command. Celtic disarray was ruthlessly seized on by Julius Caesar in Gaul (and later by Claudius's generals in Britain) in a strategy of divide and conquer that defeated the Celts in a piecemeal fashion.

During the Roman conquests of Italy, Gaul, and Britain, numerous classical references describe the appearance, weaponry, and tactics of the Celts on the battlefield. This documentary evidence has been augmented by a growing body of archaeological information from the sites of elaborate burials, battlefields, settlements, and isolated finds. Far from being a barbarian society whose methods of warfare were simplistic, the Celts displayed an elaborate understanding of military technology, colored by the rules of their own society. They emphasized personal bravery, intimidation, bravado, and ferocity over all other warlike virtues. Although the Romans ultimately conquered the Celts, this only came after a series of military setbacks.

Celtic weapons and armor were not as advanced as those used by the Romans. Although the Celts were renowned for being courageous, they lacked the battlefield discipline and technological edge that were the hallmarks of the Roman legionaries. Following the collapse of the Roman Empire, the post-Roman Celts were better equipped to confront their enemies, and even demonstrated a tactical and technological superiority that had eluded them before.

Cult of the Warrior Hero

Warfare in various forms was central to Celtic society, and classical historians have labeled the Celts a warlike people. In the first century AD the Roman chronicler Strabo described the Gauls as warlike; "the whole nation… is war mad, both high-spirited and ready for battle." Within Celtic culture the warrior was revered, and together with druids and bards he held a unique place in Celtic myth.

Previous page: A Celtic fortified center (*Oppidum*) under attack from another Celtic tribe. It was traditonal to display the severed heads of foes spitted on spears above the ramparts.

If the druids ran the religious affairs of the Celts, the secular rulers and aristocracy were drawn from among the warriors. Later Irish and Welsh chronicles reflect this esteem for warriors, who dominated a semi-feudal tribal structure where land and power were linked to prowess in combat. Archaeological evidence shows that warriors were buried sword in hand, surrounded by the panoply of warfare: chariots, armor, shield, and spear, and food and wine to sustain the warrior in the afterlife.

The importance and status of the warrior within society was evident, but it was also related to success—defending society against aggressors. The speed with which Gallic society collapsed during Julius Caesar's conquest of Gaul is linked to the loss of a whole generation of warriors on the battlefield, and Gallic disillusionment with the inability of their heroes to stop the Roman invader.

The Celts were characterized as being ferocious in battle, and fearless to the point of impetuosity. Over the centuries this developed into a cult, and influenced the tactical operation of Celtic armies for better or worse. A Roman historian writing in 189 BC said of the Galatians (Asiatic Celts) that; "they drove everything before them, and walls could not resist their fury." Caesar himself testified to Gallic courage and ferocity on the battlefield, and similar traits can be found in accounts of Celtic warriors in Roman service, in battle against Dark Age barbarians, and even in the actions of Scottish or Irish soldiers of more recent times.

Cú Chulainn's fury

One martial trait that was distinctive but not necessarily unique was blood-lust. In both classical accounts and in later Irish mythology, some warriors worked themselves into a frenzy before battle, making them formidable and almost superhuman opponents (*see pages 175–175*). In the Irish *Táin bó Cualnge*, the hero Cú Chulainn is described:

"A spasm tore through him… it distorted him, making him a monstrous thing… his head swelled and pounded."

Right: This Roman copy of the Greek sculpture known as *The Dying Gaul*, depicts a Celtic warrior, or *gaesatae*, of the 3rd century BC. These warriors fought naked except for a metal torc around the neck.

The chronicle describes him being seized by rage, and he fought like an animal. After the battle, the blood-lust passed, and he returned to his normal persona. This trait was particularly admired by the Celts; evidence to them that the warrior was the stuff of heroic myth.

During the third century BC, some Celtic warriors known as *gaesatae* fought naked, wearing nothing but metal torcs around their necks. The contemporary reliefs and sculptures of "Dying Gauls" sculpture reflect this habit, which may have had religious or supernatural overtones. This supernatural link with the warrior has a parallel in later Irish chronicles, where the tales contain numerous references to magic weapons or mystical powers.

In Celtic warfare, a fullscale battle was a rare occurrence, and among the warrior aristocracy, feasting and mock fighting was interspersed with raids on neighboring tribes or provinces, or in pre-Roman Gaul, intermittent incursions into the richer lands of the southern Mediterranean. These martial feats were duly recounted by bards, or were recorded in the later Celtic chronicles.

Personal bravery was honored above almost everything else, and accounts of Celtic warfare are scattered with references to champions and records of personal valor. This glorification of the warrior and his skills led to an emphasis on individual deeds, rather than providing for a skilled and unified military structure. The Romans adopted the reverse approach, where military skill was combined with cohesion and order on the battlefield. Heroics and recklessness had little place in the Roman army, and when the two systems clashed the Celts were annihilated.

Left: This bronze helmet from the 1st century BC, found in the River Thames, London, near Waterloo Bridge, is the only horned iron age helmet to have been found anywhere. It has repoussé decoration in La Tène style.

Below: Torcs had a religious significance for their warrior wearers. This one, found at Snettisham, England is made from eight twisted strands, and dates from just before Julius Caesar's expedition to Albion (Britain) in 43 BC.

Celtic Warfare of La Tène

Classical writers attested to the intimidating appearance of a Celtic army in battle, describing powerful men, constant noise, warlike gestures, and a barbaric fury. But faced with disciplined Roman forces, intimidation was not enough. Accounts of Roman engagements with the Celts of Italy, Gaul, and Britain provide an impression of how the Celts fought the Romans—and invariably lost.

The Roman historian Polybius describes the sight of a Celtic army in battle, when one fought the Romans at Telamon in 225 BC: *"The Insubres and Boii wore trousers and light cloaks, but the Gaesatae in their overconfidence had thrown these aside and stood in front of the whole army naked, with nothing but their arms; for they thought that thus they would be more efficient since some of the ground was overgrown with thorns which could catch on their clothes and impede the use of their weapons. On the other hand the fine order and the noise of the Celtic host terrified the Romans; for there were countless trumpeters and horn blowers and since the whole army was shouting its war cries at the same time there was such a confused sound that the noise seemed to come not only from the trumpeters and the soldiers, but also from the countryside which was joining in the echo. No less terrifying were the appearance and gestures of the naked warriors in front, all of whom were in the prime of life and of excellent physique. All the warriors in the front ranks were adorned with golden torcs and armlets. The Romans were particularly terrified by the sight of these men, but, led on by hope of gain, they were twice as keen to face the danger."*

Outdated bravado

This account provides a great insight into Celtic warfare. The reference to naked warriors (*gaesatae*) is repeated in accounts of other battles, although the practice seems to have ended before Caesar's invasion of Gaul in the mid-first century BC. Dionysus of Halicarnassus saw this as evidence of barbarian boastfulness. The noise described by Polybius is supported by other sources, and extant examples and depictions of Celtic trumpets and horns show how these instruments appeared intimidating, having long vertical stems, ending in an animal head. Livy described the Galatians in action:

"…their yells and leapings, and the dreadful noise of arms as they beat their shields in some

ancestral custom, all this is done with one purpose—to terrify their enemies."

One aspect of Celtic warfare left unmentioned by Polybius was the heritage of single combat, and other accounts describe warriors challenging their enemies to break ranks and fight man to man. In most cases the disciplined teamworking Romans ignored the challenge. The main battle line of Celts would usually be protected by a line of archers, javelin throwers, and slingers, and according to Polybius their absence at Telamon had dire results for the *gaesatae*, who were routed by missile fire.

Cavalry also played a part in Celtic warfare, and the Celts were noted horsemen. In Gaul,

Caesar recruited pro-Roman Gallic horsemen to support his army, and after the conquest of Gaul, Gallic cavalry were recruited as auxiliaries by the Romans. In Britain, chariots played a part in warfare, although they had fallen into disuse in the rest of the Celtic world before the first century BC. Archaeological reconstructions of Celtic chariots have provided useful information about how they operated, and support the accounts provided by the Romans. Usually used to augment the cavalry, chariots were utilized to harass the enemy line before it advanced, and they harried its rear afterward. The last account of chariots being used in action was at the Battle of Mons Graupius, in AD 84.

Celtic Arms and Armor

Although the Celts relied on every type of available weaponry, the principal weapon was a long, straight sword. As for armor, their smiths combined practicality with elements of purely Celtic artistry, turning shields and helmets into objects of beauty. Although well-armed and reasonably well-protected, in the end their equipment was no match for that of the Romans.

Right: Celtic shield from the 3rd century BC, found in the River Witham, near Lincoln.

Opposite: Cuirass, Hallstatt, probably 8th century BC.

Above: Sword, with typical La Tène decoration on the pommel.

After centuries of warfare between the Romans and Celts, Roman writers knew a great deal about Celtic arms and armor. The historian Diodorus Siculus was one of the most descriptive:

"For arms they have man-sized shields decorated in a manner peculiar to them. Some of these have projecting figures in bronze, skilfully wrought, not only for decoration but also for protection. They wear bronze helmets, with large projecting figures which give the wearer the appearance of enormous size. In some cases horns are attached so as to form one piece, in others the foreparts of birds or quadrupeds worked in relief… some of them have iron breastplates, wrought in chain, while others are satisfied with the arms Nature has given them and fight naked.

"Instead of the short sword they carry long swords held by a chain of iron or bronze and hanging along their right flank. Some of them have gold or silver-plated belts around their tunics. They brandish spears that are called lanciae and which have iron heads a cubit in length and even more, and a lot less than two palms in breadth; for their swords are not shorter than the spears of others, and the heads of their spears are longer than the swords of others."

Cumbersome weaponry

To the Romans, the swords and spears carried by the Celts appeared exceptional. Archaeological evidence has shown that the swords were in fact about 27 inches long, although the size increased during the first century AD. They were straight-bladed, with a single ridge. They were also well-tempered, which contradicts the claim by Polybius that they became blunt after the first blow, and bent easily. They were designed for cutting rather than for thrusting, and Dionysius of

Halicarnssus describes how they were raised up and then brought crashing down, the swordsman putting his whole weight behind the blow.

The problem was that this required space. The first century AD Roman historian Tacitus reported that British swords were long, and unsuited to fighting in confined spaces. The opposite was true of the Roman *gladius*, a short stabbing sword designed for exactly these

conditions. The other principal weapon was the spear, either a broad-bladed spear for thrusting, or lighter javelin for throwing. Spears were about eight feet long, with large heads and sockets, and metal spear butts to balance the weapon. Celtic skirmishers also used bows and slings, and archaeological examples of arrowheads and sling-stones survive.

As for armor, by the first century BC the more affluent members of a Celtic warband would be equipped with mail tunics, with rings that were riveted together. Similarly helmets were worn by the wealthy, and while most of these consisted of simple bronze or iron pieces, the decorative helmets cited by Diodorus Siculus were worn by a handful of leading warriors. A unique helmet from Ciumesti in Romania was adorned with a large bird with hinged wings. Horned helmets, as has been mentioned (*page 111*), were rare.

The Celtic warrior's equipment was completed by a shield. Livy described them as long and oblong, and this is supported by archaeological finds. Most were long oval wooden shields, with a central boss protecting a grip. Depictions of Celtic warriors suggest that these shields were decorated with painted Celtic artwork. Although their equipment was of a high quality, the technological advantages of Roman arms, armor, and their amazing artillery meant that the Celtic warrior fought on an unequal footing with his Latin opponent.

Celtic warriors faced more than sharp steel:
The ballista (below) was the Roman army's light artillery piece, with a range for its darts of about 1,400 feet.

The catapult (right) was the universal medium-range artillery of a besieging Roman army. Powered in the same way as the ballista by twisted skeins of sinew or hair, it hurled rounded stones. It came in a variety of sizes and power ranges, and could throw rocks weighing up to 220 pounds. The onager (top), known by several other names, such as the "wild ass," was a giant sling-shot, and its fierce action gave rise to its other nickname of the "scorpion." It could lob a 60-pound missile a distance of half a mile.

Dressed to Kill

When the Romans and Greeks first fought Celtic armies during the third century BC, they found Celtic warriors appeared terrifying to them; a tall, white-skinned race of barbarians who were unlike anything they had seen before. This appearance was accentuated by the way these warriors were dressed and groomed. The Celts did everything they could to create an appearance that would dazzle and intimidate the enemy.

D iodorus Siculus described the physical appearance of these warriors: "The Gauls are tall of body, with skin moist and white. Their hair is blond not only by nature but also because they practice to increase artificially the peculiar nature of their coloring. Some of them shave off their beards, but others let them grow moderately. The nobles shave their cheeks, but let their mustaches grow freely so as to cover their mouths."

This reference to hair coloring was due to the warrior practice of smearing lime paste into their hair and teasing it up, like the mane of a horse. Once again, the objective was to look terrifying to the enemy. The natural hair color of these northern European Celts was fair, ginger, or brown, the latter being the most common. To the black-haired

Below: Early La Tène chieftan and warrior (late 5th century BC), dressed in woolen garments and wearing bronze helmets.

Mediterranean peoples, all of these colors looked strange.

The Celts were taller on average than their Mediterranean neighbors, and Roman sources suggest that the Britons were generally taller than the Gauls, while the Germans beyond the Rhine were the tallest of them all. As for physical condition, Polybius describes the naked *gaesatae* as being in excellent shape, and in the prime of life. Strabo contradicts this, suggesting that the Celts had a tendency toward being overweight, and tribal laws penalized those who became too heavy. Given the demands of Celtic warfare, it seems unlikely that many warriors were overweight, especially after a season of hardened campaigning.

Colorful clothing

Roman and Greek historians described the clothing worn by these warriors. One mentioned that they: "…wear striking clothing, dyed and embroidered in many colors, and trousers that they call *bracae*. They wear striped cloaks, fastened by a brooch, thick in winter and light in summer, worked in a variegated, closely-set check pattern."

Others report that they wore thigh-length split tunics with sleeves. These tunics were probably simple shirt-like linen garments, reaching to mid-thigh. Strabo refers to "splits patterns were the most common.

Other writers refer to striped trousers, (trousers were a novelty to the Romans), and Roman cavalrymen soon adopted this practical form of clothing from the Gallic cavalrymen they recruited. As with tunics, these could be chequered, striped, or made in solid colors, or produced in undyed wool or linen.

Leather shoes were also worn extensively by Celtic warriors, at least during the late La Tène period.

Queen Boudicca is described wearing a tunic of many colors, over which a thick cloak was fastened by a brooch. Decorative cloak pins, belts, and other forms of decoration were worn by the more wealthy warriors, while golden torcs around the neck were a sign of wealth and standing in Celtic society. Other common forms of adornment were bracelets, rings, brooches, and decorative belts. Bronze and gold examples of these objects survive to this day.

and sleeves," but most depictions of Celts wearing tunics suggest a simpler design. Both long- and short-sleeved tunics are depicted in contemporary iconography. These tunics were "dyed and embroidered," making a colorful garment, similar to the Scottish Highland plaids of the modern day. Thick winter cloaks (*laenae* or *sagi*) were often made from a coarse, rough wool, with finer, thinner wool reserved for summer clothing. Once again, chequered

Late Celtic Warfare

Warfare in the British Isles during the late Celtic period cannot be viewed solely from the Celtic viewpoint. All participants—Irish, Scots, Britons, Picts, Saxons, and Angles—had their own strategic interests, but all used very similar weaponry and tactical doctrines. Archaeological and documentary information can be combined to provide a detailed view of warfare during the political formation of Britain.

Below: The Celts considered weapons a part of their life force, and devoted a great deal of atttention toward the decoration of the metal parts, such as this fine spearhead decorated in La Tène "sword" style found in the River Thames in London. Dated at between 200–50 BC, it is shown two-thirds actual size here.

Rome began withdrawing the legions from Britain to counter threats from the east early in the fifth century AD. The Romano-Britons who remained had to look after their own defense. After half a century of attempting to defend their own interests, they were forced to appeal to the Western Roman Empire for help. Rome, gripped by internecine imperial power struggles and fighting a losing battle for its own survival in the face of barbarian invasions, ignored the pleas.

Southern Britain had a limited population from which to draw fighting men, while boatloads of warlike Saxons were arriving daily. Nevertheless, evidence from the *Anglo-Saxon Chronicle* implies larger Celtic armies than recent statistical and archaeological information suggests—although probably to make the Saxon victories seem more impressive to readers. The size of the armies that fought for dominance in Britain were in fact probably small, numbering in the hundreds or low thousands. Saxon accounts of Celtic battle losses of 2–5,000 men can be reduced by at least a factor of ten. The largest armies available to commanders in Britain during the period from the sixth to the tenth centuries AD would have been little more than 4,000 men or thereabouts.

Weaponry had changed since the La Tène period. Archaeologists have unearthed a range of late Celtic and early Saxon swords, knives, spearheads, and arrows, and discernible patterns can be traced. The Saxons favored a long straight sword, similar to that used by the La Tène Celts. The term *seax*, meaning "knife" has been linked to the appellation "Saxon." It was probably seen as a weapon of the nobility, and the main Saxon weapon was the spear. Daggers and axes would also have been carried into battle. The Celts of post-Roman Britain, Ireland, and the Caledonian territories relied on weapons similar to those of the Saxons, although lighter weapons predominated in southern Britain, where Roman military weapons and methods were still used. In Ireland and Pictland, spears tended to be longer and heavier than in southern Britain, and all Celtic peoples in Britain had different types of spears for use by cavalrymen, infantrymen, and skirmishers. In the south, cavalry equipment followed the Roman model, and riders were equipped with lances and swords. Elsewhere in Britain, horsemen carried lighter and shorter spears.

Simpler strategies

The Saxons made little use of cavalry, enabling the temporary Celtic domination of the battlefield by small groups of heavily-armed cavalry. This was reputedly a military advantage exploited by the Romano-Celtic British warlord identified as Arthur, and may have been a significant factor in the creation of myths about his "knights" (the equestrian, or knightly, order having been a mainstay of Roman aristocracy).

Chariots were no longer used in the British Isles, while archery and slingshots were not mentioned in documentary sources, and no missiles have been recovered from archaeological sites. Warfare in Britain during the late Celtic period was primarily a clash between units of spearmen, sometimes supported by lighter skirmishing troops and bodies of cavalry.

While at first the post-Roman Britons retained some degree of Roman auxiliary military organization, and large numbers of experienced Roman veterans were available to train the new defense forces, Roman ways waned during the decades following the withdrawal. While mail armor was worn, its use seems to have been limited to the wealthier members of the Celtic or Saxon nobility. Although helmets such as those found at the Sutton Hoo or Benty Grange excavations were possibly worn by kings or the higher nobility, the bulk of armies during this period probably lacked any form of protective headgear.

The subtleties of the Roman military system were replaced by sheer brute force, and battles were decided more by stamina and weight of numbers than by technological advantage,

organization, or training. The Celtic warrior of this period also lacked the glamor of his La Tène ancestors.

119

DÁL RIADA

SCOTS (CELTS)

PICTS (CELTS)

STRATHCLYDE

North Tyne

● Melrose

● Lindisfarne
● Bamburgh

BERNICIA

ANGLO-SAXONS C.600

South Tyne

● Carlisle

Eden

NORTHUMBRIA

CUMBRIA

Tees

Ure

● Catterick

Whitt

Derwe

Ribble

● York

Mersey

ELMET

Ouse

Isle of Man

English settlements c.500

English expansion by 600

English expansion by 660

English territory by 800

Anglesey

GWYNEDD

● Chester

Dee

MERCIANS

Trent

POWYS

Severn

MERCIA

● Leicester

CELTS

Teme

MIDDLE
ANGLES

St. David's

DYFED

Tywi

Wye

● Worcester

Nene

● Hereford

GWENT

● Gloucester

WESSEX

● Cirencester

● Llantwit

Avon

● Bath

WEST
SAXONS

● Glastonbury

Parrett

● Tintagel

Tamar

CELTS DUMNONIA

● Exeter

● Sherborne

● Sarum
(Salisbury)

● Winchester

● Hamton

Wight

Selsey

Chapter 9

Celts and Anglo-Saxons

Four hundred years of Romanization had changed Celtic society in Britannia beyond recognition. The barbarians had become civilized. But when the armies of Rome were withdrawn, Celtic Britons faced many threats from across the Channel and North Sea. During the period from the late fourth until the mid-seventh centuries AD the unity of the Roman province of Britannia disintegrated into a series of Celtic kingdoms. With a return to decentralized government and the inevitable rise of separate armies and inter-tribal bickering, these Celtic kingdoms laid themselves open to attacks from coastal raiders crossing the Channel and southern North Sea.

The raids of Jutes, Angles, and Saxons (collectively referred to as Anglo-Saxons) had first begun during the final century of Roman Britain, but the presence of large, well-organized legions kept the pirates to the coasts and estuaries of the southeast. Within 50 years of the Roman withdrawal, however, unopposed raids encouraged greater penetration of Britain. By the mid-fifth century it was clear that the raids were not going to stop, and that they were in fact turning into an invasion. For the next two centuries, Celts and Anglo-Saxons became locked together in a struggle for survival and dominance; a struggle for Britain.

To the north and west, the Irish, Picts and Scots were largely involved in their own affairs, and only played a minor part in the conflict that raged in southern Britain. The struggle only involved them when the victorious Anglo-Saxons continued their dynamic expansion, and attempted to subdue the independent kingdoms of Scotland and Ireland.

Although the Celts of southern Britain put up a valiant opposition to the Anglo-Saxon invaders, there were simply too few Celts and too many Saxons. For the Celts, victory merely brought a breathing space, but for the Saxons, it brought new territory. The struggle reached a climax in the seventh century, when the defeat of Cadwallon of Gwynedd dashed any hope for an ultimate Celtic victory. Although the battle between Celts and Saxons would continue for several more centuries, the fate of the British mainland was sealed. The Celtic world was forever relegated to the outer fringes of the British Isles.

End of Roman Order

During the last decades of the third century AD, Roman civilization in Britain came under increasing pressure from raids by Scots, Picts, and Saxons. Roman troops were at a premium because a series of power struggles within the Empire created a demand for seasoned troops. As Roman garrisons left Britain for Gaul, the local Romano-British were forced to organize their own defenses against the new barbarian invaders.

Rome never completely conquered the British Isles, a failure that in later years came to haunt the governors of the province. Scotland, Ireland, and, to a lesser extent, Wales lay outside Roman control, and by the late fourth century their barbarian inhabitants were successfully raiding Britannia. Coin hoards in Wales testify to the plunder the raiding parties looted. The defense of the province now fell to locally raised and trained legionaries, often under the command of locally trained officers. The few "true" Romans left were, themselves, unlikely to have ever been near Rome. Some, indeed, were former barbarians. It was becoming harder to control the situation, especially when many of the legionaries had automatic sympathies with their Celtic "barbarian" cousins.

North of Hadrian's Wall the Picts and the Scots were kept at bay until 367 when an uneasy alliance with the local Romano-British fell apart, resulting in some Roman troops defecting and allowing these northern Celts to penetrate Britannia. The disaster of 367 is significant, since it was an alliance not only of the Irish, the Scots, and the Picts, but also non-Roman frontier troops who defected. Two years later, after much raiding south deep into the heartland of civilized Britain, Roman rule was restored. Stronger relations were established with the Votadani, a buffer tribe between the Picts and the wall.

Just as serious were the raids against the south and east coasts by the Saxons. During the late third century AD a chain of *Saxon Forts* was established along the coasts, to protect what had become known as the Saxon Shore.

Britannia was further weakened in 383 when Magnus Maximus took many of his garrison troops from Britannia across to Gaul. The Roman general had his eye on the imperial crown, but the gamble did not pay off. Maximus was defeated and it is unlikely that his troops ever returned to Britain. Those who had

Below: Pevensey Castle was originally a Late Roman fortification; one of the forts of the "Saxon Shore."

not followed the foolhardy general worked with local administrators to defend the borders of Roman Britain.

Vandalizing Britain

Not long after Maximus's attempt on Rome, the emperor appointed the former Vandal Stilicho to command of the Roman legions and made him responsible for the defense of the Western Roman Empire. Although Stilicho led Roman expeditions against the Picts and the Saxons, in 401 he withdrew even more troops from Britain to help defend Italy from mass Vandal invasion from the east. In 406 the Vandals crossed the Rhine into Gaul, and in 410 the last Roman troops were withdrawn to help restore the situation in Gaul. Britannia was now defenseless, and from that point on it effectively ceased to be part of the collapsing Roman world. Instead, the province became independent, ruled by a series of Romano-British chieftains.

Little is known about the first decades of post-Roman Britain, as Roman writers no longer commented on political developments in the island. Bishop St. Germanus of Auxerre left accounts of two visits he made to Britain in 428/9 and 445/6. During his first visit, life seemed to have continued much as it did during Roman times. The region was ruled by a high-king (*superbus tyrannus*) named Vortigern, which means "overlord." The bishop participated in the repulsion of a large Saxon raiding force, and his mass afterward gave the battle its name of the Alleluia victory. To St. Germanus, the battle was a clear struggle between Christians and pagans.

When the bishop returned for his second visit, Vortigern was barely in control. In the intervening 16 years the province had come under increasing pressure from Saxon, Pictish, and Irish raiders. An appeal to the Western Empire for help went unanswered, and around 450 Vortigern's Jute mercenaries mutinied. The Jutes devastated parts of southeast Britain, and Vortigern was forced to appeal to Hengist of the Saxons for help. In return for military aid, they would be granted control of a region in Kent, on the Saxon shore. Although the Jutes were defeated, the Saxons had been let in by the back door. In later Celtic annals, Vortigern was seen as a traitor who made a deal with the enemy. If the facts are examined, he may not have had any choice.

Above: A local fortification at the junction of two major Roman roads, Viroconium grew into a major British Roman city by AD 200.

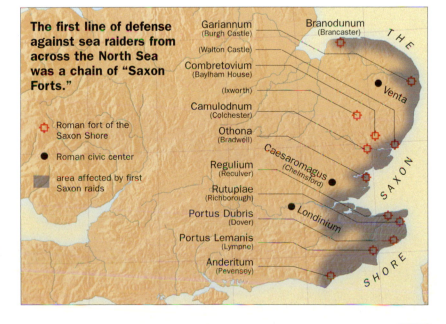

The first line of defense against sea raiders from across the North Sea was a chain of "Saxon Forts."

Gariannum (Burgh Castle)
Branodunum (Brancaster)
(Walton Castle)
Combretovium (Baylham House)
(Ixworth)
Camulodnum (Colchester)
Othona (Bradwell)
Regulium (Reculver)
Rutuplae (Richborough)
Portus Dubris (Dover)
Portus Lemanis (Lympne)
Anderitum (Pevensey)

⊕ Roman fort of the Saxon Shore

● Roman civic center

▨ area affected by first Saxon raids

THE
Venta
Caesaromagus (Chelmsford)
Londinium
SAXON
SHORE

The Sub-Roman Celts

After the withdrawal of the Romans from Britain, the former province disintegrated into a patchwork of kingdoms stretching from Pictland to the Channel, ruled by local Romanized chiefs. From a combination of documentary and archaeological evidence we can reconstruct some of this fragile political framework. These late Celtic kingdoms were to bear the brunt of the Anglo-Saxon invasions of the sixth century.

Divisions of sub-Roman Britain after AD 450.

Little is known about the structure of post-Roman Britain before the mid-sixth century. We do know that in northern Britain, beyond the ruins of Hadrian's Wall, the Picts were coming under pressure from the Scots (or Irish) colony of Dál Riada (*see pages 76–77*). From the mid-fifth century the Saxons were established in Kent, while the Jutes occupied the coast of parts of Essex. The Irish had also established another colony, this time in Gwynedd in Wales. In the rest of southern Britain, the political organization established by the Romans had been taken over by the Romano-British, referred to as the sub-Roman British from 410 onwards by modern historians. Although we cannot be certain, it appears that their territorial divisions followed the Roman diocese of the Christian Church, which in turn were probably based on older tribal divisions.

From the monk Gildas and his *De excidio et*

conquestu Britanniae written in 560, we know that the British of this time were organized into 11 kingdoms, including that of the Picts. The kingdom of Dumnonia was situated in southwest Britain, centered on the modern county of Dorset. The kingdom has been linked to the pre-Roman tribe of the Durotriges.

Below: Dumbarton Rock (Alcluyd), capital of the Celtic kingdom of Strathclyde.

Certainly old Celtic hillforts were reoccupied and turned into bastions against the advance of the Saxons.

Further to the west, Kernow (Cornwall) retained its independence from the rest of sub-Roman Britain. Another small kingdom was Gwent, the traditional home of the Silures of the Severn valley. Dyfed was the old Celtic tribal home of the Demetae, and the names have the same root. Gildas referred to King Vortepor of Dyfed as "the tyrant of the Demataeans." Further to the north the kingdom of Powys was a mountain stronghold covering central Wales, the last bastion of the pre-Roman Welsh Cornovii tribe. Ruled by King Cuneglas, the kingdom had a reputation for its military prowess. The kingdom of Gwynedd was originally an Irish colony, whose settlers dominated the indigenous population there. Gildas records that the kingdom was ruled by King Maelgwyn.

Divided and defeated

The kingdom of Elmet covered much of central Britain, and during the mid-sixth century King Gwallawg of Elmet kept the Angles of Bernicia at bay. It corresponded approximately to the tribal area of the pre-Roman Brigantes. The region finally succumbed to the Saxons during the early seventh century. To the northwest, the kingdom of Rheged was centered around the city of Caerliwelyd (Carlisle). Beyond it lay the Kingdom of Strathclyde, whose chief stronghold was the imposing rock fortress of Alcluyd (Dumbarton). For much of this period the kingdom was engaged in a defensive war with the Scots of Dál Riada. Along the southern shores of the Firth of Forth was the kingdom of Gododdin, whose king held the even more imposing hilltop fortress of Edinburgh. The Romans referred to these people as the Votadani. Beyond the Forth, the Picts of eastern Scotland and the Scots to the west have already been described on pages 74–75.

Although the sub-Roman Britons were united under the leadership of Vortigern as high-king from c.425–55, after his reign the Celtic kingdoms could not agree on an overlord. For brief periods, a number of the kingdoms united under a war leader, and the Celtic kingdoms survived, at least for a time. Given their lack of unity, one of their greatest allies was a similar lack of coordination among the kings and rulers of Anglo-Saxon England. Nevertheless, this patchwork of Celtic kingdoms would eventually succumb to the pressures exerted by Anglo-Saxon expansion.

Above: Tribal capital and fortress of the Celtic Votadani, the hillfort of Traprain Law became a bastion for the Gododdin.

Below: Edinburgh Castle was built on the volcanic plug that once housed the Celtic stronghold of Dun Eidyn, seat of the kings of Gododdin.

The Anglo-Saxons

Around AD 450, Saxon raiders established a foothold in the southeast of Britain. Over the next half century more strongholds were established along the south and east coasts, forming a chain of Germanic settlements. These early Angles and Saxons were followed by new settlers, who helped expand the limits of this new culture, creating the new Anglo-Saxon nation of England.

Right: Detail of decoration from a hanging bowl found among the Sutton Hoo ship-burial hoard, Sutton Hoo, Sussex, England.

The Angles, Saxons, and Jutes arrived in southeast Britain as raiders, then later as settlers. Their origins have been traced to northern Germany, between the Elbe and the Weser rivers for the Saxons, and from the Jutland peninsula for the Jutes. The Angles inhabited the land in between, encompassing the modern cities of Bremen and Hamburg. This development from raiders to settlers is generally assumed to have taken place about AD 450.

The Saxon chieftain Hengist was granted Kent by the sub-Roman high-king Vortigern in return for military help against the Jutes who were stationed in the region. Hengist promptly broke any further alliances with the Britons, and by the time he was succeeded by his son Ærc, Kent had become a secure bastion of Saxon power.

By about 480, the Saxon leader Ælle arrived at Selsey Bill on the Sussex coast (derived from the appellation "South Saxon"). He drove the opposing Celts into the forests of the Weald. Ælle even stormed and captured the Saxon shore fort of Anderida, massacring the garrison when they surrendered. While Sussex was consolidated into a Saxon settlement, other Saxon adventurers landed near the site of Southampton, and laid the foundations for the Saxon kingdom of Wessex ("West Saxon") in the process.

Below: This beautiful purse lid from the ship-burial at Sutton Hoo has been dated as early 7th century.

Unstoppable settlers

During the sixth century, fresh waves of settlers encouraged further expansion inland, bringing the Angles into Essex and East Anglia to the north of the Thames, and it inevitably led to the expansion of Wessex at the expense of the Celtic kingdom of Dumnonia. In 501 the Saxon leader Port landed at Portes mutha (Portsmouth), while other conquests linked the coastal settlements of Wessex with those of Sussex. A victory over the Celts by Cerdic of Wessex in 508 established Saxon control over the New Forest area, although the Celts and Saxons were still contesting the region north of Southampton well into the 520s.

This was also the period of the semi-legendary Celtic warrior Arturus (Arthur), whose victory over the Saxons at Badon (c.516) halted any further Saxon advance for a decade. In 523 the Angles regained the initiative by seizing the coastal fortress of Din Guoaroy, renaming it Bebba's Burgh (Bamborough). This formed the center of the new kingdom of Bernicia. As these Angles fought their way south along the coast, a new territory named Deira was established (from the term *dere* or "water dwellers"). Celtic resistance prevented any link between the Angles of Deira and those to the south until the later seventh century.

Other Angles continued to stream into East Anglia, which was divided into the lands of the north folk (Norfolk) and the south folk (Suffolk). To the west, West or Middle Anglia became Mercia as the Angles pushed west out of the fens toward the Trent. The river marked the border between the Celtic kingdom of Elmet and Saxon Mercia for much of the sixth century.

During the later sixth century the kingdom of the Middle Saxons (Middlesex) was founded in the Thames valley. This was significant, since it encompassed London, which finally fell to the Saxons during the middle of the sixth century. Control of London meant that the Angles and Saxons had a secure means of communication between both banks of the Thames, and consequently all the Saxon territories from Mercia to Wessex. By the time St. Augustine arrived in Kent as a Christian missionary in 596, these Anglo-Saxon territories were seen as a unified kingdom, known as Ænglaland.

Above: Gold belt buckle from Sutton Hoo, with the intricate decoration that became entwined with late La Tène Celtic ornamentation.

Below: Saxon raiders of the 5th century.

The Saxon Conquests

**Between 550 and 650, the Anglo-Saxon kingdoms of
Wessex, Bernicia, and Mercia expanded into Celtic
territories, forming a solid band of English territory
from the Firth of Forth to the Solent. Although
temporary Celtic victories delayed this expansion, the
British were unable to prevent it. By the second half of
the seventh century, Anglo-Saxons had become the
dominant force, and remained so until the Norman
Conquest of 1066.**

Saxon expansion resumed when the
Romano-Celtic warlord Arthur was killed
in battle around 539 (possibly at the semi-
mythical battle of Camlann). This had already
been taking place away from the main centers of
conflict. In 530 Cerdic of Wessex conquered the
Isle of Wight and, following his death in 534,
his successor Cynric probed north into the
modern county of Hampshire. Following the
capture of the Celtic fortresses of Sarum
(Salisbury) in 552, and Barbury Castle
(Swindon) four years later, the West Saxons
gained control of Dumnonia's eastern defenses.

The Celts were given a slight reprieve when a
struggle for power broke out among the Saxons
on the death of Cynryc of the Middle Saxons
when Æthelberht of Kent tried to grab Middlesex
from Cynryc's son Ceawlin. But by 570, the
West Saxons were ready to resume the offensive.
The following year they drove the Celts out of
the area of the modern county of Bedfordshire,
and by capturing the town of Limbury, they
expanded the borders of Saxon England so
that it stretched in a diagonal line from
the New Forest near Southampton to
the lower waters of the Trent.

Delaying the inevitable

In 577 the West Saxons launched their
decisive campaign through Dumnonia
toward the Severn. By defeating a
series of sub-Roman armies, Ceawlin
captured Gloucester and Bath,
splitting Dumnonia and Kernow off
from the rest of Celtic Britain. This
prompted a large-scale migration of
Dumnonian Celts to Armorica, which
became Little Britain (Brittany). The
remainder of Dumnonia lay ripe for
the taking.

Further forays to the north were
stopped when the West Saxons were
defeated by the Celts north of the
modern city of Oxford in 584. For the
moment, the expansion of Wessex
had been halted. This ties in with
references to a new British warlord
named Mouric. Legend has it that he prayed

to the support of their countrymen. This reflects a Saxon backlash against Christian missionaries, who were driven out of Essex around the same time, and the older form of pagan worship was certainly still practiced in Northumbria.

Æthelfrith was killed by his rival Edwin the following year, who took his crown. Edwin converted to Christianity around 625, then in the following year he led his Anglo-Saxon forces south into the Celtic kingdom of Elmet, where he defeated King Ceredig. Northumbria now encompassed much of the center of Britain, stretching from the Forth to the Humber on the east coast, and from the Solway to the Mersey on the west. By 650, similar expansion by Mercia threatened the last strongholds of Celtic power in Britain.

Left: Previously thought to be late Viking, this ship's figurehead found in the River Schelde, Belgium, actually dates from the 5th to 6th centuries. This means it is most likely to be Anglo-Saxon.

Facing: Anglo-Saxon helmet, 7th century, Sutton Hoo.

Anglo-Saxon penetration of Britain between the fifth and seventh centuries.

Anglo-Saxon conquests to 500

conquests to 650

sites of pagan cemeteries and barrows, showing extent of Anglo-Saxon penetration by end of 7th century

for a Christian victory, and by winning it at the Battle of Feathenleag (584), he ensured that West Saxon expansion northward would be halted for another 30 years.

The second dynamic phase of expansion in the Anglo-Saxon kingdoms took place in Bernicia, the struggling east coast kingdom of the Angles. In 592 Æthelfrith became the King of Bernicia, and held it against Pictish, Dál Riadan, and sub-Roman attacks. The most critical of these was an invasion by the Scots, whom he defeated in 603. He then expanded his territories to include the southern Angle state of Deira, and in 604 he formed the two kingdoms into one large kingdom, called Northumbria ("the land north of the Humber").

Æthelfrith then marched against Selyf of Powys, defeating his Celtic army near Chester in 616. Following the battle, the Saxons slaughtered a thousand Celtic monks who came

Arthur of the Britons

Of all the heroes of late Celtic Britain, Arthur is the most popular, mainly due to the semi-mythical status that later medieval authors gave him. The evidence suggests that Arthur was indeed a real person. Although not a king, he was a leading warlord who stemmed the tide of Saxon advance for a few brief years. With his death, the Saxons were free to continue their conquest of the Celtic kingdoms in Britain.

Facing: Cadbury Hill in Somerset has long been associated with Arthur of the Britons. The hill is the site of a late Celtic fortress that was occupied during the Arthurian period.

Right: Glastonbury Tor in Somerset is also the site of a late Celtic stronghold or religious settlement which has been closely associated with Arthur.

There is little hard historical evidence for the existence of Arthur. In the poem *Y Gododdin* written in the late sixth century, the defeat of the Celtic warlords was ascribed to the fact that they "were not Arthur." We know that a sub-Roman victory over the Saxons at Badon halted Saxon expansion for a generation, and the Celtic chronicler Nennius ascribes the victory to "Arthur," along with 11 others. He also describes Arthur as a "*dux bellorem*" (*lit.* leader of war, warlord).

So he was a general, not a king.

A manuscript written in the mid-tenth century claims that the Battle of Badon took place c.516, and adds that Arthur was killed together with Metraut (Mordred) in a battle named Camlann in c.537. These scanty references provide the bones on which the Arthurian legend was later laid (*see pages 176–177*).

The warlord Arthur became the leading late Celtic British hero,

and later chroniclers embellished his career until Geoffrey of Monmouth, writing in the early 12th century, made him the King Arthur of popular mythology. The name Arthur has been linked to the Romano-British name Arturus or Artorius, but it is more likely that the name had Celtic roots.

The first string of Arthurian victories over the Saxons have been traced to modern Lincolnshire, suggesting he was a local commander serving in the army of the kingdom of Elmet. His first victory was won against the Angles on the River Glein, near Peterborough. Another series of engagements was probably fought in the same area, on the south border of Elmet. After securing the southern borders of his region, the warlord marched north, to halt the incursions of Picts and Scots. He fought a battle at a fortress called Guinnion, which has never been identified.

A great strategist

Arthur then moved south again, probably to counter an Irish attack on Chester. The battle was fought inside the city, so presumably Arthur had to storm it. A second Scots threat led Arthur north again, where he halted them somewhere in the present Scottish borders. He was recalled south to face a renewed offensive by the Angles, then after securing the borders of Elmet, Arthur was ready to assist the southern Celts in their struggle against the Saxons.

In a climactic battle against the West Saxons at Badon, Arthur's Celts routed the Saxons and ensured the safety of Dumnonia for a generation. Scholars have argued over its location for years, but one of the most likely is Solsbury Hill, in the county of Somerset. In the battle, Arthur "carried the cross of Our Lord Jesus Christ" on his banners. The historian John Morris suggests that the Celts were besieged for three days by a Saxon host before Arthur could break the siege and rout the Saxons. No further Saxon incursions took place in Dumnonia for over 20 years.

Little is known about his death, apart from the brief statement about the battle of Camlann (Camluan) "…in which Arthur and Metraut were slain… and there was death in Britain and Ireland." It is likely that he died during a battle against the Scots, or even against a Celtic usurper, possibly Metraut (reflecting the actions of Mordred in Arthurian legend). One likely location for this last fight was near Hadrian's Wall, in Cumbria. The age of Arthur passed from shadowy history into legend, and the Celts in Britain were left to face the Saxons without a victorious warlord to unite them.

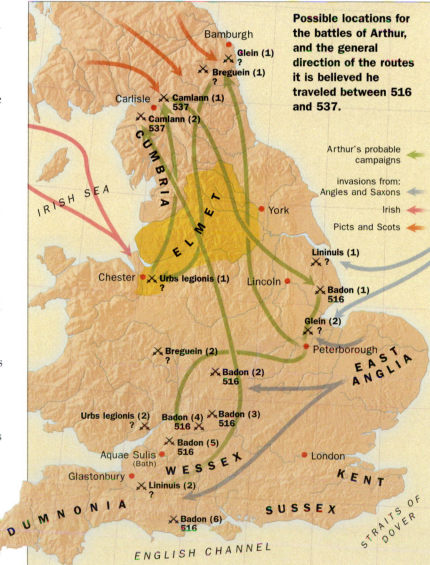

Possible locations for the battles of Arthur, and the general direction of the routes it is believed he traveled between 516 and 537.

Arthur's probable campaigns

invasions from:
Angles and Saxons

Irish

Picts and Scots

Bamburgh
Glein (1) ?
Breguein (1) ?
Carlisle Camlann (1) 537
Camlann (2) 537
CUMBRIA
IRISH SEA
ELMET
York
Lininuls (1) ?
Chester Urbs legionis (1) ?
Lincoln
Badon (1) 516
Glein (2) ?
Breguein (2) ?
Peterborough
EAST ANGLIA
Badon (2) 516
Urbs legionis (2) ?
Badon (4) 516
Badon (3) 516
Badon (5) 516
Aquae Sulis (Bath)
London
Glastonbury
WESSEX
KENT
Lininuis (2) ?
DUMNONIA
Badon (6) 516
SUSSEX
STRAITS OF DOVER
ENGLISH CHANNEL

The Celtic Twilight

For much of the seventh century the Celts continued to resist the Anglo-Saxons, engendering disunity among the Saxon leadership to buy time for their own survival. Gradually the Celts of southern Britain were forced into the Welsh and Scottish mountains, and only in Pictland did they succeed in turning the tide. By the early eighth century the Celts were a spent force, and Anglo-Saxon hegemony in Britain was assured.

Facing: More than 1200 years have passed since King Offa built his great wall to keep out the Celts. Sections of Offa's Dyke can still be traced today.

In 731 the Anglo-Saxon chronicler Bede completed his *Historia Ecclesiastica gentis Anglorum*, and he records the final struggles between the Celts and the Saxons for mastery of Britain. A century before, Cadwallon, the Celtic king of Gwynedd defeated King Edwin of Northumbria in battle at Hatfield (633). Apart from the Pictish victory over the Northumbrians at Nechtansmere in 685, it was to prove the last great Celtic victory over the Saxons.

The crown of Northumbria passed to Oswald, who raised a fresh army and defeated and slew Cadwallon of Gwynedd the following year (634). Cadwallon was celebrated by Celtic chroniclers as "the most brilliant lord king," a Celtic Christian monarch who tried to save Celtic civilization from destruction. Following his death, the Anglo-Saxon kingdom of Northumbria became the dominant power in Britain. Although Oswald was killed in 642, the kingdom continued to expand. By his death it had reached the line of the Firth of Forth, and was threatening the stability of the Picts.

Cadwallon was succeeded by his son Cadwaladr, whose policy involved encouraging Saxon rivals in Northumbria, while trying to limit the expansion of Mercia. The political rebel of the seventh century was King Penda of Mercia, whose troops had killed Oswald of Northumbria, and who made alliances with the Celtic kings of Gwynedd in order to enhance his own ambitions. He campaigned against his fellow Saxons in Northumbria and Wessex, but his plans went awry in 655, when Mercia was threatened by an invasion from Northumbria. On the eve of battle Penda's Celtic allies from Gwynedd deserted him. King Penda was slain, and for a brief period the Northumbrians controlled Mercia until Penda's son Wulfhere reclaimed his father's kingdom.

Political respite

This policy of encouraging friction between the Saxon kingdoms appeared to be working, especially since it was combined with extensive Celtic missionary work in England. This Celtic religious interference came to an end in 664, however, when the Synod of Whitby favored

Right: Remains of the 6th-century Celtic monastery at Tintagel, Cornwall. With the fall of Dumnonia to the Saxons in 690, the Cornish peninsula became the last home for Celts in southern Britain.

the Roman rather than the Celtic Church for the newly-converted Saxons (*see pages 164–165*).

In 670 Ecgfrith became the new king of Northumbria and for the next 14 years the Northumbrians would channel their military energies northward, in a struggle for control of the Scottish lowlands. Their opponents were the Picts, who survived several defeats before they finally vanquished the Northumbrians in 684. Ecgfrith was killed in the battle.

From that point on, the Saxons ceased to be a threat to the Picts, who were free to engage the Dál Riada Scots in a struggle for control of the north. In Mercia, a series of border disputes ended with peace being forged between it and Northumbria, effectively sealing the Welsh Celts into their mountain kingdoms. In 682 a West Saxon invasion took Dumnonia by surprise. Although it took a further decade to completely conquer the kingdom, the other Celtic kingdoms in the north were powerless to help.

By the early eighth century the Saxons had captured Exeter (711), and apart from in Scotland, only the Celtic kingdoms in Wales retained their independence. By this time they lacked the military muscle to attack the English, and the ultimate insult came in about 784, when King Offa of Mercia built a wall to keep the Celts penned into their Welsh mountain enclave. The struggle for Britain was lost, and the Celts became peripheral to British history, reduced to maintaining a tenuous hold on the outer fringes of the British Isles.

The Celts become peripheral to British history—England at the time of King Offa, c.780.

Offa's direct rule

Offa's overlordship

CELTS

STRATHCLYDE

BERNICIA

Bamburgh

GALLOWAY

NORTHUMBRIA

Carlisle

CUMBRIA

MAN

DEIRA

York

NORTH SEA

IRISH SEA

GWYNEDD

Chester

LINDSEY

Lincoln

POWYS

OFFA'S DYKE

MERCIA

CELTS

Peterborough

EAST ANGLIA

DYFED

TOWY

GLYWISING

ESSEX

Bath

London

Glastonbury

KENT

WESSEX

SUSSEX

CORNWALL

WIGHT

CELTS

ENGLISH CHANNEL

The location of major finds of late La Tène and early medieval Celtic art.

● La Tène Iron Age finds c.200 BC to AD 450

● Celtic Renaissance finds from 450 to 12th century

Right: From the 7th century on, the quality of Celtic artistry both in illumination of manuscripts and in metalwork grew in breadth of imagination, technique, and sheer beauty to heights unparalleled since. One of the finest examples of the late flowering of Celtic religious art is the 8th-century Cross of Cong. Made from oak, the cross is encased in copper and riveted silver. The sides are engraved with inscriptions; one refers to Maelisu, the artist who created the cross.

Birsay

Dunbeath

Rogart

Golspie

Nigg

Forre

Dunadd

Hunterston

Fahan Mura

Lisnacroghera

Dunaverney

Clogher

Drumcliff

Armagh

Keshcarrigan

Monasterboice

Moynagh Lough

Lough Crew   Kells

Cong   Moylough   Donore

Lagore   Bettystown

Clonmacnois   Ballinderry

Clonfert   Somerset

Monasterevin

Moone

Kilfenora

Durrow

Derrynaflan

Ardagh

Cashel

Inisfalen   Ahenny

Lismore

Chapter 10

The Renaissance of Celtic Art

In the 12th century, Gerald of Wales described a Celtic manuscript he had once seen in Kildare, an Irish center of ecclesiastical illumination. The work had, he wrote: "…intricacies, so delicate and so subtle, so exact and compact, so full of knots and links, with colors so fresh and vivid" that it seemed "the work, not of men, but of angels." He also recalled the story of an angel appearing to a Celtic scribe in a dream, showing him the designs he was to use in his illuminations. Even today, the beauty of Celtic illuminated manuscripts is breathtaking, and the complex and intricate designs have been copied by modern designers wishing to recapture the artistic glories of the Celtic past.

The craftsmen of this renaissance or "golden age" did not work in isolation. These artists were able to draw upon techniques and styles brought to Britain and Ireland through contact with the Anglo-Saxons, and through the Church (with its Romano-Christian symbolism. Historians have labeled this period as the Dark Ages. This appellation is rarely used today, which is just as well because it conjures up images of a stagnant period which in fact was full of progress in many areas, including artistry.

Late Celtic metalwork exhibits a complexity, artistic brilliance, and technical perfection that remains unsurpassed. These objects of gold, silver, and bronze, often inlaid with enamel or glass, were mainly designed to serve a religious function. Although designed to portray the glory of the Almighty, they also served to testify to the cultural achievement of the late Celtic world.

A Celtic Artistic Rebirth

The conversion of the Celts to Christianity marked a watershed in Celtic art, ushering in a new phase of technical excellence, artistic intricacy, and ecclesiastical patronage. Some of the most beautiful metal objects ever created were made by Celtic metalworkers between AD 400 and 1200. For this reason the early medieval period has been described as an artistic renaissance in the late Celtic world.

Right: Invading Angles and Saxons began to influence the indigenous Celtic art. The Anglo-Saxon Wilton Cross, AD 675–700.

From around AD 400 onward, the majority of Celtic artwork was religious in nature or purpose. This period coincides with the end of Roman rule in southern Britain, and the brief reclamation of the island by the Celts. With the legions gone, the resurgence of Celtic kingdoms created a growth in patronage, and the Church provided an even greater support for Celtic artists.

This was also a period of warfare and invasion, but in the wake of conflict came artistic influence. The waves of Angles, Saxons, and Jutes who landed in Britain from the fifth century onward also influenced Celtic artistic styles, bringing their own Germanic styles to those of sub-Roman Britain. For the next four centuries the Celtic and Anglo-Saxon cultures developed in parallel, and one influenced the other. In Scotland, the Picts and the Scots of Dál Riada were in an almost constant state of

conflict, but the two cultures still influenced each other, as well as their Anglo-Saxon enemies. Similarly, the Irish raiders who plagued western Britain were followed by permanent Irish settlers, who brought their own artistic conceptions to the mainland of Britain. With Irish, Scots, Pictish, Saxon, and former Roman influences merging with traditional Celtic British

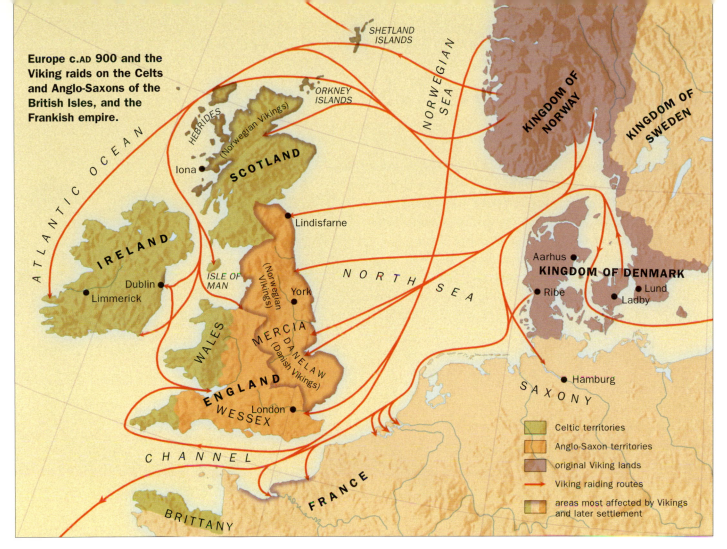

Europe c.AD **900** and the
**Viking raids on the Celts
and Anglo-Saxons of the
British Isles, and the
Frankish empire.**

SHETLAND
ISLANDS

NORWEGIAN SEA

KINGDOM OF NORWAY

KINGDOM OF SWEDEN

ORKNEY
ISLANDS

ATLANTIC OCEAN

HEBRIDES

(Norwegian Vikings)

Iona

SCOTLAND

Lindisfarne

IRELAND

Dublin
Limmerick

ISLE OF
MAN

(Norwegian
Vikings)

York

NORTH SEA

Aarhus
KINGDOM OF DENMARK
Ribe
Lund
Ladby

WALES

MERCIA

DANELAW
(Danish Vikings)

Hamburg
SAXONY

ENGLAND
WESSEX
London

CHANNEL

FRANCE

BRITTANY

Celtic territories

Anglo-Saxon territories

original Viking lands

Viking raiding routes

areas most affected by Vikings
and later settlement

artistic forms, it is hardly surprising that there
was a cultural renaissance during this period.
Even the Norse raiders of the eighth century
onward brought their own cultural influences in
the wake of the destruction they wrought on late
Celtic Britain.

Christianity as patron

The loss of Roman administrative systems and a
slow economic recovery from invasion meant
that at first there was little disposable income
available for patronage other than from the
Church. The institution relied on Celtic artisans
to ensure that devotional objects were worthy of
the Almighty. With an improvement in
economic conditions through the sixth and
seventh centuries, secular patronage of the arts
increased, although the Church remained the
principal consumer of Celtic metalwork.

Between 400–1200, external influences,
increased patronage, and improvements in metal
production and quality exerted a beneficial effect
and the nature of Celtic metalwork changed. It
became breathtaking in its intricacy and esthetic
value. Many fine examples of Celtic art have
survived, allowing us to trace the influences the
development of metalwork had during this

period of artistic renaissance.

Metalwork was not the only artistic field that
underwent this change and impetus.
Manuscript illumination provided a fresh
medium for expression, and allowed artists to
develop fresh styles while reinterpreting
Christian motifs. The people who made these
metal artifacts and illuminated pages were not
struggling artists. They were highly regarded
and well-rewarded artisans, while many of their
illuminated manuscripts have been linked to
leading members of the Celtic Church itself.

Archaeology has provided us with even more
information about these late Celtic artists.
Settlement sites have produced evidence of
metalworking facilities, and clay molds for
pouring brass into have been found as far apart
as Orkney and Ireland. Pairs of compasses used
to trace the intricate geometric patterns have
been discovered. Museums in London, Dublin,
and other cities exhibit an array of priceless
Celtic artifacts in metal and vellum. While the
earlier pre-Roman era of the La Tène Celts has
been seen as an artistic highpoint, it was
certainly equaled by the Celtic artistry of Britain
and Ireland at this time.

Irish Celtic Metalwork

In the period from the sixth until the tenth centuries, Celtic artists produced a range of objects that were directly descended from the work of earlier Gallic craftsmen. Over the centuries these Irish artists developed their skills, making their metalwork rank among the most exquisite decorative objects ever produced.

Right: The 8th-century "Londesbrough brooch" is of heavy Irish silver, cast with a complex of animal and bird motifs. It is unusual for the period in that no filigree work is used and the intricate decoration is cast rather than applied.

The technical skills needed to produce these masterpieces in metalwork had existed for centuries. Casting, engraving, raising, and tinning procedures had already been developed by the time the Romans left Britain early in the fifth century. The curvilinear low-relief patterns of the La Tène period were translated into a new form with increased complexity, and applied to a wider range of objects. These included brooches, pins, bowls, and bracelets.

In Ireland more than anywhere else in the Celtic world, artistic styles developed with relatively little interference from outside influences. Certainly Roman, Saxon, or Frankish influences would have been present, but in broad terms, Irish metalwork represents a linear development from early La Tène roots. Irish society remained relatively unchanged throughout the period from the first to the fifth centuries AD, and the advent of Christianity provided a fresh demand for metalwork. While elsewhere Celts were engaged in warfare and rebellion, in Ireland a relatively stable political climate favored patronage of the arts. The only other area in Europe to remain equally free of external influences was Pictland, and their extraordinary legacy was in stone, not in metal (*see pages 148–149*).

Work of angels

The principal qualities of Irish art of the late Celtic period are reflected in the metal objects that have survived. Stone monuments and manuscript illuminations produced in the same era are far less numerous. Celtic metalwork such as brooches, sword scabbards, and bracelets were portable, and valuable enough to hide if their security was at risk. This was particularly prevalent during the period of the Viking raids, and many caches, or hoards, were buried by their owners, and sometimes by the raiders themselves. As a result, numerous examples survive.

A recent exhibition on Irish Celtic metalwork entitled *The Work of Angels* exhibited 230 objects, the cream of the national collections of Ireland and elsewhere. Hundreds of other less dramatic pieces are also extant. Enameling was practiced in Ireland from the fifth century, and during the early Christian period its use became widespread.

Ornamentation also became more commonplace, and semi-precious stones and glass were both used extensively, usually in combination with gold filigree settings. The *millefiori* (thousand flowers) technique involved the use of glass threads of different colors, fused together and sliced to form flat inlay patterns. It became commonly used for floral decoration, such as on the Ardagh chalice and the Tara brooch (*see the following page*).

Filigree—where twisted braids of gold or silver are soldered onto the metal object—was raised to a high art form by late Celtic metalsmiths to decorate numerous fine pieces of jewelry. Another widespread techique is *granulation*, a process in which minute drops are dripped onto the surface of an ornament before it is finally soldered into place.

Above: This silver Viking hoard, found on the banks of the River Ribble, Lancashire, England, was probably buried about 905. Because much of the silver is of Irish origin, it is likely that this was the plunder of Vikings who were expelled from Dublin in 902.

Left: A brooch from the seventh century, showing off some fine filigree work, enameling, and glass inlays. Found in Baslieur, Meurthe-et-Moselle, France, this object is only 2½ inches in diameter.

The Celtic Hoards

Thanks to the depredations of Vikings, some of the greatest works of Celtic metalsmiths are still available to us today after their creators and owners buried their valuables to secure them from Viking theft. Pieces such as the Tara Brooch, the Ardagh Chalice, and items from the Derrynaflan Hoard are rightly regarded as the epitome of Celtic artistry.

Ironically, in later years, settled Vikings themselves buried valuables to hide them in times of unrest, and these hoards, or chaches, also included Celtic objects. The practice of hoarding was particularly prevalent in Celtic Ireland during the period of Viking raids. The Derrynaflan Hoard—named after the site of its discovery in 1980, at Derrynaflan, County

Above: The Tara Brooch (c.mid-7th century) represents the peak of sophistication in Celtic metalwork and ornamentation.

Tipperary—was found near an extant medieval church, which replaced one that was once part of a Celtic monastic settlement.

Although the exact reason the hoard was buried is unknown, it is considered likely that it was hidden sometime during the late ninth century. The owners were probably monks from the important monastic site where the found was made. Since the monks never

returned to reclaim their possessions, they very probably met a violent end.

The objects are of a variety of types, dates, and origins: a silver chalice, a silver paten with an accompanying stand, a plain bronze basin, and an elaborate gilded bronze sieve or strainer ladle. The chalice—a poorer piece than the paten, with crude ornamentation and clearly crafted by a metalworker who was not an expert in his field—probably dates from the mid-eighth century, while the rest of the objects were crafted c.700. Although unexceptional, it is still a striking object, as is the strainer ladle, which boasts gold and enamel decoration around its rim.

The chalice itself is similar to another example found at Ardagh in County Limerick. But by comparison with the Derrynaflan Chalice, the Ardagh Chalice exemplifies the finest of Celtic ornamental metalwork of the Celtic Renaissance period.

Creations in miniature

Many consider this chalice to be a parallel of artistic perfection to the *Book of Kells* (*see pages 162–163*). It was obviously intended to be a

liturgical object, and is composed of two quite plain bowls made from silver, one inverted on top of the other, and held together with a cast gilt-bronze collar. Two handles are mounted on the bowl, and these joints are decorated with *millefiori*-style medallions of embossed copper and silver with eloborate enameling, and fixed to the bowl by plaques enlivened by yellow, red, blue, and green glass studs. A decorative band

Left: The Ardagh
Chalice displays a
calm sanctity offset
by exuberant
decoration. It is also
a superb example of
the art of the late
Celtic metalworker.

circles the rim consisting of ten panels. The panels, separated by raised decorated studs, are incised with intricate gold filigree patterns, and a similar band encircles the base. Circular medallions on either side of the bowl add a powerful decorative touch to the chalice.

Perhaps the other most vibrant piece of Celtic Renaissance metalwork is the so-called Tara Brooch, which was actually found near the River Boyne, County Meath. Even by today's mechanical standards, the decoration on this brooch is astonishing (it is reproduced here at actual size). This superb piece of Celtic jewelry is based around a closed cast silver circle. On both its front and back a series of frames hold filigree decoration and gilt chip carvings (granulation), while a pair of enamel circles, glass and amber studs, and a sunken spiral pattern complete the striking decoration of the small object.

The brooch was worn on a tunic, probably joined together over the shoulder by a safety chain, part of which can still be seen. Birds and mythical beasts are packed into every space, recalling earlier La Tène styles and linking its design with that of the manuscript illuminations in the *Lindisfarne Gospels* (*see pages 160–161*).

A similarly exquisite brooch was recovered at Hunterston in Ayrshire, Scotland. This latter piece carries Scandinavian names scratched into its underside, reflecting the value these pieces had to Norse raiders. Numerous other examples of Celtic Irish metalwork were recovered from sites in Norway, where they had been taken as plunder.

Like the Ardagh Chalice, the Derrynaflan hoard was not a uniform set of metal objects, such as a Communion set. Indeed, such unified collections were rare. Its collective importance lies in its representation of the liturgical objects used by a prosperous Celtic church near the height of the Celtic Renaissance.

Metalworking Techniques

Celtic metalworkers used a wide variety of materials and techniques to produce their works of art. Gold, silver, bronze, enamel, and glass were all favored, and many objects were composed of multiple materials. Techniques of filigree, inlay, and gilding were highly specialized, and many of the best pieces were probably the product of several artists.

During the Celtic Renaissance in Ireland, materials were shipped from as far away as the Mediterranean. Tin was almost certainly imported from Cornwall, while Ireland itself provided a source for small quantities of gold, silver, copper, and iron. Silver and copper mines existed in medieval times, and there is some evidence that mines existed in Ireland and Scotland during the preceding centuries.

The richness of this collection of horse harness fittings (British, 1st-century AD) indicates that they belonged to a wealthy land-owner, or were part of a ritual burial for a great warrior. They are made from bronze with inlaid glass.

The red glass of Celtic enamel work was imported from the Mediterranean long after the collapse of the Roman Empire.

It had been argued that when the Romans left Britain, access to overseas materials ceased. Archaeological evidence now proves this assumption to be false, and Celtic traders developed their own links which stretched as far as Spain and the western Mediterranean. Historians also suggested that the Celts had to make do with scrap metal left behind by the Romans, or alternatively melt down existing objects. While this was certainly done, supplies of scrap metal were minimal compared with the quantities available from British mines or from imported metals. Recent metallurgical tests have revealed distinguishing features in local Celtic metalwork. For example, Irish silver was often alloyed with pure copper, while silver produced in England contained copper and bronze. It appears that there was an abundance of locally produced or imported metals available for the needs of the late Celtic metalworkers.

Simple tools, great creativity

Fragments of working drawings have been found incised on bone or slate. These were laid out using a grid, and compasses were employed extensively to produce the curving interlace of Celtic designs. Using such basic tools, the Celtic craftsmen produced these complex patterns, and their eye for intricate detail bears testimony to their skills.

Much of the metalwork of the period was cast rather than beaten, and casting molds have been uncovered throughout Britain and Ireland. Most of these molds came in two parts. A wax or lead template of the piece would be made, then pressed into the halves of the clay mold. A pouring channel would be cut in the top surface, and the template removed again. The mold was then fired, then the molten metal was poured inside it. For the most part, molds were only used once, then discarded, as repeat castings were less distinct than the original.

Another technique reserved for larger or more complex pieces was the lost-wax method. The inner template was greased and coated in clay layers, which were then fired. The inner template would melt, leaving a hollow mold. The metal would then be poured in.

A number of casting workshops have been discovered, revealing the remains of molds, crucibles for molten metal, stone crucible rests, and iron handling tongs. When pieces were hammered from wrought metal rather than cast, small hammers and stakes were used. This was a particularly common method for the production of bowls or chalices. Cast or beaten pieces were then assembled, and joined together using rivets, solder, or cement.

Mechanical joints were often used, when pieces were folded together and beaten. Rivets were the most common form of bond and, in important pieces, the rivet heads would be covered with decorative features such as roundels or bosses. The craftsmanship required to produce the best of the Celtic metalwork was extremely demanding. Given the simple tools available, their achievements are extraordinary.

Above: About a hundred bone flakes like this one were excavated from a burial mound in Lough Crew, County Meath. The decoration illustrates the compass techniques used by Irish artists in the 1st century AD.

Decoration of Metalwork

Although the construction of late Celtic metalwork pieces was technically impressive, the true glory of Celtic artistry is to be found in the decoration applied to these objects. These intricate and effervescent designs of polychrome decoration are among the most beautiful pieces of metal decoration ever produced.

Celtic metalwork was often richly inlaid with enamel, glass, semi-precious stones, or other decorative materials. The Celts had made glass from the fifth century, and a century later commercial glass workshops were in operation. Glass was not a Roman invention or exclusively used by them, and the Celts used it for the decoration of jewelry. Glass votive offerings were made in Gaul and southern Germany during the La Tène period, often produced by twisting rods of semi-molten glass into an animal shape.

The Celts were using glass inlay on bronze objects during the early La Tène period, but these early pieces used glass that was softened and then inserted into place. True enamel work involved the melting of the glass inlay. This true enameling was probably introduced to Britain by the Romans, and Irish metalworkers adopted the technique while they were still using their older semi-molten inserts. The red glass favored by late Celtic enamel workers had a high lead content, making it unstable at higher temperatures. Although this type of glass remained in widespread use, other forms more suited to melting into enamel were increasingly used during the Celtic renaissance period.

Another technique was the setting of glass into a decoration in an unmolten state. Plain or colored glass pieces were shaped, then set in the same way as metalworkers used semi-precious stones. *Millefiori* has already been described (*see page 139*), and its emphasis on multiple strands or colors of glass made it one of the most esthetic methods available. Other forms of inlay

Above: An Irish "latchet" dress fastener of the 6th–7th centuries, showing lavish use of red enamel and finely worked spirals.

were also popular, such as *niello*, a dense black metallic substance that was widely used by the Romans for the inlay of silver. Inlay is produced by cutting or casting a depression or groove into the surface of the object, and then adding the inlay material. This *champlevé* technique was favored by the Irish, while the Britons and Anglo-Saxons preferred the *cloisonné* method, where the inlay is soldered directly onto the unprepared surface.

Filigree and gilding

Even more popular than enamel decoration was *filigree*, where the ornamentation is made up from very finely twisted wire, usually gold thread. In most Irish examples, this wire is soldered onto a thin strip of gold leaf or gold foil backing plate. This in turn is sometimes mounted inward in relief so that the surface lies flush with the object, or by hammering from behind. This latter *repoussé* technique creates a decorative ridge on the object, onto which the backing plate is attached.

Another form uses a combination method. This *hollow-platform* technique involves setting a

piece of filagree decoration mounted on a relief strip of backing, which is pierced, and mounted over a flat backing plate. The filigree work is held in place by lapping the edges of the wire around the backing plate, or by stitching or even occasionally riveting it into position. One distinctive feature of late Celtic Irish metalwork is the crispness of the filigree work, with intricate designs of interwoven gold wires providing a marked contrast to the simplicity of the object being decorated.

Gilding was also practiced, and the surfaces of metal objects were tinned or plated by dipping the metalwork into a pot of molten metal. In tinning, the molten substance is tin mixed with mercury, but a similar mercury gilding technique was used for applying gold or silver gilt finishes, usually onto a bronze surface. If applied correctly, the plated surface is highly resilient. Mixing gold dust with mercury produces a coating that can be spread onto the surface with a heated spatula, then the object is reheated to burn off the mercury, which serves as a bonding agent.

Above: Irish Shrine Boss, AD 700–750. Cast from a wax or lead form in bronze and then thickly gilded. The settings once held glass, crystal, or amber ornamentation. At the top is a ring of black niello framing plain gold troughs once filled with panels of filigree.

The Influence of Christianity

At the start of the fifth century, the Irish and Welsh Celts came into contact with Christianity. For the next six centuries the religion influenced Celtic artists, and the Church was the main beneficiary of the exquisite metalwork produced during this period. Secular leaders supported the Church through grants of land, services, and presents of religious objects, creating a wealth of artwork on religious and spiritual themes.

There is little information available concerning the early spread of Christianity in Ireland, apart from the account of St. Patrick, and there is little hard evidence to support popular theories concerning how the religion arrived from the mainland of Europe. After the conversion of the Irish kings and chieftains, the secular leadership in the island supported the efforts of the Church and its missionaries. While before, only the kings and aristocrats provided patronage for skilled metalworkers and stonecarvers, from the sixth century onward the Church became the leading patron of the Celtic arts.

Even pieces commissioned by secular rulers often had a religious significance because they were designed either to gift the Church or to demonstrate the piety of their owners. This royal patronage was vital to the survival and prosperity of the Celtic Church, and their donations and the loan of skilled court artisans allowed for the production of some of the finest Christian manuscripts and religious pieces of metalwork.

Archaeologists have traced some of the leading centers for the production of high quality metalwork to the royal courts of Ireland rather than to the monasteries or Church workshops. The excavation of royal workshops at Lagore, Clogher, and Garranes in Ireland, and similar sites on the mainland of Britain indicate a high level of production, based on

Right: A reliquary is a casket for housing the relics of a saint. As such, they were invariably beautifully gilded and decorated. Many reliquaries were thought to possess miraculous powers devolved from the saint's relics. The Monymusk reliquary, shown here, was carried at the battle of Bannockburn (1314) to protect the Scottish warriors.

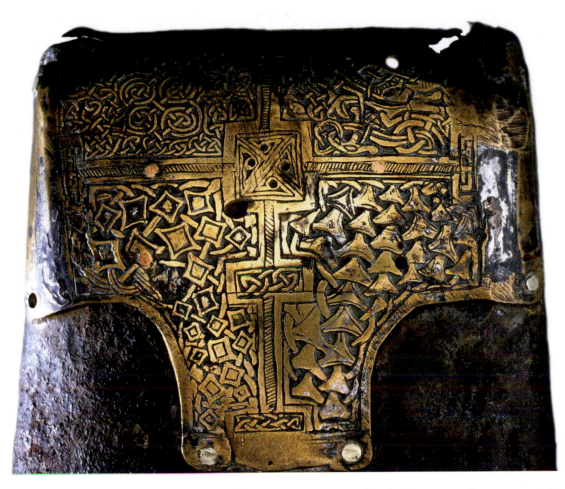

Left: Missionaries to Ireland carried a bell, usually a very humble and simply made object. St. Conall Cael's Bell from Inishkeel, County Donegal, c.600–700, is typical in that it was later embellished with ornate decoration and then housed inside an even more elaborate "shrine" dating from the 10–11th centuries.

the remains of scrap metal and broken molds in these centers.

As the Irish And Scottish economies blossomed between the seventh and ninth centuries, the kings and leading aristocrats of the region had more disposable wealth to spend on patronage of the arts, and on donations of these artistic objects to the Church.

Independent artisans

The religious metalwork assemblages recovered from Ardagh and Derrynaflan were discovered in a monastic setting, so they were assumed to have been the product of workshops attached to the Celtic monasteries. Recent archaeological discoveries have led to the realization that independent workshops existed which did not form part of religious or secular houses. These production centers were run by professional metalworkers, working independently, but relying on the patronage and orders of both ecclesiastical and secular clients.

Since the houses of both Church and State often shared the same location, it seems unlikely that metalworkers concentrated on either secular or religious subjects to the exclusion of everything else. In short, while production

centers associated with centers of power certainly produced a range of religious objects, the best late Celtic metalworkers may well have operated their workshops on their own behalf, designing their wares to suit the needs of their patrons.

Circumstances were different for stonemasons and sculptors because Church patronage was almost infinite. As monasteries and ecclesiastical churches sprang up throughout Scotland, Ireland, and Wales, clerics employed these artisans almost exclusively, and most monasteries employed their own live-in stonemasons. Many of the spectacular high-crosses of the ninth century onward are the product of stonemasons based in monastic centers such as Iona.

Whether for the stonemasons of Iona, the manuscript illustrators of Durrow, or the metalworkers of Lagore, religious belief and the patronage of the arts played an overwhelmingly important role in artistic development. Although secular art existed, and royal patronage remained significant, the Church was the major beneficiary of this production. To some extent, almost all Celtic art was influenced by Christianity, since the techniques developed to further the glory of God were also available for the embellishment of the secular aristocracy.

Stone Crosses

Throughout the Celtic lands of Britain and Ireland, large stone crosses bear witness to the conversion of the later Celts to Christianity. These are among the most commonly encountered and powerful images created by Celtic artists, and although they were often decorated using similar techniques found on metalwork or manuscript illumination, the stonemasons developed their own unique style.

In different regions of the British Isles, different styles of stone carvings predominated. In Wales and Cornwall, stone crosses were simple affairs, lacking the classical Celtic patterns of interweaving threads and floral embellishments. By contrast in Ireland, crosses of the Celtic renaissance period emphasized decoration, and references to the natural world. In Pictland and Dál Riada, decorative features were an integral part of the stone cross, and there, crosses developed into distinctive shapes where the decoration was allowed to dominate the sculpture. The trend in stone decoration evolved from the simple incising of stones to the production of bas-relief carvings. This then developed into uniquely shaped pieces of stonework comprising a third style, and although the three phases overlap, there is a generally linear chronology to their production.

The difficulties of dating

In Ireland, cross slabs are difficult to date unless they carry inscriptions as well as incised decoration. Although some extant examples may date from the seventh century AD, most were produced at least a century later. The slabs at Fahan Mura and Carndonagh were decorated with a bas-relief interlaced pattern forming a Christian cross, and may correspond to a later phase, while inscribed examples predate them. The first dateable Irish sculpture is found in Kilnasaggart, County Armagh, as it combines an inscription with an incised cross decoration. As the inscription names a historical local ruler called Ternoc whose death is recorded in the "Irish Annals," it seems likely the cross was produced before his demise in about AD 716. Incised crosses were therefore still being produced at the start of the eighth century AD. During that century, incised crosses were replaced by bas-relief ones, then by free-standing shaped stone crosses. It has been argued that these shaped stone crosses were introduced around the start of the century, as examples indicate links to Northumbrian Saxon crosses produced during the same period (c.AD 700). Their decoration is also similar to

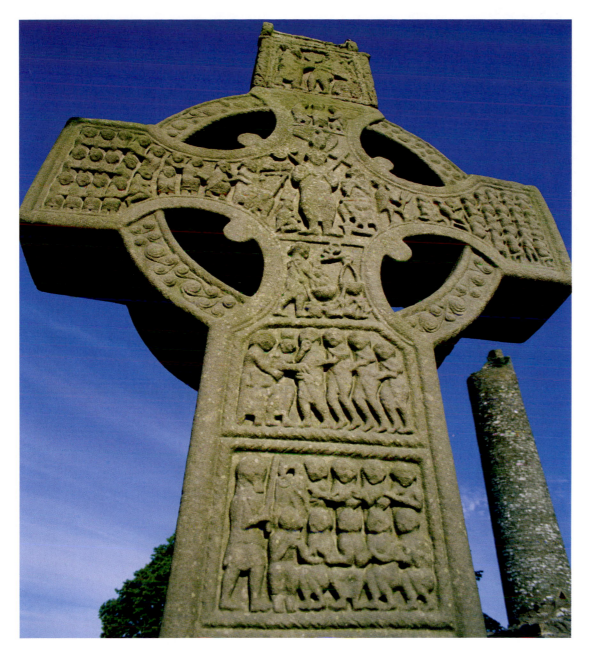

Left: Muiredach's Cross in the enclosure of Monasterboice—founded in the 5th century by St. Buithe, one of St. Patrick's disciples—is one of the finest of Irish high crosses dating from the 10th century. The west face of the cross, shown here, depicts the life of Christ, with the Crucifixion on the hub of the wheel. In the background can be seen a well preserved round tower.

decoration found in the Anglo-Saxon Lindisfarne Gospels of the same period.

The earliest fully free-standing stone high crosses come from the monastery at Iona, established by St. Columba in the center of the Irish (Scots) colony at Dál Riada. For the first time the traditions of metalwork decoration and stone carvings were combined into three-dimensional stone objects of striking beauty. One particular feature taken from contemporary jewelry production was the introduction of a central boss, resembling the setting for a semi-precious stone or piece of enamel decoration in Celtic metalwork. Other metalwork features include the use of cable beading around the edges of these stones, and the replication of filigree interlace.

The Iona crosses appear to have served as inspiration for a range of similar high crosses, although these appear to have combined this replication of metalwork with stone-carved depictions of contemporary people or events. The cross at Moone in County Kildare draws on biblical subjects for inspiration, while the North Cross at Ahenny in County Tipperary depicts a hunting scene around its base. Outside Ireland and Iona, the only Scottish cross of this type was erected at Dupplin in Tayside after the amalgamation of the Picts and the Scots into a unified Scottish people, although bas-relief and incised crosses in the region date from the Pictish period. The striking free-standing Celtic high crosses are therefore an Irish or Scots phenomenon, and represent some of the most beautiful examples of early medieval sculpture in Europe.

Facing:

A Celtic cross of the late Pictish period in the churchyard at Aberlemno in Scotland, the stone incorporates Celtic scrollwork and mythical animals with Christian symbolism.

149

The Pictish Symbol Stones

The Picts were one of the most fascinating and enigmatic peoples of Celtic Europe. They occupied the east and north of Scotland from before the Roman occupation of southern Britain until their amalgamation with the Scots in the mid-ninth century. Their greatest legacy was a large quantity of standing stones covered with symbols or depictions of people or animals, interwoven with decorative features such as Celtic scrollwork. Although these stones have been extensively studied, their true meaning remains as enigmatic as the Picts themselves.

The symbol stones have become a source of fascination for scholars. Like the Irish crosses of around the same period, the earliest carry incised decoration, usually one or more of a range of about 50 symbols. These symbols represent real or mythical animals, possible domestic objects such as a mirror and a comb, and a range of abstract designs. These symbols were not found exclusively on the symbol stones, and similar depictions are present on a handful of metal artifacts.

A survey of approximately 160 symbol stones has revealed that the symbols rarely appear on their own, but are usually grouped in pairs, one above the other. The usual combination is an animal-symbol paired with an abstract-symbol, but occasionally three or four symbols are grouped together on a stone.

There is no geographical correlation to the symbols, so it is unlikely that they have any territorial significance. It is generally assumed that these

Pictish stone monuments and sites.

ORKNEY ISLANDS

B

A

A = Aberdeen
B = Burghead
D = Dundee
E = Edinburgh
S = St. Andrew's

D

S

Dumbarton

E

Pictish symbols date from the seventh century, and although some of the animal-symbols have been linked to other Celtic representations, many are exclusively found in Pictland.

Archaeologists have grouped the stones into three categories. The first consists of non-dressed standing stones, carrying incised decoration, usually in the form of the symbols described above. A second group has been linked to the spread of Christianity among the Picts because they carry Christian crosses in relief, while the third type contains relief scenes depicting people and events. These groups are misleading, since the types overlap chronologically, just like the stone crosses in Ireland, and cannot be linked to separate phases of artistic development. Some of the symbols found on plain incised symbol stones are repeated on Christian stones. Whatever their function, these Pictish symbol stones provide scholars with more questions about the Picts than they provide answers for.

Unique symbols and figures

Some of the later, and more impressive Pictish stone sculptures can be dated to the eighth and ninth centuries. Christian symbols are widely used, and the Picts erected cross-slab monuments similar to those produced in Ireland around the same time. The difference between them is that many of the Pictish stones include bas-relief images of the mysterious Pictish symbols, of Christian and secular figures and scenes, and natural or mythical subjects.

The first development beyond simple incised carving was the production of bas-relief carvings. The most notable examples of these include the Birsay stone from Orkney which depicts three warriors, and the Golspie stone, which depicts a Pictish axeman surrounded by animals and fish. The back of both these stones carries a bas-relief Celtic cross, set against a background of interlaced decoration.

Perhaps the most celebrated Pictish stone was located in Aberlemno churchyard in Angus, and now resides in Edinburgh. One side has a bold Celtic cross in relief, surrounded by mythical animals and interlaced decoration. The reverse depicts a battle scene in bas-relief, which is believed to represent the Battle of Nechtansmere, fought between the Picts and the Northumbrian Saxons in 685. A final group are stones bearing relief crosses similar to the free-standing high crosses of Iona, but the Picts never produced the splendid high crosses of the Irish type. The Pictish stones reflect a vibrant late Celtic culture, whose artistic roots developed separately from their neighbors'. They also provide us with one of the great enigmas of the Celtic world.

Facing: The rear of Aberlemno Stone II shows Pictish huntsmen and typical Pictish symbols, including the "crescent and rod" and "double-mirror" symbols shown at the top of the stone.

Below: The rear of Aberlemno Stone I shows a shieldwall of Pictish warriors under attack from armed horsemen. It is highly likely that the stone commemorates the Pictish victory over the Northumbrians at the battle of Nechtansmere (AD **685**).

Centers of the Celtic Church, and the Roman, Irish, and Anglo-Saxon missions between 560 and 750.

✝ Irish Celtic Church foundation

▢ Celtic territories after 600

Missions, with missionary name and date, where known:

St. Columba (563) →
Irish missions

St. Augustine (600) →
Roman missions

Boniface (716) →
Anglo-Saxon missions

ATLANTIC OCEAN

ATLANTIC OCEAN

When in 617, the pagan King Aethelfrith of Northumbria is slain in battle by the East Anglian king, Aethelfrith's young son Oswald is sent to Iona for refuge, and brought up there as a Christian. In 634, Oswald returns as king to Northumbria and brings monks with him to begin converting Northumbrians to Christianity.

NORTH SEA

Birsay

Orkney Isles

Golspie

Insch

Iona

Dunadd

DAL RIADA

Dumbarton

STRATHCLYDE

Edinburgh

ST. AIDEN (627–34)

NORTHUMBRIA (634)

Lindisfarne

ST. COLUMBA (563)

ULSTER

Bangor

Whithorn

Carlisle

CUMBRIA

Whitby

Clogher

Armagh

CONNAUGHT

MEATH

Kells

Donore

Clonard

Lagore

Durrow

Man

IRISH SEA

York (625)

Lincoln

Clonmacnoise
Clonfert

Ardagh

LEINSTER

Anglesey

Gwynedd

Chester

Bangor-is-y-coed

WELSH KINGDOMS

Powys

Dyfedd

MERCIA (655)

Leicester

Peterborough

EAST ANGLIA (653)

PAULINUS (627)

MUNSTER

Lismore

Cork

Caldy Island

ST. COLUMBA (590)

Dinas Powys

Gwent

Worcester

Gloucester

ESSEX (653)

WESSEX (676)

Bath

London (604)

Winchester (676)

(Southampton)

SUSSEX (686)

KENT

DUMNONIA

Exeter

Wight

ENGLISH CHANNEL

Chapter II

Celts and Christianity

At a time when the world was being plunged into chaos by the barbarian invasions, the sub-Roman Celts of Europe retained their newly found Christian beliefs, and even brought Christianity to their Celtic neighbors in Ireland through the efforts of St. Patrick, now the patron saint of Ireland. These first missionaries fought against the druidic order to establish a religious system that was uniquely suited to the Celtic people it served. Cut off from the developments of the rest of Christian Europe, the Celtic Church developed its own idiosyncratic style based on monasteries rather than around episcopal churches.

These monastic centers provided a cultural refuge from the upheavals that bedevilled the rest of the continent, and Celtic craftsmen and scribes created devotional works in metal and parchment which rank among the most spectacular pieces of art of the early medieval world. Of all these, the illuminated manuscripts such as the *Book of Kells* have come to epitomize the cultural achievements of Celtic civilization.

The missionaries who converted the Irish were revered as saints, and their sense of purpose brought them to the Scots colony of Dál Riada, and then to the Pictish heartland of what is now Scotland. By 600 only the Anglo-Saxons of England remained pagan, surrounded by a Celtic fringe unified by religion. At a time when the English were regarded by most as barbarians, the Scots and Irish were producing some of the finest examples of artistic endeavor in the world. However, the Celtic church lacked the size and unity of its Roman rival, and when Roman Catholic missionaries converted the Anglo-Saxons, the assimilation of the Celtic church became inevitable.

Left, above: This "pound headed" Celtic cross near Perranporth, Cornwall, England, which dates from about AD 900, has a distinct shape that is very different from the contemporary high crosses of northern England and Ireland.

KINGDOM OF THE PICTS

Iona (563)

Lindisfarne (635)

Armagh
Bangor (559)
Kells

IRELAND

Whitby (Synod of 664)

NORTH SEA

Cork

SLAVIC TRIBES

WALES

ENGLAND

Caldy Island

Wilfrid (678)
Willibrord (690)

Dunwich

Bremen (788)

SAXONY

Willihed

Utrecht (696)

London

Boniface (716)
Canterbury (597)

Hampton

Columba (590)

Birinus

Augustine

Felix

Dunwich (669)

FRANKISH KINGDOM

Kaiserswerth

Boniface (723)

Fulda (744)

SLAVIC TRIBES

Echternach (698)

Mainz

Willibald

Boniface (739)

Wurzburg (742)

Killian

St. Augustine (600)

Columba (590)

Regensburg (739)
Passau (739)

Eichstatt (741)

Salzburg (739)

BRITTANY

Luxeuil (590)

Columba

Emmeram

St. Gallen (610)

Columba

FRANKISH KINGDOM

Canterbury
Dover

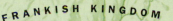

The Early Celtic Church

When Christianity became the official faith of Rome, the religion gradually spread to Gaul and Britain, although gaining widespread acceptance only after the collapse of Roman rule. Despite its religious links to the Christian world, the Celtic Church—cut off by the barbarian invasions of the fifth century—developed along its own lines, to create a version of Christianity that was unique.

Following the conversion of Constantine in 312–13 AD, the emperor adopted Christianity as the official Roman faith. With the threat of persecution finally removed, Christianity, already widespread in different regions of the empire, came into the open and began to exercise considerable power over both the government and the people of the provinces.

In the mid-fourth century a Roman Church structure was in place in Gaul and Britain, complete with bishops and an episcopal hierarchy. By the time the Romans left Britain in 410, Christianity was well-established, although the older Celtic and Roman beliefs continued to be practiced by the majority of the populace, and most especially among the military.

By the first decades of the fifth century the Irish had also come into contact with Christianity, although there is little information on this other than the writings of St. Patrick. Christian tombstones have been found throughout most of Celtic Britain which date from the fifth century and, following the conversion work begun by St. Patrick from 432, similar graves appear in Ireland. The arrival of the heathen Anglo-Saxons in Britain had little effect on the north and west of the island, where the Celtic church continued to operate.

In the English kingdoms, the local populace reverted to the worship of Germanic gods. In 431 Palladius, deacon of Auxerre became the first official bishop in Ireland, preceding the arrival of St. Patrick by a year. From that point on Ireland became the powerhouse of the Celtic Church, supplying priests and missionaries throughout the rest of Celtic Britain.

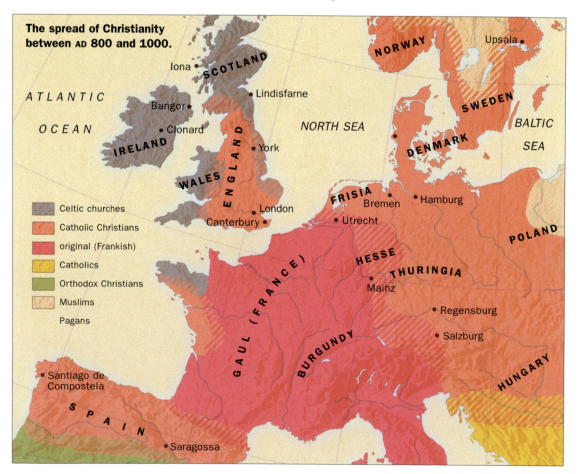

The spread of Christianity between AD 800 and 1000.

Celtic churches
Catholic Christians
original (Frankish)
Catholics
Orthodox Christians
Muslims
Pagans

End of the druids

Given the stratified nature of Celtic society, the aristocracy and peasantry appeared to have little difficulty accepting an ecclesiastical hierarchy, especially since it was structurally similar to the druidic order it was replacing. According to St. Patrick and other clerics, the new clerical order was absorbed into British society, and bishops were accorded the same positions that druid advisors had enjoyed in the courts of the Celtic kings.

However, this smooth transition may be misleading, because it is also argued that the first missionaries, in attempting to impose structures they knew from Gaul or Roman Britain, encountered problems in adapting to the specific requirements of the non-Romanized Celts. In the Romanized world, territorial diocese mirrored Roman administrative structures (naturally, since this is where they had grown from). So a territorial diocese in Gaul or Britain had a hierearcical (govermental) structure of bishop, senior clerics, and priests. And the diocese reported upward, finally to the Church in Rome.

The chronicle of a smooth transition to Christianity in Celtic Britain and in Ireland comes from the accounts of Roman Christian writers, who would want to suggest that the conversion was an easy process. But even as late as the mid-sixth century, it appears that there was no large-scale ecclesiastical structure covering all the Celtic territories. Instead, the Church was linked to individual ruling houses, with each religious center enjoying the patronage of a chief or king. In this way, the structure was more akin to the older druidic order than to the Christian Church elsewhere in Europe.

During the sixth century a new form of religious center arose: the monastic church. These were free from the territorial tethers of the ecclesiastical church, but still relied on the patronage of the Celtic rulers in whose lands the monastery was founded. Many also developed secondary sites and lands that remained linked to the main site for administrative purposes. This created a new layer of Church structure, with its own agenda.

Below: Although built in 1142 in the Norman era, the tiny church at Kilpeck, Herefordshire, England, displays extensive carvings inside and above the south door which are purely Celtic in design. Outside, along the top of the wall and around the apse, **top**, carvings of most un-Christian looking Celtic demons perch beside human and animal representations.

Monasticism

The monastic movement gained strength in the Celtic world during the sixth century. Initiated by Celtic missionaries (many of whom were made saints), the movement began in Ireland, then spread to Britain. By the end of the century monasteries dominated the Celtic church, and this helped drive another wedge between it and the developing Church in Rome.

The monastery of Iona was founded by St. Columba about AD 563, and subsequently became a thriving base for Celtic missionary expeditions into Scotland, Pictland, and Northern Anglo-Saxon England.

From the sixth century onward, the ecclesiastical administration in the Celtic world seemed to break down, and leadership of the Church was taken over by the monastic movement. The concept of monasticism was an Egyptian one, although it also had conceptual links to the older druidic *bangor* (colleges of learning). As there were relatively few towns in Celtic Britain and Ireland, ecclesiastical churches had to tie themselves closely to the seats of royal power. Monasteries, on the other hand, were founded wherever there seemed a need, although they almost exclusively enjoyed the approval and patronage of the local secular authority.

Free from administrative duties, the monks and abbots in these centers could concentrate on intellectual, artistic, and spiritual development, and on ensuring the economic independence of their own monastic site. The abbot of a monastery had far more real power than a Celtic bishop, who was little more than a spiritual adviser to a Celtic king.

Monasticism thrived in Ireland, and during the sixth century the island became a center for the dissemination and protection of the Celtic civilization. This was achieved through the recording of Celtic literature and myth, the encouragement of artistic enterprise, and the role these centers took in the spiritual well-being of the Celtic people. Monasticism was also completely alien to the episcopal Christianity that flourished in Gaul, and this inevitably led to conflict between the Celtic Church and the Church in Europe, which followed the Roman practice.

Monastic centers became linked to the production of masterpieces of Celtic art, from

religious metalwork to stone-carved high-crosses, to the masterpieces of Celtic illuminated manuscript. As centers of cultural and spiritual excellence, they have come to represent the zenith of late Celtic civilization. This success and prosperity also made them a prime target for the Norse raiders who descended on Ireland and Britain during the early eighth century.

Saintly orders

One of the leading monasteries in Ireland was at Kildare, founded by St. Brigid, while other Celtic saints were linked to the foundation of other orders; St. Brendad at Clonfert, St. Comgall at Bangor (County Down), St. Carthach at Lismore, and St. Ciáran at Clonmacnoise. St. Columba founded no less than three monasteries, at Derry, Durrow, and the great monastic center on Iona in Dál Riada.

By the mid-sixth century, many monasteries provided havens for Celtic bishops, who became increasingly eager to associate themselves with the new religious movement. When a bishop took up residence in a monastery, his duties were distinct from those of the abbot. In this way, the monastic movement came to dominate Celtic Christianity, until by the end of the century the Celtic Church was wholly monastic.

There was no overall structure. A number of independent monasteries were founded from a mother-house, and monasteries often had satellite bodies that owed allegiance. Sometimes, these were small monasteries in their own right, but often they were just a collection of small cells of solitary monks, who preferred isolation to life in a larger foundation. The monks maintained a grueling discipline, with a restricted vegetarian diet, cold-water bathing, and even self-inflicted castigation, although the nature of monastic life differed from place to place. This lack of uniformity also manifested itself in the nature of mass and the manner in which liturgical services were carried out.

This lack of unity and the absence of a central common practice created a uniquely apolitical dogma, but would also help to bring about the ultimate subjugation of the Celtic Church to the centralized, political structure of the medieval Church of Rome.

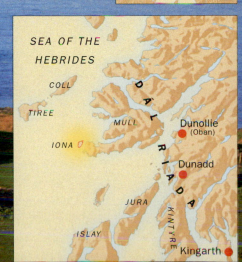

Conversion

The initial conversion of the Irish Celts to Christianity required the dominance of missionaries over druids. The victors may write history, and this struggle is recorded only in Christian annals, which provide a fascinating, if one-sided, insight into a tumultuous event in Celtic civilization. The importance of missionary work and conversion to the Celtic Church is demonstrated by the sanctification of many of these early Celtic missionaries.

T he Christian missionary Patrick converted the Irish to Christianity in the years following his arrival in Ireland in 432. The druids, closely linked to the royal houses as advisers, seers, and spiritual leaders, quickly recognized the threat Patrick posed to their power base and became his implacable oponents.

The life of St. Patrick was chronicled by two clerics, including Muirchú Mocciu Machtheni. He was born c.390 in northern Britannia, but was captured as a boy by Irish raiders. Somehow he reappeared in Roman Britain as a free man in his mid-20s, then he traveled to Gaul to study under the deacon of Auxerre.

In 432 St. Germanius of Auxerre (*see page 123*) consecrated Patrick as a bishop and dispatched him to Ireland to convert the pagans. He commenced work in Leinster, using the island now called Inis Padraig as his base. He then moved north to Ulster. Muirchú records how Patrick appeared at the court of King Loeghaire of Ulster, and was forced to counter the opposition of the king's two druids, Matha and Lochru. His annalists claim he countered them using prayer. When the druid Lucat Mael tried to poison him, Patrick removed the poison from his cup. The druid then challenged Patrick to a contest where, we are told, the druid burned to death in an ordeal from which the saint-to-be emerged unscathed.

Clearly, these Christian chroniclers based their tales on mythical-biblical events, but the antipathy between the druids and the emergent missionaries is aptly demonstrated. During his conversion work, Patrick was constantly encountering the hostility of the old religious order.

In the seventh-century *Life of St. Berach* the eponymous missionary engaged in a lengthy struggle against the druidic order. The conflict culminated when the king's military retinue, who had answered the druids' appeal for help, were rendered incapable of fighting by the power of the missionary's prayers. This miracle prompted the king to convert to Christianity, but according to the Christian annalist, the druids remained full of malice.

Founding of Iona

By contrast, St. Brigid represents a union of both religions. In the seventh-century *Vita Brigitae* the historian Cogitosus records how Brigid had a druid as a foster father and he supported her despite her Christian missionary work. He was eventually humbled by her spiritual abilities, and duly converted to the new religion.

After St. Patrick, the best-known Celtic saint is St. Columba (*Colmcille*), who founded the great monastic settlement on Iona, and brought Christianity to the Scots and Picts. He was born to a noble family in 521 in County Donegal. In his teens he entered the monastery of Finnian in County Down. In what was probably the world's first copyright battle, his disagreement with the abbot led to a ruling against Columba by High King Diarmuid. Columba led a revolt among his own O'Donnell clan, but was defeated.

Exiled, Columba sailed for Dál Riada with a band of followers in 563. He established a monastic center at Iona, courted the local Dál Riada leaders, and converted them to Christianity. His greatest accomplishment was his conversion of King Brude Mac Maelchon of the Picts, ensuring that both Celtic peoples of northern Britain embraced Christianity.

By 600, these missionary saints had converted the entire Celtic world, and although their exploits have become intertwined with myths, their remarkable achievements are self-evident. However, by the time they were ready to expand their evangelical work into heathen Anglo-Saxon England, the Roman Church was already at work there.

Facing: St. John's Crucifixion Plaque from Athlone is one of the earliest known works of Irish art with a Christian theme. Christ is portrayed nailed to the cross, attended by two angels above and two Roman soldiers, one carrying a sponge, the other a spear.

Illuminated Manuscripts

The first instances of illuminated manuscripts are during the late sixth century and reflect the establishment of monastic workshops of illumination and metalwork in Ireland, Dál Riada, and possibly also in Celtic Britain. While regarded as masterpieces, they also possess a hidden message—the Celtic church was not as isolated as its adversaries in the Church of Rome believed.

One of the earliest known examples is the *Cathach of St. Columba*, a work that was allegedly written in the saint's own hand. Most scholars now agree that it was actually produced in the early seventh century, after the death of St. Columba on Iona in 597. This psalter lacks the color and ornamentation of later works, but contains the decorative features that were to make manuscript illumination one of the lasting glories of the Celtic world.

The concept of illuminated initials originated

Below: St. Mark, symbolized by his lion, pictured writing his gospel. A page from the *Lindisfarne Gospels.*

in the eastern Mediterranean, but these late Roman works lacked the characteristic *diminuendo* (diminution) of Celtic illumination. This referred to the way the large flourish of the opening letter was reduced over the next few letters until the letter size conformed to those in the rest of the manuscript. Celtic monks produced works in monasteries on the mainland of Europe following the principles demonstrated in the *Cathach of St. Columba*, and the basic style of these illuminations was formed.

The spirals, scrolls, trumpet shapes, and *peltas* (shaped like the "spade" symbol in a card pack) of Celtic metalwork were adapted and introduced onto the page of these manuscripts. Art historians have noted the influence of non-Celtic traditions. In particular Anglo-Saxon traditions helped to shape the development of traditionally insular Irish pieces of decoration. Some manuscripts were even produced using Celtic scribes, but were designed for Anglo-Saxon religious patrons. Prime examples are the *Lindisfarne Gospels* or the *Gospel Book of Durham*. Others, such as the *Book of Kells*, demonstrate influences from Byzantium (the Eastern Roman Empire).

One of the most impressive assimilations of insular and exterior influences in Irish illumination is the *Book of Durrow*, a gospel dating from the mid-seventh century. The work is a virtual compendium of European decorative art, and while its text is drawn from the Roman world, its decorative elements are Celtic or Germanic, although Byzantine features have also been detected. Some of the symbols used to represent Evangelists have direct links with the mysterious Pictish symbols in eastern Scotland, while other decorative features have been traced to eastern Europe. Ornamental animal friezes are probably Anglo-Saxon, while other aspects are decidedly Celtic Irish.

Viking raiders

Few illuminated manuscripts of the late eighth century survive due to the destruction caused by the Norsemen. The most characteristic examples of this period are the pocket gospels, which were small enough to be carried to safety. Examples

include the *Book of Dimma*, the *Book of Mulling*, and the ninth-century *Book of MacRegol*. These pocket gospels tended to be less detailed works than the larger pieces, but are characterized by the use of simple ornamentation and vibrant colors. In the *Book of Dimma* St. John the Evangelist is associated with an eagle symbol, painted in a mosaic style, but it boasts a very Celtic decorative border.

Their cosmopolitan nature is a striking feature of these manuscripts and reflects the surprising level of contact the late Celtic Church had with the rest of Europe. While the illuminated manuscripts produced during the renaissance of late Celtic art are rightly held to represent some of the finest examples of early medieval art in the world, they also demonstrate the diversity of the Celtic Church. Far from being isolated from the rest of Europe, it was able to draw on these neighboring cultures to provide it with the spiritual and artistic inspiration it needed.

Above: The Tapestry page of St Luke's Gospel from the *Lindisfarne Gospels*.

The Book of Kells

Probably the most famous Celtic illuminated manuscript is the Book of Kells, produced c.800. Incredibly colorful and vivid, it was described by art historian Sir Arthur Sullivan as having "a weird and commanding beauty." It has captivated generations with its intricate loveliness, and serves as a window into the late Celtic world.

Facing: The Gospel of St. John's title page depicts the seated saint surrounded by intricate interwoven designs.

Below: The beautiful initial letter of the "Monogram" folio combines abstract designs with stylized human faces.

The complexity and remoteness of Celtic symbolism often makes it impossible to interpret, but when combined with discernible Christian symbolism some insights are possible. The glory of the *Book of Kells* is that it combines both pre- and post-Christian influences. Created in the late eighth–early ninth centuries, the manuscript represents the culmination of the Celtic art renaissance. On display at Trinity College Library, Dublin, it is regarded as one of the highest achievements of Celtic illumination.

Until recently the manuscript's intricate ornamentation was regarded as decorative, but detailed studies have shown that the symbolism is actually very subtle and complex. Scholars and art historians—who are still arguing over the interpretation of this late Celtic masterpiece—now consider that, although meanings have been lost over time, many are also identifiable through the study of Celtic religion and literature. This symbolism is often multi-layered, with one image evoking more than one meaning.

Some symbolism is reasonably easy to determine. In the *Christi Autem* page (folio 43),

the illumination includes air symbols (angels and butterflies), earth symbols (two cats watching two mice, or a rat eating a crust), and water symbols (an otter catching a fish). The form of the first great initial letter on the page may represent four streams of radiant energy, emanating from Christ's Godliness. Other scholars argue that it can be interpreted in the context of the Celtic religious text, which refers to "the four rivers of the virtues flowing out of one bright and health-giving paradise, irrigating the whole breadth of the Christian Church."

Uncertain origins

Most scholars agree that the manuscript was produced in Ireland, but recently one scholar came to the conclusion that it was produced in Pictland during the end of the eighth century. Arguably, there are Pictish features in the book, and Pictish influence was felt in Scots Dál Riada, and in the great monastic site at Iona. The artist may have been exposed to these Pictish influences while serving in the monastery there. It has often been suggested that it was produced in Iona, and then subsequently taken to Ireland. Wherever it was produced, it was most definitely the work of a Celtic artist of the highest caliber.

The *Book of Kells* represents a development over the earlier *Book of Durrow* in that it uses full-page illuminations, including pages depicting the Evangelists (in a symbolic form), the Temptation of Christ (known as the Temple page), the Betrayal of Christ, and the Virgin and Child. It also shows the Christ Child appearing like a miniature adult. The Virgin and Child (folio 7) is probably based on a Byzantine representation, since its features indicate an eastern Mediterranean influence.

One of the most charming features of the illumination is its light-hearted detail, such as the inclusion of animals playing, or small bearded warriors on the march. While scholars disagree on the meanings of many of its features, everyone can agree about its incredible vibrancy and beauty. The *Book of Kells* is truly one of the wonders of the early medieval age, and a splendid testament to the abilities of the Celtic monk-artists who produced it.

Iona versus Rome

By the sixth century, the Celtic Church in Britain and Ireland was thriving, but isolated from the influence of the Roman Church. Its policies and practices consequently differed from the rest of Christian Europe. Just at the time the Celtic saints completed their conversion of the Celts, the Roman Church became established in Anglo-Saxon England. Inevitably a theological struggle for dominance would ensue.

The Venerable Bede, who died in 735, left behind a unique narrative of the event that led to the assimilation of the Celtic Church by Rome. The Celtic Church's policies have been described as having a more conservative aspect than the Roman Church, and its emphasis on monasticism ran contrary to the episcopal structure that thrived in Frankish Gaul, Rome, and the Christian Mediterranean.

When Augustine arrived in England at the very end of the sixth century to convert the Anglo-Saxons, the saint-to-be discovered that the Celts of Britain were already converts. Only the heathen English retained the religions of their Germanic forebears. Augustine's mission,

Right: The holy island of Lindisfarne once contained a thriving Celtic monastic community. The buildings shown here are later medieval structures.

therefore, took on some aspects of a race against his Celtic counterparts. Whichever Christian system was successful in converting the English would gain a natural advantage through the military power of the Anglo-Saxon state. By ensuring that the English became Roman Catholics, Augustine could ensure the dominance of his doctrine over that of his Celtic rivals.

Battle for Saxon minds

The Celtic Church had already made inroads in the lands surrounding the Celtic kingdoms in Wales and in Northumbria, where monks from Iona had converted the king and his nobles. While expanding its influence, the Celtic church was also moribund, and lacked the dynamism associated with St. Augustine and his modern Roman notions of devotion. The lack of doctrinal unity within the Celtic church also made it harder to present a unified structure for the Anglo-Saxon converts to follow.

Augustine made early inroads in Kent and Essex, established a new church in London, and a religious headquarters at Canterbury. Following the death of Æthelbert of Essex in 616, both Anglo-Saxon kingdoms reverted to their old beliefs, but a marriage between the houses of Northumbria and Kent led to the arrival of Roman missionaries in York around 625.

Evidently Canterbury was active as an ecclesiastical center, despite the official policy of the Kentish court. Paulinus, Archbishop of Canterbury, converted King Edwin of

Northumbria to the Roman Church in 627, effectively preventing any further inroads into England by the Celtic Church. The pope duly made York a second archbishopric. Within two years, the death of Edwin prompted an anti-Christian rebellion. The Celtic Church was offered a second chance to fill the Christian vacuum left when Archbishop Paulinus fled to Canterbury.

In 635 Oswald seized the Northumbrian throne, and he allowed missionaries from Iona to establish a new Celtic monastery at Lindisfarne. Northumbria became Christian again, but now owing allegiance to Iona rather than to Rome. With the Celtic Church established in the north of England, and with Irish monastic settlements at Glastonbury and Malmesbury in the west, it looked as though the Roman clerics may have lost the race.

Bede explains how everything changed, starting from 663. A conflict within the Northumbrian court over the right date to celebrate Easter led to the call for a religious debate. It was convened at the Synod of Whitby (664). In drawn-out arguments the Roman Church's calendar was adopted for the dating of the Easter festival. At the time, this acceptance of a Roman preference over a Celtic one may have seemed an insignificant point. What it did, though, was mark the point at which the Church of Rome seized the moral advantage. Still lacking unity, the Celts were unable to withstand the encroachment of Roman ideas on Celtic religious practices. Over the next century the idiosyncratic Celtic church would bow to the inevitable, and region by region it would become assimilated within the Church of Rome.

Above: Canterbury Cathedral towers above the city's roofs. Founded as headquarters of the Roman Church by St. Augustine c.597, most of the building work was carried out between the 11th and 12th centuries.

Left: The ruins of Whitby Abbey, a medieval building constructed on the site of the earlier structure where the religious debate between the Celtic and Roman Churches was settled.

Chapter 12

Celtic Mythology

The Irish chroniclers of the early medieval period provide us with lists of kings, dates, and battles. What these lack is any account of how the people lived, what they believed in, and how society operated. That information comes from the great medieval works of Irish literature, written from the eleventh century onward and closely based on earlier oral histories that were passed down from one generation to the next by the late Celtic bards.

Although most of these chronicles deal with Ireland after the arrival of Christianity, some describe an earlier time, as orally recorded, when Celts were still a vibrant force outside the fledgling Roman Empire. As such these works provide us with a unique opportunity to examine the Celtic world as it existed in Gaul and Britain before the coming of the Romans.

Other works describe the pantheon of Celtic gods, although these accounts are influenced by the prejudices of the Christian scribes who recorded them. These literary works portray a world where mythical and historical figures were constantly influenced by the Celtic gods and by supernatural forces. These works also reflect the richness of Celtic life, and the unique perspective that helped create the artistic marvels of the Celtic Renaissance.

Apart from anything else, early Irish literature contains enchanting tales, and poetry that still delights the reader. These are the accumulation of centuries of stories told around the Irish royal hearths during wintertime. Their eloquence is as powerful today as when they were first told.

Celtic Ireland from 500–800, showing the major monastic centers, royal residences, and the other main sites.

monastery · royal site · other site

Fahan Mura

Lough Foyle

Derry

Aileach

Dooey

DÁL RIADA

Finn

Bann

Main

Derry

Mourne

ULADH (ULSTER)

Lough Ravel

Lisnacroghera

Lough Neagh

Bangor

Moville

Inishmurray

Lough Earn

Devenish

Lagan

DÁL RIADA

Nendrum

Lough Earn

Blackwater

Emain

Armagh

Bann

Lough Allan

(CONNAUGHT)

Lough Gara

Cruachan

Ardakillan

Roscommon

Kells

IRISH SEA

MIDHE (MEATH)

Boyne

Tara

Suck

Lough Ree

Uisneach

Lagore

Shannon

Ballinderry

Clonard

Finglas

Clonmacnoise

Durrow

Liffey

Clonfert

Rahan

Tallaght

Lorrha

Kildare

erryglass

Dunailinn

Glenalough

LAIGHIN (LEINSTER)

Clonenagh

Barrow

Nore

Slaney

Cashel

Suir

Lismore

Gods and Origins

The Celts of the La Tène period left no written record of their beliefs and history. We must look at later Irish literature of the Christian period to understand them. Some of these later sources put names to many of the old gods, and through it, elements of Celtic culture that would otherwise remain obscure are discovered.

I t is necessary to understand that a certain amount of rewriting took place to make the older myths support the framework of new Christian belief, and since much of Irish and Welsh literature available to us comes from the Celtic Church, the re-invention may at times be quite extensive. This was probably confined to references to older Celtic gods; their spiritual power was stripped away to portray them as beings who were not worshiped or sacrificed to, but who dwelt in the world of the supernatural.

Many of these gods can also be traced through archaeological remains and through Roman descriptions. For example, Dagda, father of the gods, is mentioned in Irish myth as well as in pre-Roman sources. Lugh, the sun god was also worshiped throughout Europe, and he was linked to prowess in battle, through the use of magical weapons. Numerous others indicate a common thread between Irish mythology and the gods of the La Tène civilization.

These early myths describe how the Celts arrived in Ireland, depicted as a series of invasions. In Ireland, the *Lebor Gabála* (Book of Invasions) describes these in detail. First the people of Partholón came from Spain, but all these immigrants perished. Next came the invasion led by Nemed mac Agnomain, who was so harassed by later invaders that he led his people back to Spain. He later returned and his people settled. These later invaders were the Fomori, who were succeeded by the Fir Bolg, from Greece.

Myth and fact entwined

Successive invaders have been identified with Celtic migrations by the Belgae, the Gauls, and the Dumnonii peoples. These early settlers were followed by the semi-legendary Tuatha Dé Danann, the tribes of the goddess Danu. The Tuatha conquered the Fir Bolg, then the Fomori with the help of the god Lugh, and established themselves as the dominant people of Ireland. Later Christian writers have added the Milesians as a sort of intrusion, to give the Irish Celts some classical respectability. In a climactic battle between the Tuatha and their enemies, the chroniclers introduce the whole pantheon of Celtic gods, by describing what they could do to influence the course of the battle.

Some of the gods listed in these early Celtic myths are exclusive to Ireland and Wales. For instance, Oengus Og (Angus Og) was meant to be a child of the goddess Dana, and is associated with eternal youth. Unlike the principal gods of the Celtic world, these more regional gods were linked to specific geographical locations. Manannán mac Lir came to Ireland over the sea, and has been linked to the Isle of Man. He has also been linked to the Welsh Manawydan fab Llyr mentioned in the epic mythological tale the *Mabinogion*, and may therefore represent the Irish Sea itself.

It is harder to separate Welsh mythology from Christian invention, since most works of Welsh literature were recorded much later than their Irish counterparts. They represent in part the views of the early medieval Celtic church, so the influence of the Celtic gods has been replaced by a greater emphasis on the use of magic, and there is a more clearly defined line between the human and the supernatural

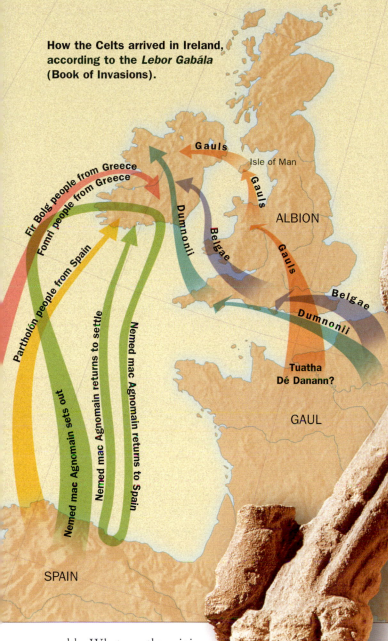

How the Celts arrived in Ireland, according to the *Lebor Gabála* (Book of Invasions).

Fír Bolg people from Greece

Fomri people from Greece

Partholón people from Spain

Nemed mac Agnomain sets out

Nemed mac Agnomain returns to settle

Nemed mac Agnomain returns to Spain

Gauls

Gauls

Isle of Man

ALBION

Dumnonli

Belgae

Gauls

Belgae

Dumnonli

Tuatha Dé Danann?

GAUL

SPAIN

worlds. Whatever the origin, these Celtic myths provide us with an insight into the belief system of the early Celts, and even though they might be tinged by later Christian influences, they are still the best source of information on Celtic belief.

Facing: God with torc and wild boar, Gallo-Roman, 1st century AD, from Euffigneix, France.

Right: A Gallo-Celtic statue of a demon eating humans, from the 1st century BC.

Life and Afterlife

Early Celtic society was agrarian, ruled by a warrior aristocracy. The most important part of their world was the cycle of life, marked by the passage of seasons and crop cycles. For the warriors, a belief in the afterlife gave them the courage to face the enemy without fear of death because their place in an idyllic afterlife was assured. Myths of Irish and Welsh chroniclers shed light on these vital aspects of Celtic belief and culture.

amalgamated with it. For some reason Samhain (now Halloween) retains its older, mythical link with the afterlife to the modern day.

This supernatural link is further reflected in the way the Celtic gods communicated with mankind. Earlier, we noted that the supposed ease with which people could talk with the supernatural world in the earlier Irish myths was replaced by a stronger delineation between the human and spiritual worlds in later Welsh writings. This has been seen as a reflection of increasing Christian censorship. When gods wanted to appear before humans, they were often surrounded by a mist, or appeared from over the sea or out of a lake, or alternatively the humans entered the supernatural world through a supernatural portal, such as a burial mound.

Celtic myth

In *Echtrae Conli*, Conn Cétchathach, the Irish high king, stands on the ramparts of Tara, surrounded by his Druids and sons. A thick mist descends, through which a horseman appears who invites the king and his retinue to follow him. They travel to a house on a plain. Inside is a girl, seated on a throne, who represents the sovereignty of Ireland. She is accompanied by the god Lugh, who is seated on another throne. The visitors are served food and drink, then the girl asks Conn the name of everyone in his party. The two deities then proceed to give Conn a list outlining the duration of his reign, and those of his successors. The gods and the house then disappear.

The mist in this story was the literary portal between one world and the next, and this device is used throughout Celtic Irish literature, such as in the account of Conn's grandson Cormac

Above: A stone Druid Circle in Kenmare, Ireland.

As we have seen, the Celtic calendar was divided into four seasons (*see pages 52–53*), and the start of each was marked by a celebration. Lugnasadh was originally the festival of the god Lugh, and traditionally associated with harvests, stock-rearing, and fire. The early Christians absorbed many aspects of pagan traditions and observances in order to offer common people continuity with the annual cycles of religious ritual, and although the origins of this festival have been obscured by Christian chroniclers, enough survives to enable us to identify the true meaning of Lugnasadh. Similarly Imbolc was altered to coincide with Easter, and Beltaine as a spring-time festival was

and his encounter with the god Manannán. The god appears through a mist "from a land where there is only truth, and there is no old age, nor decay, nor sadness, nor envy, nor jealousy, nor hatred, nor arrogance." This is the perfect description of the Celtic supernatural world, or afterlife.

For the Celts, the afterlife was invariably portrayed as a land of perpetual youth, where the flowers are always in bloom and everyone lives in peace and harmony. This "land of the ever-young" also reflects pagan Norse and Saxon versions of the afterlife, so it is a popular theme in pre-Christian belief. Faced with the prospect of an eternity in this spiritual paradise, the ever-present prospect of an early death would have seemed less of a threat to the Celtic warrior or farmer.

Above: The Celtic sanctuary at Roquepertuse dates from the 2nd century BC. Warrior skulls decorate the columns and lie piled on the ground before the shrine.

171

Early Irish Literature

Fragments of Celtic poetry exist, the literary forerunner to the great narrative works produced by the medieval Celtic church. These provide a fascinating insight into the Celtic mind, and their subtleties reflect the interwoven complexity of the late Celtic arts. Tales of the natural world, kings, gods, and mythical animals combine to produce a narrative of Celtic thought and contemporary society.

The early Celts left no written tradition behind them. The acquisition of the art of writing came late in Celtic development, largely because of druidic adherence to a strict code of secrecy to protect their own political power. This promoted and emphasized an oral transmission of history, myth, and belief. Fortunately, because this oral tradition continued for several centuries after the arrival of Christianity, some material was committed to the written word.

As a result, the Christian scribes of Ireland left behind them the oldest vernacular literature in northern Europe. Aspects of this literature, which describe Irish or Welsh society, have a direct association with the older Celtic cultures of Britain and Gaul. This Irish literary tradition is earlier, and less distorted than the Welsh works, such as the *Mabinogion*, which date from the medieval period.

The earliest Irish forms of literature are poetry, and surviving examples from the early seventh century are fragmentary at best. From the style of these works, it seems clear that they reflect the recording of poetic recitals, a first example of the passing from oral to written traditions. These early fragments are simple alliterative groupings, devoid of any rhyme or rhythm. By the seventh and eighth centuries, a more syllabic form appeared, at a time when the Celtic bards had developed their own meters.

Royal patronage

While the earliest Irish poems were concerned with mythology and the gods, later works reflected the natural world, and the Irish kings whose patronage the bards enjoyed. Works included the commemoration of a succession of the kings of Munster and Dál Riada, providing a vital source of information on early Irish kingship.

Nature and being wedded to nature was a common theme in early Irish poetry, as noted by the literary historian Kuno Meyer:

"In nature poetry the Gaelic muse must vie with that of any other nation… to seek out and watch and love nature in its tiniest and in its grandest was given to no people so early and so fully as to the Celt… it is a characteristic of these poems

that in none of them do we get an elaborate or sustained description of any scene or scenery, but rather a succession of pictures and images, which the poet, like an impressionist, calls up before us by light and skilful touches."

Irish poetry covered every topic imaginable, including the experiences of the common people who inhabited the late Celtic world. While these poems remain an important source for the feelings of the Celts, and provide us with a series of insights into the world that surrounded them, they do little to help us fill in the gaps in Celtic history created by the lack of a written tradition. For this, we have to look to Irish and Welsh prose, a source of narrative descriptions that are unique in the history of the early medieval world.

This literature usually comprised of vellum manuscripts, produced from the end of the eleventh century onward. Consequently it is not the product of true Celtic times but of medieval Celtic Ireland. Nevertheless, even the most cursory study of these documents reveals that they contain a wealth of information about the late Celtic world that is most probably applicable to that earlier pre-literate Celtic era.

Facing: Carolingian ivory panel with the Miracle of Cana (c.AD 860). The lively style and setting of this panel, which once decorated the cover of a gospel, derives from narrative illuminated Celtic manuscript style that Celtic Ireland and Britain exported to continental Europe in the early medieval era.

This page: "...to seek out and watch and love nature in its tiniest and in its grandest was given to no people so early and so fully as to the Celt..."

Early Irish Narratives

Celtic prose developed after the end of the eleventh century, but it revealed the world of the earlier Celtic people like no other source. It spoke of a world of mythology, heroes, and warriors, yet many of these accounts were linked to the early historic past.

Facing below:
In the Battle of Dun Cooley "The Hound of Ulster," Cú Chulainn, slaughtered the champions of Connaught. The Queen of Connaught sent all 29 of her sons to slay the hero. Subsumed in a rage of blood-lust, Cú Chulainn fought them from dawn to dusk, finally taking their heads. The legendary Irish hero later lashed himself to a stone pillar, **right**, after receiving the death blow, so that he would not fall as he fought to the end. Statue from the Post Office, O'Connell Street, Dublin.

Facing top: Giants' Causeway, Antrim, Northern Ireland (Ulster). Legend says that the giant Finn MacCool built a road from Antrim to Staffa in the Hebrides to reach his arch-enemy Finn Gall, another giant, but Gall tore it up into 40,000 blocks.

The first narratives produced in the Celtic world were created by Christian scribes, whose work understated the importance of the pantheon of pre-Christian gods on Celtic civilization. Set in Ireland, these tales intertwined mythology with historic fact to produce a semi-mythical past, an age before the order imposed by the Christian missionaries.

These narratives were based almost exclusively on older oral histories that had been passed down through the centuries in the immemorial style of the Celtic bards and chroniclers. Devoid of their original religious impact, they appear to be a collection of far-fetched tales, of a time when gods and monsters roamed the land. Instead, they should be read as a series of religious allegories and a set of beliefs that were misunderstood by the Celtic scribes who finally recorded them on parchment.

In the earliest works, Ireland was invaded by a race of giants, by the Tuatha Dé Danann (the forerunners of the early Celts), and a host of gods. Together, these three groups conspired and struggled until the arrival of the true Gaels (Celts). Narratives such as the *Book of Invasions*, the *Second Battle of Moytura* and *Dinnesenchas* record this mythical distant past. By the ninth century, works such as the *Dream of Oengus*, the *Táin Bó Cuailnge*, and others were being passed down as oral histories. These placed the early history of Ireland in a semi-historical context, with identifiable kingdoms, social structures, and beliefs.

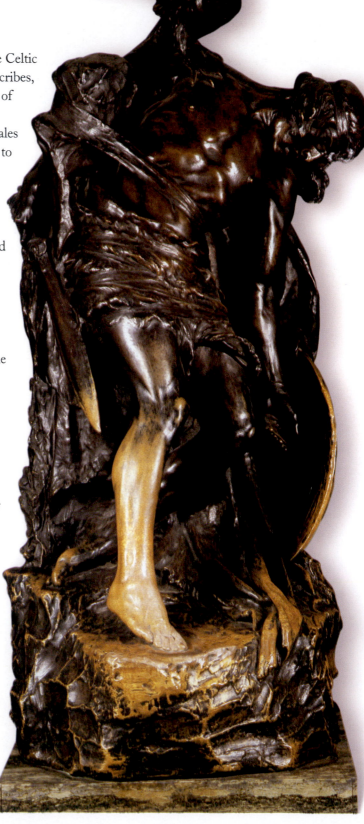

Although the Celtic deities still played a major part in the stories, they no longer retained the center stage. These works were starting to become historical narratives.

The *Táin Bó Cuailnge* (The Cattle Raid of Cooley) refers to early Irish history, and names five geographical divisions (fifths), of which four were political entities. These consisted of Ulster in the north, Connaught in the west, Munster in the south, and Leinster in the east. Recent scholarly research has placed the Ireland described in the book as existing during the fourth century AD, before the arrival of Christianity.

Fourth-century Ireland

Ireland at this time differed very little from Gaul or Britain during the late La Tène period, so the work provides an invaluable insight into the structure of general Celtic society before the coming of the Romans. It is a work that describes the kings, their warriors, the great battles they fought, and the alliances they made with each other. As such it is a political history, but one that emphasizes the importance of warfare to this warrior-society. Certainly superstition, the gods, and druids are involved in the narrative, but they are subsidiary to the humans. The Old Irish version of this classic work was written around 1100, and subsequent versions slightly modified the story. It therefore represents a narrative based on what was then a 600-year-old oral account.

Fled Bricrenn (Bricru's Feast) dates from about the eighth century, and tells of a feud between two Ulster clans. It involves Cú Chulainn, the great champion of Ulster, who also features prominently in the *Táin Bó Cuailnge* (*see pages 110–111*). The hero mixes with druids and giants, but his character also provides information on the structure of the early medieval Irish courts. Other works of the period refer back to the *Táin* and its characters, reinforcing the authenticity of its account.

These early semi-historical narratives were replaced by a series of "king accounts," which lack the social insight of earlier works. By the ninth century, written chronological accounts (backed by modern archaeological information) take over, and support the works of Irish literature in their portrayal of contemporary society. These, however, are medieval accounts, and as such are beyond the scope of this history.

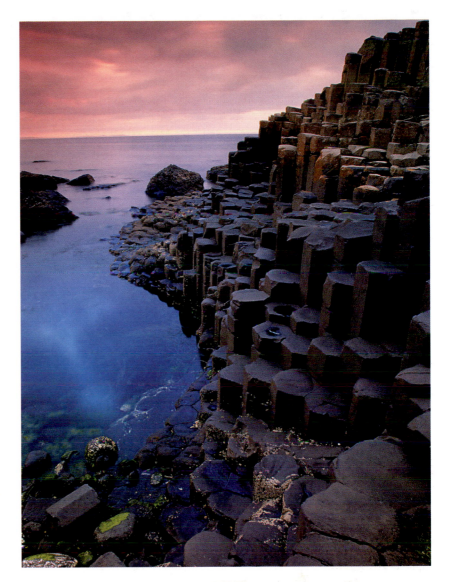

The Arthurian Legend

The romantic myth of the Arthurian legend entrances still, yet Arthur was a historic figure from sub-Roman Britain. Although many elements of the Arthurian legend—Camelot, the knights of the Round Table, the Holy Grail—are medieval creations, the military elements have some historic virtue. Ironically, the Celtic chieftain who fought the Anglo-Saxons was later personified as a chivalric English monarch.

The fragmentary evidence concerning Arthur has already been examined in Chapter nine. Most scholars now agree that he was a real person; a sub-Roman British warlord who battled the Saxons during the late fifth and early sixth centuries. The first reference to him is found in a poem entitled *Y Gododdin* written by Aneirin, late in the sixth century. While describing another Celtic warrior, it ran: "A wild boar's fury was Bleddig ab Eli… but he was not Arthur, and he fed black ravens on

Below: "Arthur's Tomb," a scene from Sir Thomas Mallory's *Le Morte d'Arthur,* painted by the Pre-Raphaelite artist Dante Gabriel Rossetti in 1855.

Catraeth's [Catterick] walls." In the *Annales Cambriae*, written about 955, the death of Arthur at the Battle of Camlann (c.539) is mentioned.

The real chroniclers of the warlord's exploits were the Celtic bards, whose unwritten tales were passed on for generations, and no doubt the tale grew with the telling. The first real written basis for the Arthurian legend came from Geoffrey of Monmouth (1100–55), whose *Historia Regnum Britanniae* (History of the Kings of Britain) portrayed Arthur as a mighty warrior king.

Geoffrey was a cleric who was born on the Welsh border. His Breton ancestors had accompanied William of Normandy during his invasion of England in 1066. He claimed his account of Arthur was simply the translation into Latin of an earlier British (presumably Welsh) book, but this original has never been found. One possible influence may have been

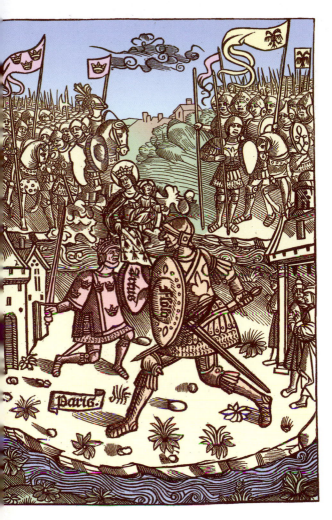

Places associated with the legend of Arthur in folklore and romance.

the precursor of the *Prophesy of Merlin*, a 15th-century Latin work translated from a tenth-century original written by John of Cornwall. Geoffrey even provided a family tree, making Arthur the son of Uther, a descendant of the Roman Emperor Constantine. Arthur's uncle was listed as Ambrosius, a prominent sub-Roman king. This established Arthur as a royal figure with a Romano-British lineage, not as a Celtic warlord. While this was a straightforward account of war, marriage, and alliances, The *Prophesy of Merlin* added the supernatural element that has come to form such an important part of the Arthurian story.

Adapting the tale

The Arthur legend came into its own when the Norman poet Wace wrote his *Roman de Brut* during the late 12th century. This romantic poem firmly establishes Arthur as a medieval king, and first mentions his entourage of knights and their round table. This was further adapted by the French writer Chrétien de Troyes, whose Arthurian romance written around 1180 converted the story to include the

courtly romance between Arthur and his queen, and added the story of the Holy Grail.

The romantic writer Layamon writing in the first decade of the 13th century added the Celtic element, which included the druid-cum-wizard Merlin, while later German writers such as Wolfram von Eschenbach emphasized the romantic and chivalrous elements of the story. The Arthurian legend appealed to medieval writers at a time when chivalric virtue was the leading subject for contemporary literature.

The *Alliterative Morte d'Arthur* (c.1360) and *Sir Gawain and the Green Knight* (c.1370) completed the transition from Celt to English warrior king, creating a world of chivalry that became inextricably linked to the Arthurian tale. The ultimate version of the tale was Sir William Mallory's *Le Morte d'Arthur* (c.1485) From that point on, the definitive version of the Arthurian legend was Mallory's. The Celtic warlord Arthur became the epitome of English chivalric virtue—a real irony considering that the real historical figure made his name fighting the Anglo-Saxons, the founders of England.

Above left: King Arthur under the protection of the Virgin Mary, fighting a giant. Woodcut from *Chroniques de Bretagne*, Paris, 1514.

OUTER HEBRIDES

INNER HEBRIDES

ULSTER

NORTH CHANNEL

S C O

REPUBLIC OF IRELAND

Belfast

Glasgow

Dublin

Edinburgh

ISLE OF MAN

IRISH SEA

WALES

Swansea

Falmouth

CORNWALL

Cardiff

E N G L A N D

E

BRITTANY

St. Malo

E N G L I S H   C H A N N E L

London

F
R
A
N
C
E

B
E
L
G
I
U
M

Paris

Chapter 13

ORKNEY ISLANDS

Kirkwall

SHETLAND ISLANDS

N D

Aberdeen

N O R T H   S E A

The modern Celtic Fringe:
the Shetland Isles; Orkney Isles;
Scottish islands, highlands,
and lowlands; Isle of Man;
Ulster and the Republic of
Ireland; Wales; the "English"
county of Cornwall; and the
Brittany peninsula of France.

N O R W A Y

The Celtic Legacy

Although the last true vestiges of Celtic culture died out in the medieval period, elements of Celtic ways survived into the early modern era. By this stage a revival of interest in antiquarianism and in the ancient cultural roots of Europe led to a reappraisal of the Celts. Although the antiquarian interest was encouraged across the continent by a string of startling archaeological discoveries, other disciplines encouraged the revival of interest in Celtic culture.

The notion of the "noble savage" encouraged a study of Europe's own pagan past, and a renewal of interest in its pre-Christian religious practices. As antiquarians marveled at the remains of a supposedly druidic society, theologians examined the nature of Celtic religion. Ironically, stone circles such as Stonehenge, which helped spark this curiosity, predated the Celts by at least 2,000 years.

Tied to this antiquarian, theological, and historical interest was a popular interest in the artifacts, artwork, and mythology of a Celtic past, brought to light by academic research. As the awareness in Celtic heritage grew, it became entwined in a growing political consciousness among the regions comprising the Celtic fringe. Although never a political movement, Celtic consciousness formed a part in the rise of national self-determination in Ireland, Scotland, and Wales. Despite this, the Celtic legacy is not about politics or regional identity. Instead, it reflects a pride shared by many northern Europeans in the achievements of their forebears. No longer considered a race of barbarians, the Celts have taken their due place among the great civilizations of the world.

D E N M A R K

Amsterdam

N E T H E R L A N D S

Post-Celtic Art

Although the "golden age" of Celtic art had ended by the 12th century, Celtic influences continued to make themselves felt in Scotland and Ireland. These post-Celtic pieces combined a simplistic Celtic artistry with influences drawn from the rest of medieval Europe. At a time when the British Isles were effectively dominated by the Anglo-Normans, this older artistic tradition helped keep alive a link with an almost forgotten Celtic past.

Independent Celtic culture effectively came to an end at the start of the 12th century. The last truly Celtic king of Scotland was Macbeth, and after his death in the mid-11th century, Scotland gradually became a state ruled by a Scottish Norman aristocracy. In Ireland, Norse occupation ended in the mid-11th century, but a wave of English and even Scottish Norman settlers continued to undermine the vestiges of Celtic identity. By the 13th century, the island could no longer be regarded as truly Celtic, since like Scotland or Wales its rulers were non-Celts.

This change also influenced Celtic art, and manuscripts produced in formerly Celtic areas were influenced more by Anglo-Norman artistic traditions than by older indigenous forms. Celtic identity had effectively ceased to exist.

The exception was in the west of Scotland, where ecclesiastical sculpture, such as tombstones and crosses, betrayed Celtic influence as late as the 17th century. However, the influence of Anglo-Saxon, Norse, and Norman art can also be detected in these works. The monastery of Iona was the leading exponent of this continued Celtic tradition, although the Argyll peninsula also retained strong Celtic artistic influences until the 16th century.

A haven for Celtic culture

This post-Celtic influence also penetrated into contemporary medieval art in lowland Scotland, and is reflected in several medieval Scottish brooches, ivory caskets, and weapons. In the Scottish Highlands, the Celtic tradition continued to influence the design of weapons until the destruction of the Highland Clan system following the Battle of Culloden (1746). Until then, Celtic interlace was found on Highland targes (shields), dirks (daggers) and broadswords (basket-hilted swords). Following Culloden, Celtic (Jacobin) artistry was viewed with suspicion by the Anglo-Scottish authorities, and it only revived as an art form in the mid-19th century.

Unlike Scotland, Wales was almost completely assimilated by the medieval English by the end of the 13th century, and Celtic culture and artwork were not tolerated by the English authorities who administered the principality. Although a handful of earlier medieval examples of Celtic stonework exist in Wales, all predated the subjugation of Wales by Edward I of England late in the 13th century.

In Ireland, Celtic culture was more deeply ingrained, and during the later medieval period the production of artwork, manuscripts, and stonework continued to draw on older Celtic influences. The most widely-known example of this post-Celtic Irish culture is the harp of Brian Boru, an instrument associated with a warlord who focused Irish opposition to Norse rule. The stunningly beautiful instrument was produced at some point between the 13th and 16th centuries, and its Celtic influence is demonstrated by the harp's interlaced ornamentation. This harp has now become the national symbol of Ireland.

Earlier Celtic religious objects were modified to suit more modern Gothic tastes, but this brutal reworking was unable to completely obscure the beauty of the original pieces. Other objects were almost purely Celtic, such as the 14th-century Domnhnach Airgid shrine, or the 15th-century book satchel designed to hold the manuscript of the *Book of Armagh*. Art historians identify these two pieces as being representative of an early Gaelic Revival, which spanned the 15th to the 17th centuries. Influenced by a hardening political resistance to outside interference in Ireland, the movement sought inspiration in older Celtic artwork rather than the Anglo-Norman medieval influences. These Irish craftsmen were rejecting external threats to Irish culture as well as to its political identity. They were keeping the older Celtic traditions alive.

The Celtic Revival

Two succeeding esthetic movements revived interest in the Celts. In the 18th century, antiquarians and historians portrayed their Celtic forebears as "noble savages," and the study of the Celtic past became socially acceptable. Queen Victoria's love affair with all things Scottish led to a Celtic artistic revival, and paved the way for a reassessment of Celtic cultural identity.

Although a handful of 17th-century antiquarians described aspects of the surviving evidence of Celtic culture, the true revival of interest in things Celtic came

Below: One of several reconstructed Celtic sites, this village near Quin, County Clare, Ireland is a popular attraction for tourists with an interest in the Celtic past.

in the mid-18th century. Inspired by Rousseau's notion of the "noble savage," European historians began to re-examine their own "savage" forebears. Although the interest was created through contact with the North American Indians, it was felt that anthropological information from America might have parallels in the barbarian cultures of the primitive Europeans. While antiquarians looked at Neolithic monuments such as Stonehenge and Celtic hillforts like Maiden Castle with a renewed interest, academics studied surviving Celtic artifacts for clues about the mysterious people who created them.

Around the same time both theologians and antiquarians tried to reassess the importance of the druids in the world of the Ancient Britons or Gauls. Lacking other sources, a romantic impression of the druidic order was created based largely on classical references. The 17th-century antiquarian John Aubrey linked the druids with Stonehenge in his unpublished thesis *Monumenta Britanica*, and a century later the theologian William Stukeley in his *Itinerarium Curiosum* of 1742 tried to link together stone circles and druidusm with Old Testament patriarchal Christianity.

Although this connection between druids and stone circles has long since been discredited, the two phenomena remained linked until the 19th century. A cultural myth was created around the druids, and in 1781 the Ancient Order of Druids held their inaugural meeting. This semi-masonic order continued into the 20th century, and helped propagate interest in druidism, religious mysticism, and pagan worship. Today, druidism is linked to a late 20th century interest in alternative religions, such as New Paganism, Wicca, and Shamanism. Popular among supporters of the alternative new-age culture, druidic worship is still practiced.

Reasserting a Celtic identity

In Wales, a revival of interest in the Welsh language and literature during the late 18th century led to a reappraisal of Celtic culture. Here, where the druids had always been closely linked with the Celtic bards, it was logical that a body would support the survival of Celtic literature and song. This led to a revival of interest in the Welsh language, and the creation of the *Eisteddfod* (Assembly), where the old Celtic tongue is celebrated in song and poetry, and which in turn has encouraged a reawakening of Welsh identity.

An Irish Celtic revival developed in Ireland during the 19th century, its inspiration partly inspired by a political opposition to English dominance. Ironically, in Scotland the same revival was brought about by the enthusiasm of Queen Victoria for all things Scottish. While the Gothic revival in England influenced art and architecture, the Celtic revival led to a politically inspired cultural movement in Ireland, spawned by the Catholic Emancipation Act of 1829. Irish antiquities were studied, together with the surviving illustrated manuscripts to create a new appreciation of Celtic culture.

Original design by William Morris for one of the woodcut initials used at the Kelmscott Prss — To Eric G miller from S C Cockerell christmas 1920.

While archaeologists across Europe began to uncover the wonders of the Celtic past reflected in the artifacts left in grave sites, historians sought to find out more information about the Celts themselves. As public exposure to Celtic history and access to the museums containing artifacts grew, a popular demand for information blossomed. Irish mythology was widely read for its Celtic allusions as much for its romantic qualities, and artists began to copy the Celtic artwork they encountered in museums. By the start of the 20th century, a Celtic cultural revival had re-established an awareness of Celtic culture. Meanwhile, the seeds of a Celtic political re-awakening were also being sown.

Above: This design for a printed decorative initial by William Morris was produced during the early 1890s, but draws on the earlier Celtic tradition of illumination for its inspiration.

The Celtic Fringe

The Celtic Fringe has been identified as the six "Celtic nations" of Scotland, Ireland, Wales, Brittany, Cornwall, and the Isle of Man. These regions were the last bastions of Celtic civilization, and consequently led the way in the Celtic cultural revival of the 19th century. Inspired by this shared identity, the inhabitants of the Celtic Fringe have also been feeling their way toward a collective Celtic identity, both as individual nations or regions, and as members of a wider culture.

Below: Drivers entering Wales across the border with England will immediately notice that the Welsh language takes precedence on the roadsigns.

The celebrated Celtic Historian Peter Beresford Ellis, writing in 1985, spoke of a "Celtic Revolution," where a change in the attitudes of the Celtic peoples in the Celtic Fringe was leading to a reassessment of their own political and cultural identity. However, there is no Celtic state, and the six "nations" he identifies share no political unity. Ireland and Scotland are culturally very similar, yet divided by religious belief. Both Cornwall and Brittany are intrinsic provinces of England and France respectively, and any suggestion of an effective move toward self-determination is ludicrous.

This said, Scotland, Wales, and Northern Ireland now have a level of political self-determination that would have been inconceivable a decade or two ago. Nationalist movements in both Scotland and Wales are now an established part of the politics of both countries. Increasingly, Scots see themselves as Scottish first, and British second. Does this reflect a political opposition to the British Union, or is it a reflection of an increased awareness in a Celtic identity?

As mentioned earlier, the term "Welsh" is derived from the Anglo-Saxon *weahla* (foreigner), and Cornwall comes from "land of the foreign kerns" (or Irish). Brittany means "land of the Britons," while Scotland is named after the Irish settlers who colonized the west of the country in the early medieval period. Although the names

reflect a sense of difference, the political and cultural assimilation of these regions with their neighboring English (Anglo-Saxon) or French (Frankish) neighbors has been almost total. Despite this, all these regions share a unifying cultural entity, with their own artistic, social, and historical sensibilities.

Survival of Celtic languages

In Scotland, the Highland and Lowland division meant that until recently, only the Highlanders were considered Celtic (or Gaelic), and in remote corners of the Highlands and Islands, Gaelic was spoken in addition to Scots-English. Although writers such as Robert Burns helped establish recognition for the Scottish tongue as a culturally distinct dialect, it is nevertheless an Anglicized language. Scottish Gaelic

Irish still retain their opposition to Gaelic, and treasure their political adherence to Britain. Since the independence from Britain of Eire (Republic of Ireland), Irish Gaelic has been recognized as the official national language, while English is the official tongue in Ulster (Northern Ireland).

For the Welsh, the revived interest in the Welsh language that came with the advent of institutions like the *Eisteddfod* (*see page 183*) developed rapidly after 1945, and today Welsh is a compulsory subject in schools, while all

is the direct ancestor of the Scottish accent, but it remains a foreign language to the vast majority of Scots.

Irish Gaelic was always spoken in Ireland, but English became the dominant language, its use encouraged by political administrations and the Church. The Gaelic tongue continued to be spoken in rural Ireland, however, and formed a focal point for the Irish independence movement from the 19th century onward. The exception was Ulster (Northern Ireland), which was essentially a Protestant Scots colony. These Scots-

government forms, road signs, and even television channels and some publications are bilingual.

The smaller regions of the Celtic fringe maintain independence movements. In Brittany the Union Democratic Bretonne has campaigned for self-determination with partial success, although the region's linguistic assimilation is as complete as Scotland's. Any future political union of the Celtic Fringe is extremely unlikely. Nevertheless, their shared cultural consciousness is a tangible force.

Above: The annual Eistedfodd at Llangollen attracts music lovers from around the world to celebrate this most Celtic of festivals.

Celtic Consciousness

What is it to be a Celt? Has the term any relevance today, or does it refer to a European civilization that has been lost with the passage of time? In the past decade, an upsurge in regional national identity within the British Isles has been mirrored by a similar increase in Celtic identity. Have Celtic consciousness and regional awareness any relevance in the 21st century?

Below: Celtic religious traditions like the rag trees still seen today as far apart as Cyprus and Ireland, are echoed in modern Christian rites like the Christmas tree, **right**, adorned with trailing and hanging "votive" decorations.

People are sporting Celtic symbols, or are otherwise identifying with an ancient Celtic past wherever you look. This interest is partially inspired by the intriguing and hauntingly beautiful examples of Celtic art in the world's museums. It also manifests itself in a sense of heritage. While many condemn the film *Braveheart* for its lack of historical accuracy, few Scots were unmoved by the film's sentiments. It played on dormant emotions, pitting Celt against Anglo-Saxon, and represented a late-blooming resurgence of

independent Celtic spirit. It also has something to do with romanticism, looking back to an uncomplicated age of chivalry in much the same way that the Arthurian legends did for previous generations.

The Celts of today are not just the indigenous inhabitants of the Celtic Fringe, of Ireland, Scotland, Wales, Cornwall, the Isle of Man, and Brittany. Millions identify with this "Celtic consciousness" through their spiritual beliefs, their traceable ancestry, their artistic temperament, or simply by a feeling of independence. The Celts were a people who constituted one of the great world civilizations, and who formed an important role in the development of Europe. They were also all but crushed by a series of conquerors who brutally imposed their will on them, and tried to eradicate all traces of their language, culture, and belief. The resurgence of the small Celtic nations in recent years has inspired the renewal

of "Celtic consciousness." The recent opening of the Scottish and Welsh parliaments marked a turning point in the history of the British Isles, and a shift in the attitude of their constituent peoples.

Celtic heritage

In *The Rise and Fall of the English Empire* (Medusa Press, London, 1976), the historian Francis Ripley argued that there never was a British Empire. The Anglo-Saxons invaded Britain and conquered the indigenous Celts. Although unable to eradicate all the Celtic peoples in Britain, they formed a dominant power-base, which became England. Ripley argued that the Anglo-Saxons never lost their imperial dynamic, continuing their policy of conquest and annexation until the present day.

Following what the Anglo-Saxon hegemony called the "unification" (the Celts would have called "annexation") of Scotland, Wales, and Ireland with England, the homogenous term "British" was re-invented. The first conquests of an "Anglo-Saxon Empire" were her Celtic neighbors. The "island race" of Winston Churchill never existed, because "British" really meant "English," or "English-dominated." For the Scots, Welsh, and Irish, national identity is strongly intertwined with their Celtic consciousness. It is inevitable that as national identity takes root, so will this Celtic identity.

It is unlikely that there can ever be any political or even social re-establishment of a unified Celtic power. The world has opened up its frontiers through technology and travel, so that today, Wales has a population that can trace its ancestry to every continent on the globe, and comprises a mixture of all of the world's races. There are no Celts or Saxons anymore, just people. What can and is happening is an increasing awareness of the richness of the Celtic heritage, and an understanding of the important part the Celtic peoples have played in the creation of the modern world.

Above: Modern-day druids perform a ceremony at Stonehenge during the summer solstice. Awareness of a Celtic heritage is evidenced throughout the countries of the Celtic Fringe.

Museums & Further Reading

The following European museums contain important collections of Celtic artifacts. Remember that not all objects might be on display at any one time. Serious students are recommended to contact the museum before visiting.

Austria
Steiermärkisches Landesmuseum Joanneum, Graz
Keltenmuseum, Hallein
Naturhistorishes Museum, Vienna

Czech Republic
Národní Múzeum, Prague

Denmark
Nationalmuseet, Copenhagen
Forhistorisk Museum, Moesgard

France
Musée Granet, Aix-en-Provence
Musée Archéologique, Châtillon-sur-Seine
Musée Bargoin, Clermont-Ferrand
Musée Archéologique, Dijon
Musée de la Civilization Gallo-Romaine, Lyon
Musée de la Archéologie Mediterranéenne, Marseilles
Musée de Millau, Millau
Musée Historique et Archéologique de l'Orléanais, Orléans
Musée des Antiquités Nationales, Saint-Germain-en-Laye, Paris
Musée de Bretagne, Rennes
Musée Saint-Rémi, Rheims
Musée Archéologique, Alise-Sainte-Reine
Musée Archéologique, Saintes

Germany
Rheinisches Landesmuseum, Bonn
Römisches-Germanisches Museum, Koln
Landesmuseum für Vor- und Frühgeschichte, Saarbrücken
Schleswig-Holsteinisches Landesmuseum, Schleswig
Württembergisches Landesmuseum, Stuttgart
Rheinisches Landesmuseum, Trier

Ireland
Cork Public Museum, Cork
National Museum of Ireland, Dublin
Trinity College Library, Dublin

Luxemburg
Musée National d'Histoire et d'Art, Luxemburg

Spain
Museo Arqueológico, Cordoba
Museo Arqueológico Nacional, Madrid
Museo Arqueológico, Numantia

Switzerland
Musée Schwab, Beil
Bernisches Historisches Museum, Bern
Musée Cantonal d'Arquéologie, Neuchâtel

United Kingdom
University Museum, Cambridge, England
City Museum, Carlisle, England
Norwich Castle Museum, Norwich, England
Ashmolean Museum, Oxford, England
British Museum, London, England
Corinium Museum, Gloucester, England
Guildford Museum, Guildford, England
National Museum of Scotland, Edinburgh, Scotland
Kelvingrove Art Gallery and Museum, Glasgow, Scotland
Tankerness House Museum, Kirkwall, Orkney, Scotland
National Museums and Galleries of Wales, Cardiff, Wales
Oreil Ynys Mon, Llangefni, Anglesey, Wales

Suggestions for further reading

ALCOCK, LESLIE Arthur's Britain Penguin, London, 1971
ARMIT, IAN Celtic Scotland B.T. Batsford, London, 1997
BRUNEAUX, JEAN-LOUIS The Celtic Gauls, Numismatic Fine Arts, Los Angeles, 1988
CHADWICK, NORA The Celts Penguin, London, 1971
CUNLIFFE, BARRY The Celtic World, Constable, London, 1992.
CUNLIFFE, BARRY The Ancient Celts, Oxford University Press, Oxford, 1997
CUNLIFFE, BARRY Iron Age Britain, Batsford, London, 1995
ELLIS, PETER BERESFORD Celt and Saxon, Constable, London, 1993
ELLIS, PETER BERESFORD The Ancient World of the Celts, Constable, 1998
ELLIS, PETER BERESFORD The Celtic Revolution, Y-Lolfa, Tal-y-Bont, 1985
ELLIS, PETER BERESFORD Dictionary of Celtic Mythology, Constable, London, 1992
ELUÈRE, CHRISTIANE The Celts: Conquerors of Ancient Europe, Abrams, New York, 1993
GREEN, MIRANDA The World of the Druids, Thames & Hudson, London, 1997
GREEN, MIRANDA Dictionary of Celtic Myth and Legend, Thames & Hudson, New York, 1992,
HARBSON, PETER Pre-Christian Ireland, Thames & Hudson, London, 1988
HUBERT, HENRI The Rise of the Celts, Constable, London, 1987
JAMES, SIMON The World of the Celts, Thames & Hudson, New York, 1993
LAING, LLOYD Celtic Britain, Routledge and Kegan Paul, London, 1979
LAING, LLOYD & JENNIFER The Picts and the Scots, Sutton, Stroud, 1993
LAING, LLOYD & JENNIFER Art of the Celts, Thames & Hudson, London, 1992
LEHANE, BRENDAN Early Celtic Christianity, Constable, London, 1994
MARKLE, JAN Women of the Celts, Cremonesi, London, 1975
MARKALE, J. Celtic Civilization Payot, Paris, 1976
MEGAW, RUTH & VINCENT Celtic Art, Thames & Hudson, London, 1989
O'RAHILLY, THOMAS Early Irish History and Mythology, Dublin Institute, Dublin, 1946
POWELL, T.G.E. The Celts, Thames & Hudson, London, 1980
RANKIN, H.D. The Celts and the Classical World, Croom Helm, London, 1987
RITCHIE, W.F & J.N.G. Celtic Warriors, Shire, Aylesbury, 1985
SHARKEY, JOHN Celtic Mysteries: The Ancient Religion, Thames & Hudson, New York, 1975
STEAD, I.M Celtic Art, British Museum Publications, London, 1985
THOMAS, CHARLES Celtic Britain, Thames & Hudson, London, 1986
WILCOX, PETER Rome's Enemies: Gallic and British Celts, Osprey, Oxford, 1985
YOUNGS, SUSAN (ed) The Work of Angels, British Museum, London, 1989

Late Celtic Timelines

58–50 BC Caesar fights Gallic War.

AD 43 Roman invasion of Britain under Emperor Claudius.

54 Claudius persecutes Druids in Gaul.

60 Romans attack Druids on Anglesey.

69 Druids rise against Romans in Britain.

c.400 Saxons, Irish, and Picts begin invasions of southern Britain. Irish establish colonies in Wales and Scotland.

410 Emperor Honorius withdraws legions from Britain. Roman officials are expelled, and a native government established.

425–450 High King (*Superbus tyrannus*) of Britain identified as Vortigern ("overlord").

429 Bishop Germanius of Auxerre makes first visit to Britain and leads "Alleluia" victory against Saxon raiders.

430s Uí Néill clan rises in Ireland.

430 Palladius, Deacon of Auxerre, sent by Rome as bishop of Irish Christians.

432 British Celt, Patrick, sent as missionary to Ireland. Starts conversion of the druidic schools of Ireland to monastic schools.

435 Tibatto leads movement for Armorica's independence from Roman Gaul.

438 Ireland's civil law, the *Senchus Mór*, is codified, according to the *Annals of Ulster*.

446 British appeal to Aetius, commander of the armies of the Western Roman Empire, for aid against the Saxons. Vortigern employs Jute mercenaries to help against the Saxons.

449 Jute mercenaries employed by Vortigern stage a mutiny led by Hengist and Horsa. Start of the Celt-Jute war.

c.450 Cunedda and his sons leave the territory of the Gododdin (Votadani) and eject Irish settlers from Gwynedd. He establishes the Gwynedd dynasty.

460 Major Celtic victory over Jutes at Richborough. Jutes confined on Isle of Thanet.

Ceretic of Strathclyde receives letter from St. Patrick. Patrick writes his *Confessio* (autobiography).

462 Death of St. Patrick.

463 Death of Loeguire Mac Néill, High King of Ireland. Succession of Lugaid Mac Loeguire.

465 Jutes break out from Thanet.

470 Fergus Mor Mac Eirc of the Ulster Dál Riada crosses to Britain and forms a new Dál Riadan kingdom in Kintyre.

473 The Jute Hengist and son Aesc secure major victory over Celts.

477 Aelle and sons lead Saxon settlement at Selsey Bill.

491 Aelle and his South Saxons, after 14 years of fighting, reach Pevensey and destroy it.

495 Cerdic and his son Cynric land near Southampton and begin to establish a West Saxon kingdom.

6th century First extant remains of literature written in Irish and Welsh. Irish hymns sung in Latin.

c.500 Start of the British Celtic migrations to west of Britain, to Ireland, to Armorica (Brittany), to Galicia and Astrurias, and to areas such as Brittenburgh (on the Rhine). Arthur of the Celts achieves 12 listed victories over the Saxons.

508 West Saxons under Cerdic defeat Natan-leod, local Celtic ruler in New Forest area.

514 Stuf and Whihtgar reinforce Cerdic.

c.516 Arthur achieves most famous victory over the Saxons, at Badon. Saxon advance halted for a generation.

522 Brendan establishes Clonfert abbey.

523–550 Angles seize fortress of Din Guoaroy and establish a settlement called Bebba's Burgh (Bamburgh), which forms center of a kingdom called Bernicia.

c.537 Defeat of Arthur at battle of Camlann. Arthur and Metraut slain.

552 Celtic defeat by West Saxons at Old Sarum (Salisbury).

554 Comgall founds monastery of Bangor in Ulster.

558 Childebert of the Franks makes war on Armorica (Brittany). Chonoo, king of Armorica, resists. Hostilities continue until 630.

560 Gildas, British Celtic monk, writes *De Excidio et Conquestu Britanniae*, only major contemporary source for the history of the period. Death of Cunomoros (King Mark of Cornwall).

563 Arrival of Colmcille, exiled from Ireland, in Dál Riada.

566 Gildas on a visit to Ireland. He exchanges Isidore of Seville's encyclopedia for a copy of the *Táin Bó Cuailnge*.

568 Athelberht of Kent defeated by West Saxons.

570 Death of Gildas in Brittany.

571 West Saxons invade mid-Britain.

574 Colmcille ordains Aedán Mac Gabhráin as king of Dál Riada.

575 Convention of Druim Cett (Co. Derry) attended by Colmcille and Aedán. High King of Ireland recognizes Dál Riadan rights.

577 West Saxons defeat Celts at battle of Deorham, reach the River Severn, and capture several Celtic cities including Gloucester.

578 British Celtic migration to Brittany transforms Celtic Armorica, now called "Little Britain." Dumnonia, Cornouaille, and Bro Erich emerge as small kingdoms in Brittany.

589 Death of Dewi Sant (St. David) in Dyfed.

590 Urien of Rheged besieges Angles in Lindisfarne, slain in battle there.

c.590 Attack of the Gododdin on Catraeth (Catterick).

c.593 Death of Ceawlin of West Saxons after being deposed.

596 Pope Gregory sends Augustine as

missionary to Aethelberht of Kent.

603 Aedán Mac Gabhráin of Dál Riada defeated by Aethelfrith at Degastan.

604 Aethelfrith of Bernicia unites Bernicia and Deira into Northumbria.

607 Death of Sinlán moccu Min, abbot of Bangor and Irish chronicler.

608 Death of Aedán of Dál Riada.

615 Selyf, king of Powys, slain in battle at Chester. Massacre of 1000 monks from Bangor by the Saxons.

616 Christian missionaries chased from Essex after death of King Saeberht. Most Saxon areas converted by St. Augustine revert to pagan worship, except Kent.

617 Aethelfrith slain by Raedwald of East Anglia at battle of River Idle. Edwin becomes king of Northumbria. Aethelfrith's three sons take refuge on Iona and are brought up as Christians there.

625 Elmet is incorporated into Northumbria and settled by Saxons after last Celtic king, Ceretic (Caradoc), is driven out. Edwin marries Aethelburgh, sister of Eadbald of Kent, and is converted to Christianity by Paulinus.

625 Foundation of Abernethy by Irish nuns under patronage of Nechtan, king of Picts.

628 Mercia defeats Wessex at Cirencester. Cadwallon of Gwynedd and Penda of Mercia form alliance against Edwin.

633 Edwin of Northumbria slain in battle by Cadwallon, king of Gwynedd, at Hatfield.

634 Oswald, son of Aethelfrith, leaves Iona to become king of Northumbria and begins converting Northumbrians to Christianity.

635 Irish monks flourish in Northumbria, and establish monastic centers.

635 Borders of Brittany are agreed by treaty with Dagobert, king of the Franks.

637 After a defeat by the Irish high king, Dál Riadan territory in Ireland is lost.

638 Northumbria attacks Celtic Edinburgh.

642 Oswald slain by Maserfeld at town now named Oswestry.

655 Celtic Gwynedd withdraws from alliance with Mercia; King Penda is slain at Winwaed Field and Mercia is ruled by Northumbria. After three years, Penda's son Wulfhere leads rebellion and seizes throne of Mercia.

661 Irish missionaries in all Saxon kingdoms.

664 Synod of Whitby, discussing differences in Roman and Celtic practices, favors Rome.

672 Major Synod of Saxon Church at Hertford.

681 Jarrow founded. Bede enters new monastery.

c.685 *Beowulf* is written, although only eighth-century copies now survive.

688–705 Ine, king of Wessex, expands further into Dumnonia.

697 Law of the Innocents promulgated by Adomnán is intended to protect non-combatants during war. Popular among Celts but ignored by Saxon kingdoms.

c.700 Golden Age of Irish literature.

711 West Saxons capture Exeter.

713 Northumbrian war on Picts ended by treaty.

715 Mercia raids Wessex.

722 Battle of River Camel. Cornish and Dumnonians defeat Wessex.

c.725 Irish monks reported in Iceland and Faroe Isles.

731 Bede completes *Historia Ecclesiastica Gentis Anglorum* shortly before his death in 734.

757 Civil war in Mercia brings Offa to power after Aethelbert of Mercia is murdered

768 Welsh kingdoms accept Roman Church's dating of Easter (process begun in Whitby, 664).

776 Kent throws off Mercian control

778 Offa invades Wales, raiding into Dyfed.

779 Offa is regarded as supreme king of Saxon kingdoms.

c.780–806 *Book of Kells* begun on Iona and completed at (or taken to) Kells in Ireland.

c.784 Offa builds dyke to cut Wales off.

790s Viking raids on Ireland, Iona, Lindisfarne, and Skye.

802 Vikings burn Iona.

807–14 Abbot Cellach abandons Iona and builds new church at Kells.

816 Irish missionaries prohibited from preaching within English kingdoms at Council of Chelsea.

838 Wessex defeats Celts of Cornwall and remnants of Dumnonia.

839 Viking victory over Picts.

841 Thorgil establishes Norse (Viking) kingdom of Dublin.

843 Wessex is beaten by Vikings at second battle of Carhampton.

846 Charles the Bald signs treaty recognizing the independence of the Breton kingdom. Brittany retains its independence until 1488.

847 Kenneth Mac Alpin is recognized as the king of Dál Riada and of the Picts.

853 Mercia and Wessex attack Powys.

888 Alan I of Brittany defeats the Norse.

c.900 *The Voyage of Brendan* is written, suggesting that Brendan may have reached the New World.

907 Vikings capture Nantes and threaten rest of Brittany.

913 Vikings devastate Brittany.

916 Codification of laws throughout most of Welsh kingdoms.

918 Norse defeat Irish high king near Dublin.

931 British Celts driven from city of Exeter by Athelstan. The River Tamar is accepted as the border between Cornwall and Wessex.

937 Alliance of Celts fails in final attempt to drive Saxons out of Britain. Borders between Saxon and Celtic kingdoms become set along approximate modern borders between England, Scotland, and Wales.

Index